UNDERGRADUATE TEXTS IN COMPUTER SCIENCE

Editors
David Gries
Fred B. Schneider

Springer Science+Business Media, LLC

UNDERGRADUATE TEXTS IN COMPUTER SCIENCE

Joseph Bergin

Data Structure Programming

With the Standard Template Library in C++

With 49 Illustrations

 Springer

Joseph Bergin
Department of Computer Science
Pace University
New York, NY
USA

Series Editors
David Gries
Fred B. Schneider
Department of Computer Science
Cornell University
Upson Hall
Ithaca, NY 14853-7501
USA

On the cover: Cover photo taken by Richard Embery/FPG International LLC.

Library of Congress Cataloging-in-Publication Data
Bergin, Joseph.
    Data structure programming : with the standard template library in
C++ / Joseph Bergin.
        p.   cm. — (Undergraduate texts in computer science)
        ISBN 978-1-4612-7223-6   ISBN 978-1-4612-1630-8 (eBook)
        DOI 10.1007/978-1-4612-1630-8
        1. C++ (Computer program language)   2. Data structures (Computer
science)   3. Standard template library.   I. Title.   II. Series.
QA76.73.C153B457   1998
005.7'3—dc21   97-45234

Printed on acid-free paper.

Production managed by Natalie Johnson; manufacturing supervised by Jeffrey Taub.
Photocomposed copy prepared using Springer's svwide style macro.

9 8 7 6 5 4 3 2 1

ISBN 978-1-4612-7223-6

Preface

In this book we are about to study how data abstraction, and data structures programming with the Standard Template Library can empower our programs. The Standard Template Library (STL) was developed at Hewlett-Packard, based on the work of Alexander Stepanov and others. Libraries similar to this have been developed for other languages such as Ada and now Java. C++ however, has been special in that the standard for the language has evolved specifically to support generic programming as seen in the STL.

The Standard Template Library provides a solid basis of fundamental abstract data types and algorithms that are commonly needed in many software projects. It combines efficiency of implementation with the safety of compile time type checking of arguments. Once a student learns to use the library, it will no longer be necessary to rebuild common data types such as lists and expandable arrays for each new project. The STL provides these and many others without the compromise in efficiency that is the usual trade-off for generality.

In many places in this book we shall speak about "the" implementation of the STL. This is not precisely true as the STL is not defined in terms of an implementation, but in terms of a specification of behavior and efficiency. Other implementation strategies can be used than the ones that we detail here, provided that they meet the specification. What we are actually describing is the so called "reference implementation" of the STL that was developed at Hewlett-Packard as the library standard was being developed.

Our technique for teaching data structures along with the STL is to develop C++ classes and functions that are similar to, though simpler than the reference implementation. In some cases our sample implementation does not meet all of the STL requirements, and we will point out the serious discrepancies as we go along. It is our belief that students can learn from working with these simpler implementations and that they will give appropriate background for examining the actual implementation if that is deemed necessary. Some of the "simpler" implementations are actually quite sophisticated—more so than is found in some books intended for this level.

There are some places where, in a sequence of exercises, each depends on the earlier ones. This is a good place to put a team of students to work implementing different parts based on prototypes agreed upon as a group.

The Standard Template Library

Complete documentation of the STL can be found in the current C++ standards document (see reference [13] in the Bibliography) and from:

Alexander Stepanov and Meng Lee
http://www.cs.rpi.edu/~musser/stl.html
look for doc.ps.gz

The STL code shown in this book is taken from the Hewlett-Packard version of STL that is used as the basis of many commercial versions of the library. This material is:

Copyright (c) 1994
Hewlett-Packard Company.

Permission to use, copy, modify, distribute and sell this software
and its documentation for any purpose is hereby granted without fee,
provided that the above copyright notice appear in all copies and
that both that copyright notice and this permission notice appear
in supporting documentation. Hewlett-Packard Company makes no
representations about the suitability of this software for any
purpose. It is provided "as is" without express or implied warranty.

Reference versions of the STL may be obtained over the internet from David Musser at address
ftp://ftp.cs.rpi.edu/pub/stl/
or from Hewlett-Packard at ftp://butler.hpl.hp.com/stl/

The software written specifically for this book may be obtained from
http://csis.pace.edu/~bergin/stl

Acknowledgments

Carroll Zahn showed me the alternate representation of lists discussed in Chapter 7. David Musser answered many questions by email concerning the state of the standard. Hewlett Packard and Silicon Graphics provided interesting implementations of the standard that are worthy of study.

Dedication

To my teachers,
my colleagues,
and my students.

Joseph Bergin
Pace University
New York City

Contents

Chapter 1
Data Structures and Algorithms

1.1 Data Abstraction and Encapsulation

Niklaus Wirth, the creator of Pascal, Modula-2, and more recently, Oberon, once wrote a book entitled *Data Structures + Algorithms = Programs*. A key idea of that book is that data structures and algorithms must work together to produce a result. Further, the thesis is proposed that data structures and algorithms must be developed together, and, using modern languages, should be packaged together as a unit of functionality.

As an example, the built-in floating point types of C++, such as float and double, come packaged within the language with a set of operations that manipulate them. Operators such as operator+ and operator< are intrinsically bound to and indispensable from the values on which they operate. One of the great strengths of the C++ language is that it permits the programmer to create data types and bind them to operations so that they operate with all of the ease and power of the built-in types.

The idea of a data abstraction has three parts. First there is a set of values to be manipulated. The internal structure of these values is not of interest and may be hidden from users. For example, the internal representation of the data type double is only infrequently of interest to the programmer. These values are taken as atomic, or indivisible. The second part of the definition of a data abstraction is a set of operations that manipulate the values. The internal workings of the algorithms is also not of interest to the user, only the specified results that the operations promise to provide. Again, the internal operations of operator* are not as important to the user of doubles as the fact that the operator approximates the true mathematical result of a multiplication. The third element of a data abstraction is a set of rules that define the operation of the operators. An example here would be a specification that sets out the limits of the approximation of the multiplication of two doubles.

Question: What are all of the operators that C++ provides for type double?

The process of packaging the data and the operations of a data abstraction together into a single unit is called *encapsulation*. Most modern computer languages provide some means of encapsulation. Object-oriented programming employs one kind of encapsulation; namely that of packaging up the data and the operations that manipulate it into objects. These objects communicate with each other at run time by requesting the execution of operations of one another.

One sort of data abstraction that is often of use in programming is that of a set. A set is a container of values of some kind. As a container we need to insert values into it and to check if a given value is stored. We also need operations for common set functions such as union and intersection. The computer representation of the set values is not of particular importance as long as it is adequate to support the specifications of the operations. Some representations won't do, however, since one of the specifications of an operation will probably involve the speed with which an operation can be carried out. Some representations will not be sufficiently efficient to support this part of the specification. To be specific, we might want to specify that deletion from the set be achievable in constant time, independent of the size of the set. We might desire this to be true if the use of the set is within a program in which deletions must be done frequently. This requirement might greatly restrict what implementations we might choose, but if the specifications can be met, the user does not need to be aware of the details of the implementation. For example, an implementation that required that each item in the set be examined to find the one to be deleted would not be suitable if deletions must be done in constant time.

There are lots of categories of users, of course. The user of a spreadsheet program is, perhaps, not especially aware of the details of computer programming, and may have little interest in how a logarithm is implemented, or even that a power function is implemented using logs. Most software, however, is written to be used by other programmers. This is because most software is built by more than one person in a team. Most of the programmers are providing components to be used by other programmers to build the overall product. Most of the time we will use the term *user* for another programmer who must use the products of a programmer in his or her own work.

In fact, it is desirable that the user of sets not be aware of the implementation of either the values or the operations. This will be especially true if the set abstraction is to be used in a very large project developed by many people, even more if the set data type is to be used in several projects over a long span of time. The reason for this is the inevitability of change. Problems change over time and software must be built in such a way as to permit changes to the programs themselves. The main difficulty in exposing the details of an implementation to a user is that of *coupling*. When a user knows the details of an implementation, he or she may somehow take advantage of those details. If these details change, as they probably will, then the software built subsequently will also need to be modified. This is very undesirable. We should be able to build programs out of independent parts, so that replacing one part with a functionally equivalent part will not require modification of the parts that depend on it. This can be achieved only if the details are effectively hidden from users.

An analogy can be made here with hardware integrated circuits (ICs). Engineers build electronic equipment from off-the-shelf components based on the specifications of the signals that can be expected on the various pins of the IC. The internal wiring of the circuit is not of importance, only the overall effect as presented to the external interface, namely the pins. This greatly decreases the complexity of design, and increases its modularity.

This de coupling of the parts of a software project can be enhanced if the details are actually hidden from other programmers so that they can be manipulated only by the operations provided. This is called *information hiding* and is an important feature of modern computer languages.

In C++ we would build a set data abstraction by encapsulating the details within a Set class. The public members of the class would be the operations on our sets, and the private members would be the implementation details. The users of our abstraction would use the class to create objects of type Set and would manipulate the sets by requesting execution of the operations such as union and intersection. We will take up the details of classes later in this chapter and the details of sets in a later chapter.

Since sets need to be able to store different kinds of things, and since it is not very productive to define a set as containing only a single kind of thing (int set, or float set), we would like to be able to define our set abstraction independent of the type to be contained therein. In C++ we may use templates to provide parameters to our abstractions, so that they may be specialized when used and do not need to be rewritten for each different use.

The Standard Template Library (STL) is one of the standardized components of the C++ language. It provides a large set of data abstractions such as set, list, and stack that have proved useful in many different kinds of applications. These abstractions are all presented as templates so that they may be specialized in many ways when needed by users (other programmers) without being modified. The STL also has a large number of algorithms for manipulating the provided abstractions using techniques of proven efficiency and generality.

1.2   Classes, Data Abstraction, Encapsulation, and Information Hiding

The main means of encapsulation in C++ is the class, which evolved from the C struct or the Pascal record idea. The main difference between classes and more primitive records is that classes also define functional elements as well as data elements. Thus we have Wirth's *Data Structures + Algorithms*. In C++, classes are types. Values with a class type are called *objects*. Since a class defines both data and functional elements, each object has both data and functional elements. Therefore, instead of the data being treated as passive, to be acted on by functions, the data (i.e., objects) are treated as active since they have functional parts.

Here is a very simple class that encapsulates the idea of a die. Dice usually come in pairs, but we shall implement only a single die. Most dice are small cubes with a different number of spots on each face. They are used in board games to generate player moves. We will use a die to generate random values that we will store in some data structures seen later so that we may test those structures. First we present the class declaration, which defines what functions are available for use in a Die. The class declaration also shows the variables that are used to implement a Die.

```
class Die
{  public:
      Die(unsigned int faces = 6);

      int roll();
      static void randomize(int seed = 0);
   private:
      unsigned int _faces;
};
```

The class is divided into public and private sections. The private section here contains only a member variable _faces. We intend to be able to create dice with any number of faces: even physically impossible numbers of faces. The public part contains a constructor Die(int) and two member functions: roll() and randomize(int). Function randomize is marked static. The constructor will automatically be called whenever we create a new **Die** object. It just sets the _faces variable to its parameter. We provide a default value of 6 for this parameter, so that the user can create a standard six-sided die by creating a Die but without giving any parameter. For example,

```
Die standard;      // Creates a 6 sided die.
Die special(12);   // Creates a 12 sided die.
```

The definition of the constructor follows. Notice how the member variable is initialized between the parameter list and the (empty) statement part.

```
Die::Die(unsigned int faces)
:  _faces(faces)
{
}
```

To roll a die, we call the standard function rand() that is exported from <stdlib.h>. We take the remainder modulo the number of faces, which gives a number between 0 and _faces - 1. We finally add one to this result and return it.

```
int Die::roll()
{  return rand() % _faces + 1;
}
```

The way that rand() works, each time we re run our program we will get exactly the same random numbers. This is useful while testing, but if we really want random numbers, then we must *seed* the random number generator. We do this by calling the function srand(int). This is the purpose of the randomize member function. We randomize with the user's parameter, or, if that is zero, we use the system clock to give us a seed. The type time_t and the function time() are exported by interface <time.h>.

```
void Die::randomize(int seed)
{   if (seed == 0)
    {   time_t now = time(NULL);
        srand(now % 32763);
    }
    else
        srand(seed);
};
```

Each Die object will contain a _faces variable and will have access to a roll() function. Once we create a Die object named standard, we can roll it with `standard.roll()`, as in

```
cout << standard.roll();
cout << special.roll();
```

The constructor and the static function are not available in the same way. Constructors are called implicitly when we declare variables of class type. Static member functions are not part of the objects of the class, but part of the class itself. If we want to execute the static randomize function of the Die class, we need to say something like

```
Die:: randomize();
```

What follows is the definition of a StopWatch class that we shall use to empirically determine the running time of certain algorithms. The class depends on a built-in interface <time.h> that comes with C++. The StopWatch class is user-defined and can be found in the interface StopWatch.h.

```
class StopWatch
{   public:
        StopWatch();
            // Start a new timer at system
            // reference time
            // (UNIX and PC: GMT 0:0:0 Jan 1 1970)
            // (Macintosh: Midnight Jan 1 1904)
            // The resolution is one second.

        StopWatch (const StopWatch &d);
        ~StopWatch();
        StopWatch & operator =
            (const StopWatch &d);
        time_t start();
            // Returns the absolute time of start.

        time_t stop();
```

```
                    // Returns the absolute time of stop.

              time_t mark();
                    // Returns the absolute time of mark.
                    // Prints (cout) the elapsed time
                    //     (seconds) since start
                    //     and the elapsed time since last
                    //     mark.

              void reset();
                    // Resets all times to system reference
                    // time.
           private:
              time_t _startTime;
              time_t _markTime;
              time_t _stopTime;
       };
```

Every class has a name and a feature list. The features, called members, may be either variables, such as _startTime, or functions, such as stop(). Each object created from this type definition will have all of these features.

Some of the features are declared public and some private. The public members are accessible to other program sections. The private members are available only within the code of this class. Here all of the variable members are private, which is the usual case, and all of the functions are public, which is common, but not universal. This visibility control is up to the creator of the class. Thus, within a class, we see both encapsulation and information hiding.

Some of the class features are special in a number of ways. Here we have two constructors, which are functional members that have the same name as the class. We also have a destructor, that has the name of the class preceded by the "~" character and no parameters. Constructors are not contained within the objects, but are used to create the objects themselves. When we include a constructor in a class, we provide the means of initialization for objects so that each object we use will always be in a consistent internal state. This construction by a member of the class is needed since it is the data members that need to be initialized, but they are private and not accessible to client code, including the main function that drives our computation.

Note that some of the parameters of member functions are marked const. This simply means that the function will not attempt to modify them. It will then be possible to pass constants as well as variables for the real parameters (arguments) when the functions are called.

This class illustrates the standard idiom of C++ encapsulation by providing two constructors, a destructor, and an assignment operator. This class is actually too simple to require all of this. They would be required if the class managed any dynamic memory. If the user does not provide them, then standard versions will be provided by the compiler.

Here we have two constructors. The first has no parameters, and constructs a Stop-Watch from standard values—here the system clock. The second constructs one Stop-Watch as a copy of another. The constructor with no parameters is called a *default constructor* and is needed by the C++ system as well as by users. If no constructor is provided by the programmer, then C++ will provide a default constructor. The constructor that copies an object of the same type is called a *copy constructor*, and it will also be provided if the user provides no constructors at all. The copy constructor is needed by the system whenever we call a function and attempt to pass a StopWatch object as an argument. The provided copy constructor just copies the individual fields from one object to another. The provided default constructor merely gives default values to contained objects.

Destructors are called automatically by the C++ system when an object is no longer available. They provide the means for a programmer to specify clean up processing done when an object is destroyed. When you declare a StopWatch object as a local variable within a function, the variable has a lifetime that is the same as the running time of the function. When the function returns, all of its local data cease to be. The system will call destructors on all of your local objects at this time. Objects created on the free store using operator new, and objects declared to be static are handled differently, as will be seen later. The system will provide a destructor if the programmer does not, though this provided destructor will take no actions other than to call destructors of any other objects that are contained within the one being destroyed. This will be the case if one object has members of class type.

The StopWatch class also defines a new version of the assignment operator, `operator=`, so that the programmer can specify what will happen when one StopWatch object is assigned to a StopWatch variable. This ability to give operators new meanings for new kinds of data is what makes it possible for C++ objects to behave just as built-in values do. We could, for example, provide a difference function representing the (last mark time) difference between two StopWatch objects. We could use `operator-` to implement this operation. The system will always provide operator= if the programmer does not. It provides for memberwise assignment of the members of the object.

Most of the operators of C++ may be given new meanings. This mechanism is called operator overloading. One small weakness of the implementation of operator overloading in C++ is that it is not possible to change the precedence or associativity of the operators when giving a new version. In particular operator= has relatively low precedence and it associates from the right. All overloaded versions of this operator will behave in the same way.

In the above class declaration, we have omitted the definitions of the member functions. Some programmers prefer to include these definitions with the classes themselves and others prefer to list them separately in an implementation file. For example, in the separate file StopWatch.cpp, we have

```
StopWatch::StopWatch()
:   _startTime(0),
    _markTime(0),
    _stopTime(0)
```

```
{
}
```

and

```
time_t StopWatch::stop()
{  _stopTime = time(NULL);
   return _stopTime;
}
```

When defining member functions, constructors, and destructors separately, we must give the class name as part of the definition, using the scope resolution operator:: as well.

We create a new StopWatch object by using the name of the class as a type in the usual way. The constructor will be called as part of the execution of this object creation.

```
StopWatch myWatch;
```

We operate on an object by sending it a message consisting of the name of one of its member functions and any needed parameters. The result of the message will be the result of calling the member function:

```
time_t now = myWatch.start();
```

Philosophically, we treat the execution of one of the member functions as if it were executed by the object itself acting as if it were a computer. Therefore, we say that my-Watch receives the start message and executes the start member function, returning the start time to the message sender. Thus we think of the sender of a message as a client, and the object that receives the message as a server that provides information to the client.

Destructors are not called directly. The system sees to their execution when an object ceases to exist. Objects that are local to a function are destroyed when the function exits. Static objects are destroyed when the program terminates. Finally, objects created on the heap are destroyed when the user uses the delete operator.

If we look back at the constructor definition above, we see that the member variables of the class are initialized in a special section, outside the statement part, introduced by a colon symbol. We give the name of a member variable and, in parentheses, the values that we want it to have. This initialization syntax is used only in constructors.

Another thing to keep in mind when defining classes is that if you don't include a public section, then everything is automatically private. This is rarely, though occasionally, useful. As a point of style, we name classes with capitalized words, member functions starting with a lowercase letter, and member variables beginning with an initial underscore character. This particular style isn't necessary, though it does make it easier to see what things are when reading code. Some style is very important to the readability of your programs. The standard template library itself uses a different capitalization convention. There, the class names are not capitalized, just as the built-in type names of C++

are not capitalized. We also use a style in which all grouping symbols such as "{" and "}" either line up horizontally on the same line or vertically.

Exercise. Examine the rest of the code of the StopWatch class provided with the code that came with this book. Devise a test of the code and run it. One way to do this is to take a program you have written previously and "instrument" it with one or more Stop-Watches to time its behavior. You will need to include StopWatch.h, of course, and link to StopWatch.cpp.

Here is another class that we shall use in future chapters. Class CountedInt defines very simple objects that merely keep a value that remembers the order of creation of objects of the class. This class contains a static data member c. Such a variable is not a member of each object of the class, as there is only one such variable for the entire class and all objects in the class have access to it. Notice that such a member must be initialized outside the class but at the global level. The scope resolution operator "::" must be used to access c. Static data is also called *shared* data, since it is shared among objects within a class. In this example, we have included the definitions of the member functions and constructors within the class itself.

```
class CountedInt
{  public:
      CountedInt(int x = 0)
         :  _order(c++),
            _value(x)
      {
      }

      CountedInt(const CountedInt& count)
         :  _order (c++),
            _value (count._value)
      {
      }

      CountedInt& operator=
         (const CountedInt& count)
      {  if(this != &count)
         {  _value = count._value;
         }
         return *this;
      }

      int getValue()const{ return _value; }

      void setValue(int v){ _value = v; }
```

```
        int getOrder()const{ return _order;}

    private:
        int _value;
        int _order;
        static int c;
};

int CountedInt::c = 0;
    // Initialize c from class CountedInt.
```

This class shows additional features as well. First, it is possible to give default values to parameters of functions in C++, including member functions. Here we have given the constructor CountedInt(int) a default parameter value of 0. This means that if we use the constructor and don't give an argument, then the value 0 will be assumed for x. This also means that this constructor serves as a default constructor, since it may be called without arguments.

Within the assignment operator=, we have used the reserved term this. Variable this is a pointer variable that points to the object that received the message that caused this code to be executed. It stands for the object in control of the computer at that time. The assignment operator = is treated as a message to the object on the lefthand side of operator =, with the object on the righthand side treated as a parameter. Here we check to see if this is the same object as count, by comparing this to the address at which count occurs. If they are the same, then this isn't really the assignment of a different object, so we do nothing. Otherwise we make the object known as this a copy of the parameter object. But since the assignment does not result in a new object (we had two objects before the assignment and we have two objects when we are done), we don't give a new value to the _order member variable. It retains the value that it had. The return statement returns the object to which the variable this points. Pointers and addresses will be taken up in detail in the next chapter.

Also note that two of the member functions are marked const by including this reserved word after the parameter list. This means that the member function will not try to modify the object this. In other words, it won't directly or indirectly modify any of the member variables of this class.

The copy constructor also illustrates that private features of a class are not private to the objects in the class only. They are really private to the member functions of the class. Therefore, within the class we may refer to the _value and _order members of any of the objects of the class, including those of the parameter object named count.

Exercise. Test the above class. Make certain that you have tested all constructors and member functions. Is it possible to modify the member variable _value from main?

1.3   Derived Classes. Object Orientation

In C++, one class can be derived from another, called the base. The meaning of this is that the derived class has all of the public features of the base class and may add additional features. We say that the derived class *inherits* the features of the base. The derived class can also give new procedure bodies to any of the member functions of the base class. This is not exactly the same as overloading, in which we have several functions in a class with the same name but different parameters. Here we have only a single function in different classes with the same parameters, but different implementations in the base and in the derived class. This is called overriding.

For example, suppose that we are building a spreadsheet program. We will use some container to hold the individual spreadsheet cells. It might be advantageous to (a) define the cells as a class, and (b) make the container hold pointers to this class. The cell class can define properties common to all spreadsheet cells, such as a getValue function. We can then derive additional classes from this cell class for the different kinds of cells in the spreadsheet. Some cells hold just a numeric value (NumericCell) and some hold a formula to be evaluated (FormulaCell). Each of these classes will define its own version of get-Value. The spreadsheet can then hold pointers to any of these specialized cells.

```
class SpreadsheetCell
{   public:
        SpreadsheetCell(...);
        double getValue();
    . . .
}


class NumericCell: public SpreadsheetCell
{   public:
        NumericCell(...);
        double getValue();
    . . .
}


class FormulaCell: public SpreadsheetCell
{   public:
        FormulaCell(...);
        double getValue();
    . . .
}
```

Notice that we declare the base class of a new derived class after a colon. We also make the inheritance public. This means that a client of the NumericCell class, for example, will be able to utilize features of the SpreadSheetCell class as well. Inheritance can also be private, though it is seldom used.

Derived classes do not have access to private members of their base classes. Some-times it is desirable to give derived classes access to some features that are not publicly visible. C++ provides an additional level of visibility control called protected. A protected member is visible to its own class and to any derived class. Some programmers make the implementation variables of a class protected. Others prefer to leave them private and to provide access functions to them. These access functions may be public or protected as necessary, depending on the specific needs. This latter method lessens the likelihood that a change in one class will necessitate a change in another class, even a derived class. For example, each cell of a spreadsheet has some format that is independent of whether the cell is numeric or formula. Assuming that we also have a Format type defined, we might have something like the following in our SpreadSheetCell class:

```
class SpreadsheetCell
{  public:
      SpreadsheetCell(...);
      double getValue();
   protected:
      Format getFormat();
      void setFormat(Format newFormat);
   private:
      Format _format;
   . . .
}

class NumericCell: public SpreadsheetCell
{  public:
      NumericCell(...);
      double getValue();
   . . .
}

class FormulaCell: public SpreadsheetCell
{  public:
      FormulaCell(...);
      double getValue();
   . . .
}
```

The derived classes will have access to getFormat() and setFormat(). This means that the member functions of these derived classes may call the protected functions, and may directly refer to protected variables if there are any. The ordinary clients of the cells will not have such access.

The best way to use inheritance is to conceptualize relationships between different kinds of data in your program. If one kind of data seems to be a specialization of another kind, then the more specialized kind is a good candidate for a derived class and the more generalized kind a good choice for its base class. Inheritance models specialization well and other relationships poorly. In particular, it models part relationships badly. An automobile is made up of parts: body, frame, engine, wheels, and so on. We don't use inheritance to model this relationship, however, but member variables. An Automobile object has a body member, a frame member, etc. On the other hand, there are different kinds of automobile engines. It might make sense to have a base class Engine, with derived classes for HighPerformanceEngine, Diesel Engine, and whatever other kinds are necessary.

The Standard Template Library does not depend heavily on object-oriented features of C++. Relatively little inheritance is involved in this library. In contrast, other libraries use inheritance extensively, some to the extent that every class is derived from a common base class. Some other object-oriented languages (Smalltalk, Modula-3, Java) make this a requirement, in fact.

Exercise. Suppose in a software library we needed both an Integer class and a Fraction class. Is either of these a good candidate for a base class of the other? Explain your answer thoroughly. Consider both the concepts involved and the use of the classes.

1.4   Templates

Templates are another important means of providing abstractions in C++. They permit us to define entire collections of functions or classes at once and then tailor them for use as needed. The STL depends fundamentally on this facility, as you can guess from the name. The basic idea of templates is that they allow us to write functions and classes in a very general way and then specialize them when they are actually put to use.

In C++ there are two different kinds of templates: *function templates* and *class templates*. Function templates are used when the same algorithm can be applied to different kinds of arguments. Class templates are used when the same class structure can utilize different types in the same way.

The most commonly seen example of a function template is one that defines the algorithm for swapping the values of two variables. As an ordinary function, if we want to swap the values in two integer variables we would write the following:

```
void swap(int& a, int& b)
{   int temp = a;
    a = b;
    b = temp;
}
```

We desire to generalize this, of course, since exactly the same algorithm works for floats, or indeed any assignable data types. We can do so with a function template as follows:

```
template <class T>
void swap(T& a, T& b)
{   T temp = a;
    a = b;
    b = temp;
}
```

To define this template we have done two things. We replaced all occurrences of the type int with a *template parameter* symbol T, and we indicated that we wanted a function template instead of a function by including the template preamble to the function definition. In this context, the template parameter T is defined in angle brackets, "<" and ">," and it is preceded by the word *class*. This use of class is not related to classes as defined above, but simply means that the parameter is required to be a type.

A function template defines a family of functions, one for each possible set of values of the parameters. Yes, you can have several parameters. We use such a function template simply by calling one or more of the functions that it defines. For example,

```
int x = 5, y = 3;
swap(x, y);
float r = 5.2, s = 1.1;
swap(r, s);
```

The system will create two different functions for us using the function template. These *template functions* will be able to swap ints and floats respectively. The function template mechanism is a function factory facility, since it creates functions as needed.

Class templates are used when we write one class that must depend on another type, but that other might be different for different uses. For example, a set needs to contain objects of some kind, but what kind is of little importance when we define what we mean by a set. Therefore, instead of defining set as a class, it would be better to define it as a class template, and let the user decide what kind of object should be put into his or her sets.

Extending the example above, in which we built a class of counted ints, there was no reason that we needed to restrict ourselves to type int. We could instead have provided a class template so that we could count creations in any kind of values. Consider how we do this. First we come up with a name: CountedValue. Then we decide on a name for our parameter: V. Then we replace all occurrences of int that refer to the value collected, by the parameter V and precede the whole by a template preamble. We will have a few difficulties in this particular case.

```
template <class V>
class CountedValue
{   public:
        CountedValue(V x)
        :  _order(c++),
           _value(x)
```

```
    {
    }

    CountedValue(const CountedValue& count)
    {   _order = c++;
        _value = count._value;
    }

    CountedValue& operator=
        (const CountedValue& count)
    {   if(this != &count)
        {   _value = count._value;
        }
        return *this;
    }

    V getValue()const{ return _value;}

    void setValue(V v){ _value = v;}

    int getOrder()const{ return _order;}

  private:
    V _value;
    int _order;
    static int c;
};
```

The first difficulty is that it is harder to give default values to parameters here, since we don't know their types when we write the template. One possibility is to use V() as the default value, as this syntax will construct a default value of type V, provided that V is a type that provides a default constructor.

To use a class template, the user must explicitly give a value to the template parameter. For example,

```
CountedValue<int> cvi (5);
CountedValue<double> cvd (4.1);
```

will define a new counted integer value and a counted double. Note that these objects are from two different classes. A class template creates classes. The template mechanism for classes is a type manufacturing facility.

The second difficulty concerns the initialization of static data, such as our variable c. We can't provide for this in general, as we don't have template variables. We need to explicitly initialize these values for each class that we intend to instantiate. This must be done before we can execute the above definitions of cvi and cvd. Since the static variable is private, this initialization must be done at the global level, outside of any function:

```
int CountedValue<int>::c = 0;
int CountedValue<double>::c = 0;
```

This is not much of a problem in practice, as static members are quite rare in C++.

What types may be substituted for template parameters? C++ does not in itself place any restriction on the type that may be used to instantiate a class template. However, the code of the template itself may place restrictions. Some of these restrictions don't look like restrictions at all until you really understand the working of C++, and especially its constructors and operator structure. For example, in the template CountedValue, the parameter V appears once as the type of a parameter. This means that we may pass such a value, which requires the presence of a copy constructor. If we attempt to instantiate CountedValue with a type that does not support copy construction, then we will fail, with a compiler message. All of the built-in types do support copying and most user-defined classes will also. Some classes purposely fail to provide this mechanism. Such classes can't be used with our CountedValue template.

Question. What other restrictions do we impose on type V in the CountedValue template?

It is very important to realize and remember that C++ templates impose restrictions on template parameters only through use of those parameters. This is very different from the types given to function parameters in which the restriction is made by the type system and not by the uses to which the parameter is put. So, when we define a function and say that one of its parameters must be of type int, then no values are possible except int values (and those compatible with int). The restriction on the parameter is not there because we happen to use an int operation, but because the declaration itself imposes it. This is not the case with template parameters.

It is possible to define class templates (but not function templates) in which the parameters are values rather than types. One example simulates Pascal's range type. A range is an integer value (more generalized in Pascal, actually) that has legal values only in some fixed range, such as the integers between 10 and 20, inclusive. We can give the Low and High bounds of the range as template parameters. We present an excerpt from this class template here:

```
template <int Low, int High>
class Range
{ public:
     Range(int v = Low)
      : _value(v)
     { if(Low > High)
           userERROR("Illegal Range type.");
       if(_value<Low || _value>High)
```

```
        userERROR("Range error.");
    }

  Range<Low, High> & operator =
      (const int v)
    { if(v<Low || v>High)
        userERROR("Range error.");
      _value = v;
      return *this;
    }

    int first(){return Low;}

    int last() {return High;}

    operator int() // Produce an int
    {   return _value;
    }

    . . .

  private:
    int _value;

}; // Could provide additional operators.
```

Then a range variable would be created with

```
Range<10, 20> x = 10;
```

If the appropriate operators are included, then all changes to the variable can be checked for the validity of the new values. We can therefore guarantee that x is always within range.

Newer versions of C++ even permit template parameters to have default values. For example, we could give the range variable defaults that make them equivalent to ints with the following:

```
template <int Low = minint, int High = maxint>
class Range
{ . . . }
```

If available, default template parameters apply also to type (<class...>) parameters. The STL depends on this feature, and if it is not present, the STL can be only partially implemented.

There is one special difficulty with using templates, especially if you are a novice. Since templates are not compiled until they are actually used by a program, it is both difficult to test a template and difficult to read the error messages produced by compilers when you make errors in a template definition. To test them correctly, you need to test every part with a variety of different arguments so that you don't make subtle assumptions about the requirements of the template. A minimum test for a template intended to be used with most (or all) types uses a built-in type such as int, a pointer type such as char*, and a user-defined struct or class type.

The error message problem is especially frustrating. It is often difficult to decide what to do when you get an error message in a template. Often the errors are caused by inconsistency between the features of the argument type and the needs of the template. For example, if a certain operator is applied to a value of the template parameter type within the template, then that operator must be supplied by the actual argument used to instantiate the template. It is worth the effort to construct an example in which this is not the case, so that you see the message that will be produced by your compiler in this situation. For example, with the following function template:

```
template <class T>
void junkt(T t) {cout << *t;}
```

and the instantiation/call

```
junkt(5);
```

one of my compilers flags an error within the template (not the call) that indicates that a pointer or an array is required. The problem is not in the template, but in the call, however. Yes, a pointer or array is required to de-reference, but that is obvious. What the compiler did not do, however, was show me which of possibly several instantiations (calls), caused the message to occur.

1.5   Which Data Abstractions Are Useful?

The question posed in the title of this section is without a complete answer, as it is limited only by human ingenuity. Any time we can think of a binding of data and operations, with rules defining the behavior of the operations, we have a good candidate for a data abstraction.

One set of abstractions used frequently today defines modern computer interfaces: the so-called GUIs or Graphical User Interfaces. Window is one abstraction in this set. The data elements define rectangular regions of a display. The operations open, close, paint, and move these regions, as well as adorn them with controls. The controls themselves form another subset of the abstractions of a GUI. The data define current settings and default behavior of things like scroll bars or buttons. The operations connect the user's movements with the mouse to changes in the display. It is not our purpose in this book to take up the details of such data abstractions.

Another class of abstractions define numeric objects of various kinds. for example, int and float are built-in data abstractions in C++ as well as in many other languages. A user-defined abstraction could be built to define rational numbers (fractions) made up of a numerator and a denominator. Another could define complex numbers with real and imaginary parts. Here the operations would be mostly arithmetic. We would want operator+ and operator<, for example.

Similar to this, and very useful in C++, is a String abstraction, that makes manipulation of character strings less error-prone and more convenient than is possible when using char* values. For example, we could overload operator+ to provide a string catenation operation, as is done with the built-in string class of C++.

Some abstractions come from the problem domain in which we happen to be working. For example, a game programmer might want an abstraction of a game board. This abstraction would allow for user pieces to be moved according to rules of the game. A programmer developing medical systems might attempt to build an abstraction of an automated pharmacy that would dispense drugs based on symptoms of patients. In the aircraft industry, programmers use abstractions of aircraft flight surfaces and behaviors. These kind of abstractions are quite specialized to a single industry, or even to a single project.

One very useful class of data abstractions is that of *containers*. A container contains values of some kind, or references (actually pointers) to values of some kind. An example of a container is a set. Another kind of container is a list. The difference between a set and a list is that a list imposes a physical, though not necessarily a logical, ordering on the elements that it contains. A set imposes nothing on the values it contains other than the fact of containment. We have a lot to say about containers, as they are one major component of the Standard Template Library. In some other libraries, containers are called collections—they collect values. It turns out that containers are closely related to other data abstractions called iterators. Iterators are used to refer to the individual elements of containers and to provide the means of applying operations to the contents of containers. Think of some numbers written on a blackboard at the front of a room as being a container. Think of sitting a few feet away with a laser pointer (a finely focused light beam) that you can use to point to any one of the numbers. You can point to only one at a time, but you can easily move the pointer from number to number. To add up all the numbers, you could start with a running sum of zero and then point to each of the numbers in turn, adding that number to the running sum. When you had visited (iterated over) each of the elements exactly once, you would have the sum. Yes, iterators do something like what is done with integers and for loops. That similarity is part of the design of iterators.

1.6   Abstractions Provided by the STL

The data abstractions provided by the Standard Template Library fall into several categories. First there are the container classes and their iterators. The algorithms that manipulate containers are a separate category. Additionally, there are function objects, adaptors, and allocators. Function objects give us a way to specify characteristics of the objects stored in containers. Adaptors modify either the interface or the behavior of some other component, and allocators give us control over how the system allocates space for our objects. While there are many parts, they all revolve around the container classes, and the other components merely support containers. There are eight basic container types of two kinds. The sequential containers are arrays, vectors, deques, and lists. The associative containers are sets, multisets, maps, and multimaps. In addition, adaptors may be used to transform these containers into three additional forms: stacks, queues, and priority queues. There are versions of the STL that also include hash table containers. For the rest of this chapter, we will examine these container-based data abstractions conceptually. We will look at each of them again in detail in a later chapter. We will also look at how some of them might be useful in developing programs of various kinds.

Arrays represent densely stored blocks of cells of some type. The dense storage permits any individual cell to be quickly accessed. Arrays in the STL are the built in arrays of C++. They have fixed size. The dense storage permits the system to compute the actual position of any cell from its relative position in the container. Because of the speed of retrieval, arrays support many sophisticated algorithms efficiently. Arrays are the abstraction of choice if the problem requires fast retrieval, or the data must be sorted into logical order. Arrays are discussed in detail in Chapter 2. Much of the STL can be considered to be a generalization of features of arrays. The main operations on arrays are storage into and retrieval from a cell indicated by its relative position in the storage. In an array A, the first cell is denoted A[0]. If the array has n cells, then the last cell is A[n-1]. Arrays are used throughout computer science for many tasks, including the implementation of other structures. Two dimensional arrays are just arrays in which the elements stored are also arrays. A spreadsheet is just a two-dimensional array. A graphics screen is a two-dimensional array of picture elements or pixels.

Vectors are similar to arrays except that they may be enlarged at one end to hold additional data. They may also be shrunk at that same end. They support efficient retrieval, though not quite as efficiently as arrays. Vectors support the same algorithms as arrays and a few more that require variable size containers. In addition to the storage/retrieval operations of arrays, vectors support the push_back(T) operation that extends the length of the vector and inserts the (template parameter) value at the end. Similarly, pop_back() will remove the last item, shrinking the size of the vector. Vectors are used in graphics to hold lists of figures to be drawn or lists of points to be connected.

Deque, pronounced as in "deck of cards," sometimes spelled dequeue, is an acronym for double-ended queue. A deque is also similar to an array except that it can grow and shrink at either end. The dense storage again permits rapid retrievals. Deques permit push_front() and pop_front() in addition to vector operations.

Lists don't use dense storage. Instead the cells of a list are linked together using pointers or addresses of logically adjacent cells. The individual cell of a list may be physically anywhere in memory. From a given cell it is efficient to access only the immediately preceding and the immediately following cells, if any. This means that some algorithms are not appropriate for lists, as the accessing of elements would be too inefficient. On the other hand, lists make it possible to insert values efficiently between existing values, which is an expensive operation with Vectors and Deques. Therefore Lists are used where we desire the maximum flexibility in insertion and deletion of cells at any point in the container. An algorithm will be efficient on lists provided that we can execute the algorithm by processing the elements in the order of the cells in the list. Otherwise, it is likely to be very inefficient. Because it is sometimes necessary to sort lists into a given, logical order, and because the generalized algorithms appropriate to Vectors and Deques would be inefficient on Lists, the List class template defines a sort member function that works well on lists, but would not work well on those other types. Lists are much more useful than this brief introduction suggests. They are used extensively in artificial intelligence and they permit highly complex programs to be written. The language lisp is built of sophisticated uses of lists.

Among the sorted associative containers, sets are intended to behave like the sets of mathematics. We can form unions and intersections, for example, as well as insert and remove elements. Multisets are similar except that they permit an element to be contained several times, while a set permits an element to be present only once if at all. Sometimes multisets are called bags.

A map container is a set of pairs of a certain kind. These pairs consist of keys and associated information, where the key is used to define uniqueness of pairs. A pair is said to *associate* the additional information with its key. Sometimes these pairs are called associations. Generally, two pairs are considered equal if their keys are equal. A set of these, a map, therefore implements something like a dictionary where the keys are the words to be looked up and the information is the definitions. An alternate name for map is dictionary, in fact. A map can also be thought of as implementing a function, where the set of keys is the domain and the set of information values is the range. Because of the equality relationship on pairs, if a map contains (1,2) and we wish to insert (1,3), then (1,2) must be removed since a map is like a set, and (1,2) and (1,3) are equal.

A multimap is like a map, except that a given pair may be present more than once, or more precisely, two pairs with the same key may be present at the same time. Therefore (1,2) and (1,3) may be in a multimap simultaneously. Maps and multimaps implement simple kinds of databases in which we store and later look up data according to its keys. Maps and multimaps are used extensively in artificial intelligence and in logic programming. The programming language Prolog depends fundamentally on the idea of a map.

A stack, which can be formed from a vector, deque, or list by applying an adaptor, is a container in which all insertions and retrievals are at one end. The push operation inserts an item at this end and the pop operation removes the most recently inserted item. A stack implements a storage strategy called last-in, first-out, or LIFO. Stacks are used extensively in programming and are indispensable in compilers and in the management of runtime systems. We can often do processing on complex data structures such as trees and certain kinds of graphs by employing stacks.

A queue is a container that supports insertions at one end and deletion at the other. Queues may be effectively created from deques and lists by applying an adaptor. Queues are used in operating systems programming and in simulations of complex systems in which events occur at random times and must be handled in the order in which they occur, but in which a time delay may occur before they can be handled. We simply insert the events in a queue when they occur and remove them when we are ready to handle them. Queues have a protocol called first-in, first-out, or FIFO.

Priority queues are similar to queues except that the item that is removed is not the item that has been in the queue for the longest time, but the one with the largest value. The values are considered to be priorities and we always remove the item of highest priority. Priority queues can be efficiently created from vectors and deques by applying an adaptor. Priority queues are used in operating systems to keep track of user jobs that are waiting to execute. We always run the job with the highest priority when a processor becomes available. The previously running job is returned to the queue, perhaps with an adjusted priority, if it has not completed when it was interrupted.

In the STL, containers are homogeneous. This means that they store elements of the same kind. The type of element stored in a container is specified by its template argument. Thus we have list<int> and list<Window>. Because of the object-oriented features of C++, it is possible to store things in containers that are not precisely of the same kind, but of related kinds. To do so, however, requires pointers. This will be taken up in the next chapter.

1.7   Summary

Make certain that you understand each of the following terms:

array
base class
class
class template
constructor
containers
copy constructor
coupling
data abstraction
default constructor
deque
derived class
destructor
encapsulation
function template
information hiding
inheritance

instantiation (of a template)
iterators
list
map
multimap
multiset
overloaded operator
override
priority queue
private member
protected member
public member
queue
set
stack
static member
vector

1.8   Exercises

1. A standard list of ints may be defined by using

```
#include <list.h>

list<int> testList;
```

Try the following code:

```
#include <iostream.h>
#include <STL.h>
#include "stopWatch.h"

StopWatch watch;
list<int> ml;

void main(void)
{   watch.start();watch.mark();
    int pwr = 1;
    for(int i = 0; i < 50; ++i)
    {   ml.push_back(pwr);
        pwr *= 2;
    }
    list<int>::iterator w;
```

```
for(w = ml.begin(); w != ml.end(); ++w)
    cout << *w << ' ';
cout << endl;
w = max_element(ml.begin(), ml.end());
cout<< "Max is: "<< *w <<endl;
cout << "Size is "<< ml.size()<<endl;
watch.mark();
int query;
cout<< "Enter a positive number. "<<endl;
cin >> query;
query = abs(query);
int count = 0;
for
( w = ml.begin()
; w != ml.end() && *w < query
; ++w
)
++count;
if(*w != query)
{   --count;
    --w;
}
cout   <<"two to the "<<count<<" = "
        << *(w)<<endl;
}
```

Some entries produced by the above may be unexpected. Modify the above code to erase them.

Use push_front instead of push_back. Modify the query so that it is consistent with this change. We want to return the largest power of two that is not greater than the query.

What happens when you make the following errors? Run the code and verify your answers.

```
#include <iostream.h>
#include <STL.h>

StopWatch watch;
list ml;

void main(void)
{   watch.start();watch.mark();
    cout << ml.front() << endl;
    ml.pop_back();
    ml.pushBack(123);
}
```

2. Create a template class to define a die, in which the number of faces of the die is an integer template parameter rather than an argument to a constructor of an individual die. What tradeoffs are there between the two approaches?

3. Add a member to the die class to obtain the number of faces of the die. Make this a function. Don't just make the number of faces a public member variable.

4. Add a member function to the die class to obtain the value of the last roll without rolling it again. What else do you need to add to the class to make this feasible?

5. Prove that the static variable c in the counted value class is always equal to the number of counted values that have been created since the beginning of the program.

6. Add another static variable to the counted value class that is always equal to the number of counted values in existence in the program. Recall that destructors are called when an object is deleted for any reason. Give the class a member function so that the value of this variable may be obtained.

7. Write a program that rolls a standard (6-sided) die 720 times. (a). How long does it take for this program to run? Use a StopWatch object to find out. (b). How many 6s do you get in 720 rolls? How many do you expect to get?

8. How many pairs of 6s do you get in 720 rolls of a die? A pair of 6s is defined to be a 6 on an odd-numbered roll and another on the next even-numbered roll.

9. How many pairs of 6s do you get in 720 rolls of a die? A pair of 6s is defined to be a six on any roll and another on the next roll. Note that four 6s in a row would be counted as three pairs.

10. Save 120 rolls of a die in a list<int>, using push_back to insert new items. Then write out the list to see what it contains. Use an iterator to write it out. How long does this take? Repeat with a vector<int>. If you don't see any difference in time, try it with 1200 rolls instead. What can you conclude about the relative performance of lists and vectors?

11. Save 120 rolls of a die in a list<int>. Use the sort member function of list to sort your list. Write out the contents using an iterator. The prototype is:

```
void list<int>::sort()
```

How long does the sort take? How long does it take to sort 1,200 items in a list?

12. Save 120 rolls of a die in a vector<int>. Use the generic algorithm sort to sort your list. Write out the contents using an iterator. The prototype is

```
void sort(iterator first, iterator afterLast)
```

How long does the sort take? How long does it take to sort 1,200 items in a vector?

Chapter 2
Programming with Arrays and Pointers

In this chapter we will learn about programming with arrays and pointers. In the Standard Template Library, arrays and pointers are one fundamental component, though they are unchanged from standard C++. Most of the major features of the STL are generalizations and abstractions based on features of arrays and pointers.

2.1   Arrays

An *array* is a block of memory consisting of several items of the same kind. These items are called components of the array. The components are arranged sequentially, one after the other, in computer memory. The computer will store the array with no wasted space in a single block of data as in Figure 2.1. This storage method is sometimes called *dense* or *contiguous* storage. An array has a fixed number of components, defined at the time the array is created.

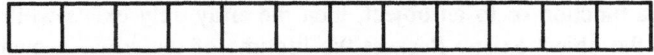

Figure 2.1. An Array.

There are two ways to define an array in C++. We are required to give the type of components of the array as well as its length in the definition. The easiest is to use a definition like the following, which defines an array of 12 doubles.

```
double monthlySalary[12];
```

This definition actually defines two things, which are most often treated as if there were only one. The first thing created is the array itself. If doubles require 4 bytes of storage, then this array will require a single block of 48 bytes. The second thing created is the address of this block. The address of the block is also the address of the first component of the block. The name monthlySalary actually has a value equal to this address. The location of a component of an array is called a *cell*. The individual cells of the array are named monthlySalary[0] through monthlySalary[11]. See Figure 2.2. These cells are variables like any other and can hold a value that can be changed. monthlySalary itself is a constant, meaning that it will always refer to this same block of data. Notice that the length of the array is 12, and, since we start with a cell numbered 0, there is no cell numbered 12. But note that monthlySalary[12] is the address of the location immediately following the array.

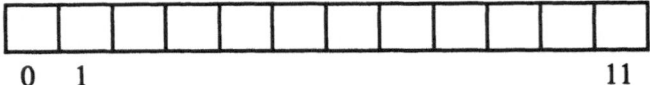

Figure 2.2. An Array with markings indicating cell numbers.

When used as a cell number, an integer is called a *subscript*. This comes from mathematical usage that would probably write A_i, for the computer scientist's A[i]. A subscript is also called an *index*.

A very common pattern of use of arrays is the following for loop, which reads 12 doubles from the standard input and assigns them to the 12 components of the array:

```
for (int i = 0; i < 12; ++i)
    cin >> monthlySalary[i];
```

Notice from the above that subscript expressions may, in fact, be variables. They may also be arbitrarily complex integer-valued expressions. C++ has no restrictions here.

The location of the block of data defined by the array definition is up to the compiler to arrange. If an array definition appears at the global level or is marked static, then the block will continue to exist as long as your program continues to run. If the definition is local to a function or to an object, then the array only exists while the function is running or the object exists. Because the lifetime of the array is managed by the system, such data are often called *automatic*. This applies to all data, not just to arrays.

Be careful with array definitions. The following defines a single double (called a *scalar* to distinguish it from an array) and an array.

```
double thisMonth, monthlySalary[12];
```

One of the important things to remember about arrays defined as above is that their sizes are determined at compile time. It is not legal to use a variable expression as the size of an array defined in this way.

2.1.1   An Example. A Guessing Game

Suppose we are building a game program in which the player guesses integer numbers. Suppose that the game needs to remember the guesses made by the player in the order that they are made. One way to do this is to create an array whose length is the maximum number of guesses allowed, together with an auxiliary variable called an index.

```
long guess[ 10 ];
int nextGuess = 0;
```

Then, when a guess is made by the player, we execute

```
guess[ nextGuess ] = playerGuess;
nextGuess++;
```

which first uses that value as a subscript into the array to determine the component into which we save the player's guess and then increments the index. We can, of course, combine these two statements into the single one:

```
guess[ nextGuess++ ] = playerGuess;
```

Finally, we can process all of the guesses actually made with

```
for(int i = 0; i < nextGuess; i++)
    ... guess[ i ] ...
```

For automatic arrays the built-in function `sizeof` will tell us the number of bytes required by the array. We can apply `sizeof` to either a value, such as a variable, or to a type. If we want the number of components, we can divide the size of the array by the size of the component.

2.1.2   Another Example. Array of Objects

Often we want to create arrays in which the components are to be a user-defined type, especially a type defined by a class. There are special requirements that enable this to be done. C++ requires a class used in this way to have a default constructor: a constructor with no parameters. Since all classes should have such a constructor anyway, and since C++ will provide one if you don't provide any constructors at all, this is a light requirement.

Recall the CountedInt class from Chapter 1. This class has a default constructor since we may call one of the constructors with no arguments. Now we can fill an array with CountedInt values and look at what we have.

```
void main()
{  CountedInt All [10];
        // The default constructor is called for each cell.
    for(int i = 0; i < 10; i++)
       cout << All[i].getOrder() << endl;
}
```

Exercise. Test the above code. First anticipate what it will produce. Were you correct?

2.2   Pointers and Arrays

The second way to define an array actually splits the definitions of the two parts (name and block) into two definitions. We may define a variable that will be used to refer to an array of doubles with

```
double* dailyCosts;
```

Here, the variable dailyCosts is defined to be a **pointer** variable. While pointers can be used in many ways in C++, one of the most important is to make them "point to" arrays. Note that dailyCosts is a variable, not a constant, and so it could hold different values at different times. The above declaration does not give it any value, however. It is useful to give every variable some value, and C++ provides a value named NULL for use in initializing pointer variables. This is normally just the constant 0, but it guarantees the pointer has a specific value that can be tested. A better definition of dailyCosts would be

```
double* dailyCosts = NULL;
```

This both defines the variable, and initializes its value. This looks like an assignment, but it is technically not. It is an initialization.

None of the above defines an array, just a variable that could be used to refer to an array. We could actually define such a variable and make it point to our monthlySalary array with

```
double* someSalary = monthlySalary;
```

This assumes that monthlySalary was previously defined. This defines someSalary as an alias of monthlySalary, and someSalary could be used just as monthlySalary is used. An alias is a name that refers to the same thing, usually a variable, as another name. Note that someSalary is a variable, while monthlySalary (as a name) is a constant. We could set the sixth monthly salary using an assignment such as

```
someSalary[5] = 1200.0;
    // Set the sixth monthly salary.
```

However, since someSalary is a variable, it can be used to refer to any array of doubles (or to any single double, for that matter). One way to make someSalary refer to an array is to create the array at run time. The computer reserves a large amount of storage in a structure called the *free store* or *heap*, which can be used to create new values as the program runs. We always refer to values in the free store with pointers, though pointers may refer to locations elsewhere as well. We create these values in the free store by using the C++ operator new. Operator new creates variables that are called *dynamic*. The lifetimes of dynamic values are determined by the programmer, they are not automatic.

```
someSalary = new double[6];
```

creates a new array of 6 doubles on the free store and assigns a value to someSalary, which is the address of, or a pointer to, this block of data. This is shown in Figure 2.3. Having done this, someSalary[0] through someSalary[5] are defined and legal, though the computing system will not be able to detect an expression like someSalary[8] as an error. An important lesson to learn about arrays is that the legality of subscript expressions is up to the programmer to guarantee. The system provides little help here.

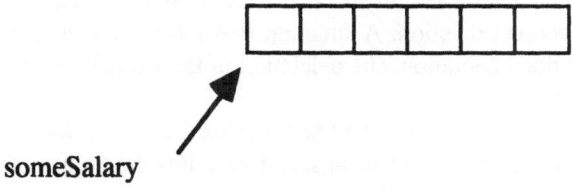

someSalary

Figure 2.3. A pointer variable and the value it points to.

The C++ system does not guarantee a particular layout of memory, so the following may not work exactly as shown, but some variant will. Suppose we define two automatic arrays with

```
long array1[5], array2[5];
```

Then array1[9] might well refer to the same component as array2[4]. This would be the case if array2 were laid out exactly after array1 in the memory.

Exercise. Try the above on your computer and report on what you learn.

We need to distinguish between the pointer variable that refers to an array and the array itself. Given the above, someSalary is an automatic variable that refers to a dynamic value. If someSalary were local to a function, then its lifetime would end when the function returns. The array itself, however, continues to exist until the programmer deletes it using something like

```
delete [] someSalary; // Delete an array.
```

The delete operator is the inverse of new. It returns previously defined free store values to the heap. Note that delete is used for other values besides arrays. To use the above, however, we would need to write it in a place where the name someSalary is defined. It is possible for a dynamic value to outlive the variable used to create it. Consider the following:

```
double* getNewSalaries()
{   double* result = new double[12];
    for(int i = 0; i < 12; ++i)
        cin >> result[i];
    return result;
}
```

This function creates and returns an array. Notice that the variable `result` is automatic and ceases to be at the end of this function. The array itself, however, is returned to the caller. Actually, the array itself isn't returned. A pointer to it is returned. The array itself just continues to exist in the free store. It is then the responsibility of the caller to see to its eventual deletion. A function that returns a new dynamic value should clearly say so in its documentation, since deletion of the value becomes the responsibility of the caller.

Automatic arrays in C++ may be initialized with constant values. Suppose, for example, that we need an array of strings, and we know the values of these strings in advance. Then we may define and initialize the array at once with something like

```
char* days[ ] =
    {   "Sun", "Mon", "Tues", "Wed",
        "Thur", "Fri", "Sat"
    };
```

Here days is an array of seven strings (char *). Note that we let the system count the length of the array for us. We could have made it explicit by writing the seven between the brackets also. The system will create the array defined by the initializer and make days a constant pointer to it. We could write out the contents of this array with

```
for(int i = 0; i< 7; ++i)
    cout << days[i]<<endl;
```

We cannot initialize dynamic arrays in the same way. The problem is that a dynamic array must exist before we can give its components values, while an initialization such as the above must exist before the pointer that is to refer to it. In particular, the following will not work.

```
long* values = new long[5];
    // Create a new dynamic array.
values = { 2, 3, 5, 7, 11 };
```

At the end of this sequence, `values` will be pointing to a static array and the dynamic array on the free store has no pointer pointing to it. It is a lost block in the heap that cannot be recovered while the program runs. In general, you should never follow a free store allocation by an assignment to the same variable. Between such statements you should either delete the item or create an alias, so that you always have at least one should either delete the item or create an alias, so that you always have at least one pointer to each free store item. This is true of arrays as well as other things in the free store.

If you define an array dynamically, the sizeof function won't tell you the size of the array if you apply it to a pointer to the array. This is because you are asking for the size of a pointer (often 4 bytes), not the size of the array. Therefore, the sizeof(days) will probably be 4. If you ask for sizeof(*days), you will likely get 1, the size of a char. The best way to know the size of a dynamic block is to remember it when you allocate it. Save the length you use in a variable.

2.3   Pointer Arithmetic

If we have a pointer variable, we often need the thing that it points to. The prefix operator `*` is called the dereferencing operator, and it will give us the value to which a pointer points. For example, in the above string example, the array variable days is a pointer that points to the beginning of the array. In other words, it points to its first component (days[0]). Therefore, *days and days[0] may be used interchangeably.

We can also always create a pointer value. Suppose that we have a double value salary. We can create a pointer to it with &salary.

```
double salary = 4500.00;
double* aliasOfSalary = &salary;
```

Now salary and *aliasOfSalary are variables that refer to the same entity, namely the 4500.00. Thus the following will increase the salary by 2000.

```
salary += 1000.00;
*aliasOfSalary += 1000.00;
```

Thus "&" and "*" are inverse operators. One gives us an address from a value, and the other a value from an address.

We can apply the above to arrays and array components as well.

```
double* sal = &monthlySalary[4];
```

gives us, in sal, the address of monthlySalary[4]. Notice that we are using two operators in this expression, operator& and operator[]. The latter has the higher precedence, so this is the address of monthlySalary[4], not the fifth component of &monthlySalary (which doesn't really exist since &monthlySalary isn't an array).

Some arithmetic operators can be applied to pointers. In particular, an integer may be added to or subtracted from any pointer, and the difference between two pointers (to the same type of thing) may be computed. The meaning is illustrated in the following examples:

```
long values [ ] =
   {   10, 20, 30, 40, 50,
       60, 70, 80, 90, 100
   };
long* somewhere = values;   // Points to the 10.
somewhere++;                // Points to the 20.
cout << (*somewhere) + 2;      // Prints 22.
cout << *(somewhere + 2);      // Prints 40.
cout << *somewhere + 2;        // Prints 22.
cout << *(somewhere + 22);
   // Prints garbage outside array.
cout << somewhere - values;
   // Prints 1; the number of components
   // between the two values.
cout << *somewhere - *values; // Prints 10.
```

Note that the addition operator has lower precedence than the dereferencing operator. We can generate a pointer to the cell immediately following our array values with

```
long * afterEnd = &values[10];
```

or equivalently with

```
long * afterEnd = values + 10; // See below.
```

It would not be safe to de-reference this pointer, but we shall see that we will eventually need this value in the STL.

If we have an array A, then A is a pointer and the expression &A[i] is exactly the same as the expression A+i. In fact, the *pointer duality law* specifies the equivalence of these two expressions. Note that A+i does not refer to a location i *bytes* past the beginning of A, but the location i *components* after A. This will be true independent of the component type of the array. The pointer duality law can also be written as A[i] is equivalent to *(A+i).

Using the pointer duality law implies that the following for loop will process all of the elements of our array, values.

```
for(long* p = values; p < values + 10; ++p)
   cout << *p;
```

What can happen if you are not careful about your array subscripts and equivalent pointer expressions? That depends on whether you are reading values or writing them. If you are reading values from the "array" and your subscript does not fall in legal bounds, then you will get a value, but the value will be meaningless. The computer will interpret the values retrieved as if they had the component type, but, of course, they may not. It is for this reason that (a) you get garbage, and (b) it is hard to recognize it as such, since it has the correct form.

If you are attempting to place data into the array (write the array), then the situation is much worse. If you write into a valid cell then you change it, of course. If you write into an illegal cell, one outside the legal bounds, then you change something. That location in the computer memory is probably being used for something else, and when the value of that item is later retrieved, it will not have the last value that was correctly placed into it, but some value placed by our incorrect reference. There is no guarantee that the value written has the same type as the value read, but any sequence of bits can be interpreted according to (nearly) any type, so the user of that other data item will find a legal value, but the wrong value.

In the worst case, on some computers you can do serious damage by making illegal array references. For example, on many small computers, a technique called memory-mapped I/O is used in which physical devices such as disks and printers are installed in such a way that they look just like memory. They are controlled by "writing" into their device control registers, which are just memory locations. If an out-of-bounds array reference were to accidentally write to a device register, that device would do something. Perhaps, if it were a disk drive, it would erase that disk. This would be a very unhappy event.

A few final words on pointer arithmetic. Notice that it is *bidirectional*. You can subtract from a pointer just as you can add. Therefore, continuing the above examples, `afterEnd - 1` is a pointer to the last cell of our array.

Actually, pointers are more than just bidirectional. They are actually *random access*. This means that from a pointer to any cell in the array, we can move immediately, in one step to any other cell. For example, suppose that `third` is a pointer to the third cell of some array. Then `third + 5` is automatically a pointer to the eighth cell, if such exists. Using the pointer duality law, if A[i] represents the third cell, then A[i+5] represents the eighth. In either case we can move from any cell to any other, without visiting the intervening, or any other, cells.

Finally, we may subtract two pointers into the same array. Thus, again referring to the array values from above, `afterEnd - values` is the number of components of the array: 10. Note again that it is not the number of bytes of storage occupied by the array. Indeed, some computers are not even byte-oriented. Rather, it is the number of cells between the two pointers.

2.4   Arrays with More than One Dimension

In C++ multiple dimension arrays are not technically possible. It is, however, possible to define arrays whose components are arrays, and this has much the same effect. We can give an alternate definition of our days array with

```
char days[7][5] =
    {  "Sun", "Mon", "Tues", "Wed",
       "Thur", "Fri", "Sat"
    };
```

Here we have an array of 7 arrays, each of 5 characters. We describe the array as "7 by 5" or as having 7 rows and 5 columns. See Figure 2.4. We need the "inner" arrays to hold 5 characters, since Thur has four letters plus the terminating null character. The extra character is wasted in the other names, except Tues, of course. In C++ we may have an arbitrary number of dimensions in this way, but be careful, since the size of the resulting structure is the product of the sizes in the individual dimensions and the size of the ultimate component type, here char. A large number of dimensions could result in a very large structure, even if the length in each dimension is small. Sometimes an array with two dimensions is called a matrix.

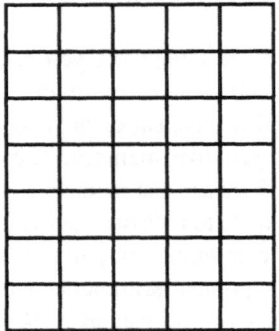

Figure 2.4. A Matrix with 7 rows and 5 columns.

This new declaration of days defines a slightly different structure than the original, however. In this new definition it is clear that there are a few wasted bytes, since each interior array is required to have five, though most of the values stored require only four. In the original, this wasted space will not be present. The former method of definition is somewhat more flexible because it admits components of differing sizes. The first definition of days defines an array whose components are pointers to characters. The second defines one whose components are arrays of characters. Similar, but not quite the same. Use sizeof to discover the difference.

Just as we can get access to the individual strings by indexing, we can also get access to the individual characters, though we need to use double indexing.

```
days[ 2 ] [ 0 ];   // Refers to the T of Tues.
days[ 5 ] [ 2 ];   // Refers to the i of Fri.
days[ 4 ];         // Refers to the array
                   // containing Thur.
```

Exercise. Prove that if array has declaration:

```
int array[A][B]
```

that &array[m][n] is the same as array + B*m + n.

2.5   Putting It Together. An Application

One of the topics in artificial intelligence is machine learning. In this section we present a simple game that learns from its mistakes. It is almost too simple to be called artificial intelligence, but it is only intended to introduce you to the concept and to show programming with arrays.

The French Military Game is played on a graph with 11 nodes, numbered 0 to 10. The game has two sides: the Police and the Fox. The Fox has only one piece that begins the game at cell 5. The Police has 3 pieces, originally at 0, 1, and 3. The Police moves first and the players alternate. On a turn each side may move one piece along one of the arcs. The object of the Fox is to reach cell 0. The Police, who may only move vertically and to the right, has the objective of trapping the Fox against a side wall For example, if the Fox is at 6 and the Police at 3, 5, and 9, then the Police wins. If the Fox reaches cell 0, then it wins. A game with over 20 moves is forfeited to the Fox. (The Fox is a spy, trying to elude the Police and reach its base.) Play the game a few times with two human players to get a feel for it. Note that there is only one side for the Police , not three separate players. When the Police moves, it may move only one piece.

```
      1--4--7
     /|\ | /|\
    / | \|/ | \
   0--2--5--8--10
    \ | /|\ | /
     \|/ | \|/
      3--6--9
```

In this computer simulation, the computer plays the Fox. Initially the computer plays randomly, with a bias toward moving left. However, the Fox learns from its mistakes and after only a few games it becomes nearly impossible for the human player to win.

To represent this game board, we use a two dimensional array of integers as shown below.

```
0 2 2 2 0 0 0 0 0 0 0
1 0 2 0 2 2 0 0 0 0 0
1 2 0 2 0 2 0 0 0 0 0
1 0 2 0 0 2 2 0 0 0 0
0 1 0 0 0 2 0 2 0 0 0
0 1 1 1 2 0 2 2 2 2 0
0 0 0 1 0 2 0 0 0 2 0
0 0 0 0 1 1 0 0 2 0 2
0 0 0 0 0 1 0 2 0 2 2
0 0 0 0 0 1 1 0 2 0 2
0 0 0 0 0 0 0 1 1 1 0
```

This is a definition of the board. It has 11 rows and 11 columns, one for each cell in the graph. A zero at a row, column entry indicates there is no arc from the row entry to the column entry. A nonzero entry indicates an arc, hence a possible path for the Fox. The Police can't travel all arcs in all directions, so a 2 is used to show a legal Police move. The 2 on row 1 (the second row, since they are numbered from 0) and column 2, indicates it is legal for the Police to move from cell 1 to cell 2. Such an array is called an adjacency matrix, since it defines which cells in a graph are adjacent (have arcs between them).

We can store this game board definition in a file of 121 integers. This file is read in at the beginning of play and stored in a two-dimensional array.

The key to the learning aspect of this game is that there are only 165 legal positions for white, and 11 positions for black. During one play of the game, the computer keeps a record (in an array) of all of the positions that occur.

A single game is stored in a two-dimensional array with 20 rows and 2 columns. Column 0 is used for a Police position (a number from 0 to 164), and the second column is used to store the Fox position (a number from 0 to 10).

At the end of the game it updates a 165×11 matrix of weights, increasing all the weights of positions occupied if the computer won, and decreasing them if it lost. When the computer tries to choose a move, it consults this table and chooses one with the highest weight value. This means that the complete results of all positions of all games played can be summarized in a rectangular array of 165×11 integer entries. Finding a best move is just searching for the maximum value in a portion of an array. Very simple.

The Police position is translated into a number by computing $2^a + 2^b + 2^c$, where a, b, and c are the cell numbers occupied by the Police. Since no two Police pieces can occupy the same cell, and since they are all less than 11, the maximum value of this is $2^9 + 2^8 + 2^{10}$ and no two positions result in the same value. Only 165 different values actually occur. (The number of ways to choose 3 items from a set of 11 without replacement, in the language of combinatorics. $165 = (11!) / (3!)(8!)$) The 165 different values of this sum are all between 7 and 1792. These are stored in another array. We search this latter array for a Police position value and the cell number in which we find the result is used as a row index into the memory array.

From this description you can try to build the game.

2.6   How the STL Generalizes Arrays and Pointers

In the Standard Template Library there are several other data structures that have components. These data structures are called, collectively, containers. Each of them has some feature different from arrays. Vectors are like arrays except that their length may be changed. Deques can grow also, but at either end. Lists do not use dense, contiguous, storage. Sets don't have a linear or sequential structure. There are several other container classes as well.

Pointers are generalized in the STL to objects called *iterators*. An iterator has the property that it refers to a specific location in a container, and this location may be moved by doing simple arithmetic operations. One of the features of iterators in the STL is that they may be used with `for` loops in a way completely analogous to the way we use pointers and `for` loops with arrays. Some iterators, like pointers, are bidirectional. Some iterators, like pointers, are random access. Other iterators are more restricted, such as forward iterators that can only move in one direction through their container. Different kinds of containers support different kinds of iterators.

The algorithms provided by the Standard Template Library for the manipulation of containers are all defined in terms of iterators. In other words, to manipulate a container using one of these algorithms, we pass the algorithm one or more iterators over that container. This philosophy that the algorithms are defined in terms of the iterators, rather than the containers themselves, makes it possible to write the algorithms in a very general way. In particular, an algorithm that works for lists may well also work for sets or for vectors. Finally, this philosophy makes it possible for these same algorithms to work with the built-in arrays of C++, as well as the components of the STL proper.

2.7   Some Common Problems. Searching and Sorting

When we save data in some container, we often want to retrieve the values we have stored. The efficiency with which we can do this is greatly determined by the ordering of the data within the container. Sorting is the problem of putting a collection of data into some particular ordering or relationship. Searching is the retrieval process itself.

2.7.1   Linear Search in Arrays

One common problem that occurs in dealing with arrays is that of searching for an element that may or may not be in the array. `While` loops are especially helpful in this. Suppose we have an array A in which we are certain that a value x occurs, and we would like to know the cell number in which it occurs. The following loop will tell us.

```
int i = 0;
while(A[i] != x) i++;
```

This loop exits as soon as A[i] == x and so we have the desired index. If we are not certain whether x is in the array or not, however, we need to be a bit more careful to avoid searching past the end of the array. The following will serve, where we replace lengthOfA with the actual length of the array A.

```
int i = 0;
while (i < lengthOfA && A[i] != x) i++;
```

The test for the length must be made first, so that we can guarantee that an index used to retrieve a value (A[i]) represents a legal subscript. C++ will guarantee that if i >= lengthOfA, the second test will not be evaluated and the loop will exit. This is the advantage of short circuiting the evaluation of Boolean expressions. The value is returned as soon as enough of the expression is evaluated to make the answer clear. The same is true of the OR operator | |. Note that in this search, if the item is not present, the value of i will be left at lengthOfA. This can be tested. Remember that when you write a loop with a compound exit condition such as we did here, when it exits, you don't know which condition caused the exit. Therefore, an additional test after the loop is often required.

A for loop can also be used in conjunction with the break statement.

```
for (int i = 0; i < lengthOfA; ++i)
    if ( A[ i ] == x ) break;
```

This loop will also exit with either A[i] containing the desired value or the index equal to lengthOfA.

Exercise. Use the pointer duality law to change the above for loop into an equivalent one that uses pointers instead of subscripts.

The above process is called sequential search, since we look for the item of interest sequentially, starting at the first component. If the array is long, then this can take quite a while. It is possible to search faster if the array is sorted, as we shall see.

2.7.2   Selection Sort

Next we attack the problem of putting an array in order, assuming that the elements in the array are *sortable*. To be sortable means that the elements of the component type must support operator<. This is certainly the case for the built-in types of C++ and it may be true for user-defined types, since it is possible for the programmer to give alternate definitions of operator< for user-defined data. As we shall see later, there are other ways that a type can be made sortable.

One of the simplest algorithms for sorting is called selection sort. The idea behind selection sort is to remove the smallest element from the array, then sort the remainder with the same process, and then attach that smallest element back to the beginning. The picture in Figure 2.5 should help.

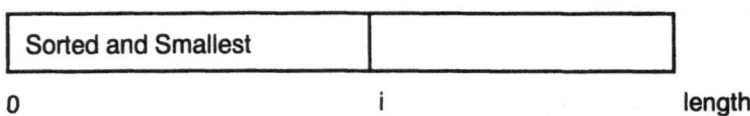

Figure 2.5. Selection sort, outer loop.

This is intended to be a picture of the sort function in the middle of its operation. The implication is that there is an index i, somewhere between 0 and length-1, and all cells strictly to the left of cell i have been sorted and also contain the smallest values in the entire array.

Each array picture that we draw, called an *array section*, is intended to represent the state of some array, part way through an algorithm. Usually they represent the state of some loop or recursion partly completed. The above picture actually represents a for loop with control variable i in the middle of its execution, as we shall see. When we put a value below the rectangle representing the array, we intend it to represent a subscript. When it is inside the rectangle, it represents a value. A vertical bar in the rectangle separates the array into two parts that may have different characteristics. If something is known about the elements in some section, then we write a description within the rectangle. The positioning of subscripts and vertical lines is significant and in the above case, the fact that the subscript i is to the right of the vertical line indicates that the description "Sorted and Smallest" applies only to subscripts 0 through i - 1. A statement, such as the one defined by Figure 2.5 is called an *invariant* because it's truth will not change. We will keep it true throughout our process.

Our job is to complete the process by getting i up to value length-1 so that the part to the left will be the entire array except for one cell. Since that part is sorted and since its values are no greater than the value in cell i = length - 1, then the entire array is sorted, which is our aim. The problem then is how to get this figure true, keep it true, and get i up to length - 1.

First, it is easy to make this picture true. All we need to do is to set i to be 0. Since there are no cells to the left of i = 0, it is certainly true that it is sorted. Likewise, nothing in the left part is any larger than anything in the part from i through length-1, since there are no cells at all in that left part.

The goal of getting i up to length - 1 can be achieved if we keep increasing i as we progress. We will use a for loop to do this for us. The part about keeping the picture in Figure 2.5 true is the challenging part, and this is where the original idea comes in.

What we want to do is to find the smallest value in the part i...length-1 and move it to cell i. Then, when we increase i, the picture is still true. Make sure that you understand why before you read further.

To handle this last part of the task, it will be helpful to consider the picture in Figure 2.6.

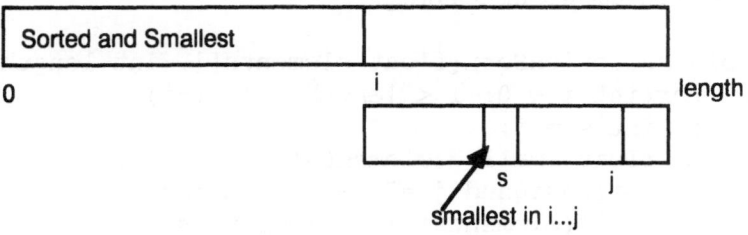

Figure 2.6. Selection sort, inner loop.

The implication here is that we have a picture of the portion between i and length - 1. In this section we have an index j and an index s, and cell s contains the smallest element in the section between i and j. If we can get this true, keep this true, and get j up to length - 1, we will have found the smallest value in i...length - 1. We can then swap cells i and s to achieve our goal of getting the smallest value to cell i. We can make this picture true initially just by setting s and j to be i and keeping an auxiliary value named small to hold the smallest value discovered so far: the one in cell s. We can get j increased with a for loop. We can keep the picture true just by setting s to j whenever we discover a value at j, smaller than the value at s as we move j along. This leaves us with the following code for the selection sort. Note that the only requirement we make on the type to be sorted is that it support operator<.

```
const int length = ...;
float elements[length];
...
    void selectionSort()
    {   for(int i = 0; i < length - 1; ++i)
        {   int s = i;
            float small = elements[s];
            unsigned j;
            for(j = i + 1; j < length; ++j)
                if(elements[j] < small)
                    // operator< used.
                {   s = j;
                    small = elements[s];
                }
            elements[s] = elements[i];
            elements[i] = small;
        }
    }
```

This is not a very good function, since it will only sort an array named elements, and only if its length is named length and only if it contains floats. We can do better. One way is to pass in the array to be sorted along with the length, so the function sorts its parameter instead of a global value. That would certainly be an improvement. In C++ this would look like the following.

```
void selectionSort(float elements[], int length)
{   for(int i = 0; i < length - 1; ++i)
    {   int s = i;
        float small = elements[s];
        for(unsigned j = i + 1; j < length; ++j)
            if(elements[j] < elements[s])
            {   s = j;
                small = elements[s];
```

```
        }
      elements[s] = elements[i];
      elements[i] = small;
   }
}
```

This is much better, but we still can sort only floats. One way to improve this further is to turn it into a function template. The result won't be a function, but a means of creating functions as needed.

```
template < class T >
void selectionSort(T elements[], int length)
{   for(int i = 0; i < length - 1; ++i)
   {   int s = i;
      T small = elements[s];
      for(unsigned j = i + 1; j < length; ++j)
         if(elements[j] < small)
         {   s = j;
            small = elements[s];
         }
      elements[s] = elements[i];
      elements[i] = small;
   }
}
```

Note that here, both occurrences of the type float have been replaced by a reference to the template parameter T. This parameter is a type. Later if we need to sort an array of ints, then the system will use this function template, with T equal to int, to create a sorting function for us. It will also be used to create a different function that will sort floats if we need it. The compiler sees to this creation (instantiation) of functions from the template by examining which functions we make use of in our code. This instantiation of template functions from function templates is automatic, but note that it requires the system to create different functions for different values of the template parameter.

```
int intArray[6] = {5, 4, 3, 6, 2, 1};
float floatArray[5] = {1.2, 3.4, 2.5, 0.4, 1.1};
selectionSort(intArray, 6);
selectionSort(floatArray, 5);
```

One requirement that the writer of a function template must remember is that the template parameter must appear in the parameter list of the function itself. This is the means that the compiler uses to determine which template function to create. It is not enough to specialize the return type or the body of the function. The template parameter must appear in the function parameter list.

Another means of improving on our selection sort algorithm is to include it as a member function in a class. Suppose we build a class Array to provide additional support that C++ arrays do not have. For example, our Array class could provide bounds checking which C++ does not do for built-in arrays. This class would actually be a class template rather than a class, with the element type (component type) as the template parameter. If this were the case, and it is attractive to do, then we might consider making selection sort one of the member functions of this class. In this case, the array `elements` would be one of the member variables of this class, implementing the class with a built-in array.

These last two solutions, a function template or a member function, are both great improvements over our original version, but note that they still have a restriction. They can only sort arrays. In the function template case, we have used an array declaration as the type of one of the parameters. If we have a member function of class Array, we are obviously restricted to sorting objects of that type.

However, if we apply the pointer duality rule uniformly, we can remove even this requirement. We are going to change selectionSort again. Suppose we pass in two pointers, one that points to the first component of the array and one that points just after the array. A typical call might look something like the following:

```
int elements[20];
int * start = elements;
int * after = elements + 20;
selectionSort(start, after);
```

To make this work, we change the prototype of the function template to

```
template < class T >
void selectionSort(T* start, T* end)
```

Now, selectionSort can sort elements without referring to an array directly in any way. The important thing to recognize is the pointer duality law, which states that if A is any pointer to the start of an array, then A[i] is equivalent to A + i. The replacements we shall make are defined as follows:

replace   elements[s] by *loc or equivalently &elements[s] by loc
replace   elements[i] by *where
replace   elements[j] by *inner

See Figure 2.7 and compare it to Figure 2.6.

This gives us the following version, which no longer makes reference to any array, only to pointers that point in to the array.

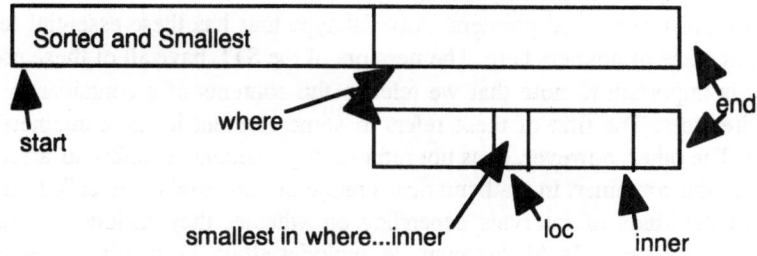

Figure 2.7. Selection sort, inner loop with pointers.

```
template < class T >
void selectionSort(T* start, T* end)
{  for(T* where = start ; where < end ; where++)
    {  T* loc = where;
       T small = *loc;
       for
       (  T* inner = where + 1;
          inner < end;
          inner++
       )
          if(*inner < *loc)
          {  loc = inner;
             small = *loc;
          }
       *loc = *where;
       *where = small;
    }
}
```

The algorithms of the Standard Template Library are all defined using this last idea. While it is entirely equivalent to the above when we are sorting arrays, the fact that the algorithm doesn't refer directly to arrays but only to pointers means that the same algorithm can be used for other structures that have the property that they can be referred to by pointers. Do note, however, that this last version is not nearly as easy to read, especially for novices. Being less easy to read and understand, it is more likely to have an error.

What essential features of pointers have we used in the above? All we need to do is examine the uses. We have applied `operator++` to the pointer variables in several places. We have used `operator*` to de-reference the pointers in several places. We have used `operator<` for pointers (as well as their de-referenced values). We have assigned one pointer value to another with `operator=`. We have done pointer arithmetic (e.g., `where + 1`). Finally, we have implicitly assumed that if we execute `start++` sufficiently often, then eventually `start < end` will be false. The implication of all this is that we don't even need pointers. Any datatype that has these essential features could be used in place of pointers here. The iterators of the STL have all of these properties.

It is important to note that we refer to the contents of a container in the STL using two iterators. The first of these refers to some element in the container: its "first" element. The other, however, does not refer to any element. It refers to a location "past the end" of the container. In mathematics, a range of real numbers is called an interval. There are several kinds of intervals depending on whether they include or exclude their endpoints. The interval [a, b], for example, includes all of the numbers between a and b, including both of these values, as well. This is called a "closed" interval. The open interval (a,b) excludes both endpoints, but contains the values strictly between a and b. The half open interval [a,b) includes a, but excludes b. In the STL we uniformly use something like this half open interval to refer to our containers, except that the "end points" are iterators, rather than numbers.

It is also possible to sort an array into decreasing order, in which the largest value is first, rather than last. To do so we replace operator< with operator> of course.

2.7.3   Binary Search

Once an array is sorted, it is possible to search it much more efficiently than if it is not. One commonly used mechanism is called binary search, which is similar to a guessing game that you may have played. One player announces that she has thought of a number, say between 1 and 100. The other players guess what the number is, and for each guess the original player informs the guesser whether the guess is correct, too high, or too low. A correct sequence of guesses can arrive at the remembered number quite quickly. In fact, if the number remembered is between 1 and 1 million, it only requires about 20 guesses to arrive at the answer.

The correct next guess, of course, is halfway between the largest previous guess that was too low, and the smallest previous guess that was too high. So your first guess in the 1...100 version is 50 and if that is too high, you next try 25, which if too low, you next guess either 37 or 38, etc.

In binary search over a sorted array, we first look in the cell in the middle of the array. If that is the desired value we are done, but if that value is larger than the one we seek, then, since the array is sorted, the desired value must be to the left (assuming the sort was increasing). Binary search is called binary, by the way, since it splits the portion of the array yet to be searched into two equal parts at each step. In other words, each failure reduces the remaining work by a factor of 2.

Here is a recursive version of binary search over an array. It returns the cell number in which it finds the item, or an arbitrary cell number if the target is not present. Because the process is recursive over a portion of the array, we must pass parameters to indicate the subscript bounds of the search.

```
template<class T>
unsigned int binarySearch
(  T* elements,     // Array of Ts.
   const T& t,
       // Searching for t in elements.
   unsigned int first,  // Starting here.
   unsigned int last    // Ending here.
)
{  if(first >= last) return first;
   unsigned int mid = (first + last)/2;
       // Middle of the array.
   if(t == elements[mid]) return mid;
   if(elements[mid] < t )
       return binarySearch(t, mid + 1, last);
   else
       return binarySearch(t, first, mid - 1);
}
```

Exercise. Modify binary search by applying the pointer duality law throughout. The parameters of your modified version should be the target plus two pointers, one to the first cell of interest, and the other to the location just after the last. It should return a pointer to the cell that contains the value if found, and an arbitrary pointer into the array otherwise. Be careful about the translation of mid. Test both the original version and your new version.

2.7.4 Quicksort

Quicksort is called quick because it sorts faster than sorts like selection sort. This is because it does more work each time it scans the array. In particular, what we will attempt to do is to use a linear scan of the array to establish the truth of the logical statement embodied in Figure 2.8.

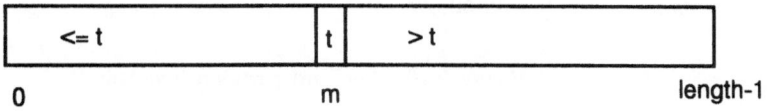

Figure 2.8. Quicksort partition.

The idea here is to split the array approximately in the middle around a value t with the property that all values to the left of t are less than or equal to it, and all values to the right are strictly larger. Once we establish this "partition step" we will then recursively repeat the process on the two side pieces: the piece from 0 to m-1 and the piece from m + 1 to length - 1. Since this is to be done recursively, and since we need to say in the recursion step what the limits of the sorting are to be, quickSort will need to have two parameters so that we may pass in these bounds. We can establish our plan in an outline as follows:

```
quicksort(first, last) is
    if (first < last)
            partition, finding m
            quicksort(first, m-1)
            quicksort(m+1 last)
```

There are a variety of ways to carry out the partition step. One of the clearest and easiest follows. What we will do first is establish the truth of Figure 2.9.

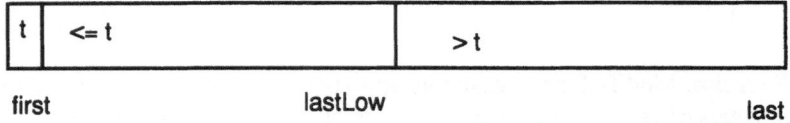

first   lastLow   last

Figure 2.9. Quicksort partition postcondition.

This will be a bit easier to do, since we know where the special "pivot" value will be: always in cell first. Instead of m, we now use an index named lastLow, that marks the cell in which we find the last "small" value. Note that if we can establish the truth of Figure 2.9 then a swap of cells first and lastLow will establish Figure 2.8.

To establish Figure 2.9, we will carry out a process described in Figure 2.10.

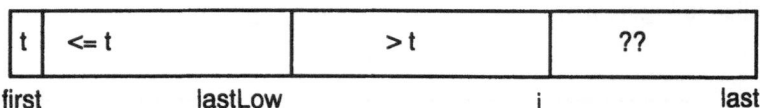

first   lastLow   i   last

Figure 2.10. Quicksort partition invariant.

What we do here is to use an index i, which we move along so that it is eventually equal to last. Cells between first+1 and lastLow are <= t, those between lastLow+1 and i are > t, and we don't know about those beyond i, since we haven't examined them yet. We make this picture true initially by setting i and lastLow to be first. Then all parts are empty except the first cell and the "??" part. We get i to be last eventually, by increasing it in a for loop. We keep Figure 2.10 true in the following way. Each time we increase i, we examine the new cell i. If its value is > t, then nothing needs to be done. On the other hand, if it is <= t, we can increase lastLow and then swap cells i and lastLow. This will reestablish the truth of 2.10 for the new i. Putting all of this together, we arrive at the following code for quickSort. We employ an auxiliary function swap that exchanges the values of two cells.

```
template<class T>
void swap(T* elements, int i, int j)
{   T temp = elements[i];
    elements[i] = elements[j];
    elements[j] = temp;
}


template<class T>
void quickSort
(   T * elements,
    unsigned int first,
    unsigned int last
)
{   if(first < last)
    {   T t = elements[first];
            // t is the pivot.
        unsigned lastLow = first;
        unsigned i;
        for (i = first + 1; i <= last; i++)
            if(elements[i] < t)
            {   ++lastLow;
                swap(lastLow, i);
            }
        swap(first, lastLow);
        if(lastLow != first)
            quickSort
                (elements, first, lastLow - 1);
        if(lastLow != last)
            quickSort(elements, lastLow + 1,last);
    }
}
```

Note that the portion of this algorithm up to the recursive calls is the **partition** step, and its result (Figure 2.8) is called a partition of the array.

Exercise. Modify quickSort by applying the pointer duality law throughout. Your function should have two parameters. They are pointers to the beginning and the "after" position, as usual. Test both the original version and your new version.

2.7.5   The Efficiency of These Algorithms

After correctness, the most important aspect of any algorithm is its efficiency. There are two aspects to efficiency, namely the efficiency of the algorithm itself and the efficiency of its implementation. It turns out that the latter measure is not nearly so important as the former and merely requires that the programmer take care not to execute unneeded instructions. The essential efficiency of the algorithm itself is much more important, as it sets limits that no details of implementation can overcome.

Efficiency can be measured various ways. One measure is the space required. If an algorithm is written to run on a multiprocessor system, then the number of processors required may be an important measure. Usually, however, efficiency means time efficiency. How much time can we expect an algorithm to take to complete?

It must first be recognized that this question cannot be answered in specific, concrete, exact terms. Computers differ in their speeds. Disk drives have differing transfer rates. Multiuser computers have different loads that affect the speed of programs running on them. Most importantly, each time we run a program, we likely do so with a different set of input data. This can have a large effect, and we expect that a run with a small amount of data will be faster than one with a large amount of data.

Therefore, efficiency is always expressed in terms of some measure of the input requirements (size of the data) or the resources required (memory, processors, etc.). Here we will consider only the time efficiency of our algorithms as a function of the size of the input data. We also adopt a measure that will be independent of the speed of a particular computing system on which a program implementing the algorithm might be run.

Some algorithms always take the same amount of time when run on a given system in a given start state (system load, available memory, etc.). For example, an algorithm that returns the first element of an array can be expected to run in constant time independently of the size of the array. However, an algorithm that uses a simple `for` loop to sum the elements of an integer array must visit each cell of the array, so we expect that its running time will be proportional to the size of the array, approximately doubling if we double the size of the array. But this doubling isn't a precise measure either, since any such algorithm will have a certain amount of overhead (initializing the sum, etc.) that must be done no matter what the number of data items that it processes. Therefore, for example, summing an array of two items using our for loop algorithm will not run exactly twice as long as when applied to one element. However, between 1000 and 10,000 elements, the time will be very nearly related in a 1 to 10 ratio, since this fixed overhead will be *amortized*, or spread out over a large number of repetitions.

In order to be as precise as possible when presenting the run-time characteristics of an algorithm, we resort to a mathematical means of expressing the upper and lower bounds of functions, here the running time, as a function of the amount of the data processed. What we do, essentially, is to compare the running time function to functions of well known behavior, such as polynomials, logarithms, and exponential functions. These functions have been extensively studied and characterized using calculus. When the value of function g is always less than the value of function f for a given input x, we say that f dominates g, or gives an upper bound for g. If, on the other hand, function g is always greater than function h at each point of the domain, we say that h forms a lower bound of

g. If functions f and h are also quite close together at all input values, then we have pinned down the behavior of function g quite well.

Computers run relatively fast today, so the behavior of an algorithm on a small amount of data is only seldom of interest. For most algorithms, the time is nearly instantaneous. The problem gets interesting only when the data set gets large, the time gets long, and we reach the limit of how long we are willing to wait for an answer. So, we are usually willing to ignore the bounds problem for small inputs. With all of this in mind, we can give a definition of a precise measure of the upper bound of a function, in terms of another function.

Let f and g both be functions of an integer variable. We say that function g is $O(f)$, read "big oh of f," provided that there is an integer M and a constant C, such that for all $x > M$, it is true that $g(x) <= C \cdot f(x)$. The purpose of M is to ignore small values of x (the size of the input in our application). In effect, this lets us ignore the fixed overhead of the algorithm. The purpose of C is to provide a constant of proportionality that lets us ignore the specific speed of processors. Different systems will just have different values of C.

Note that if our running time is $O(f)$ for some function f, this just means that the running time for input size n is less than some multiple of $f(n)$ for all n that are relatively large. It might be nearly $C \cdot f(n)$ or considerably less. To get a sharp estimate of the running time, we also need a lower bound.

Lower bounds are expressed quite differently, though it sounds similar. We say that a function g is $\Omega(f)$, read "big omega of f," if there is a constant C such that for any integer N there is an $n > N$ such that $g(n) >= C \cdot f(n)$. Said another way, g is bigger than a fixed multiple of f for infinitely many values. All this means is that it is sometimes large, not that it is necessarily always large. In terms of running time, this means that for some sets of inputs, the program will run for a long time and that this behavior will be observed for more than just a finite number of values.

Normally, however, when we give a "big oh" bound for a function, we mean that the running time is indeed close to that bound. So, while it is technically true to describe a function as $O(x^2)$, when it is also $O(x)$, that won't normally be done. Note that if a function is big O of some polynomial function, then it is also big O of x^n, where n is the degree of that polynomial, since any given polynomial of degree n is $O(x^n)$.

We call an algorithm linear if it is $O(x)$, since $f(x) = x$ is a linear function. An algorithm that is $O(x^2)$ is called quadratic. One that is $O(x^3)$ is cubic. As one extreme, an algorithm with constant running time is $O(1)$, and at the other extreme an algorithm is called exponential if it is $O(2^n)$. Exponential running time algorithms take extremely long to execute on large sets of data, as illustrated by the following exercise. Another commonly used bound function is the logarithmic function $\log_2(n)$. An algorithm with such a bound is described as logarithmic.

Exercise. Suppose that you have an exponential algorithm that takes 1 second to complete if the size of the input is 16 items. For each additional item the time doubles. How much time does it take on a set of 64 items? Suppose your computing cost (cost of time and depreciation on the machine plus electricity consumed) is one penny for 16 items. What does it cost for 64 items using the same formula?

The sequential search algorithm presented above is linear, of course. The number of steps it executes is directly proportional to the length of the array, as can be inferred from the use of the `for` loop. Likewise, the selection sort algorithm is quadratic, since it contains two nested loops, each of which is linear. In general, algorithms built out of loops are relatively easy to analyze for their runtime bounds. Recursive algorithms and some others are a bit more challenging.

One means of analyzing the running time of an algorithm is to write down an equation that describes the running time and then solve it. Even though we know that sequential search has linear running time, let us use this technique to analyze the efficiency as an illustration of how to go about it.

In sequential search we look at one item in a set of n and if that is not the target of the search, we still need to examine n-1 others. Therefore, if there is a single item in our container we take one unit of work to verify whether or not that item is the target. If there is more than one item, say n, then the work required is one unit to check the first item plus the work required for the other n-1 items. If we write down this work equation, where W_n represents the work done for n items and W_{n-1} the work for n-1 items, we get the following.

$$W_n = 1 + W_{n-1}, \text{ if } N > 1 \text{ and } W_1 = 1.$$

Equations like these are called *recurrence relations* because they are recursive definitions of a value. As in all recursive systems, note the necessity of a base (non-recursive) case to which we reduce.

We can solve this by repeated substitution, replacing a work term on the righthand side by its definition using this formula itself. Notice that we start with n-1 on the right and a single 1. If we substitute the meaning of $W_{n-1} = 1 + W_{n-2}$ into the above formula, we get

$$W_n = 1 + (1 + W_{n-2}) = 2 + W_{n-2}$$

If we repeat this, we get

$$W_n = 2 + W_{n-2} = 3 + W_{n-3} \ldots = n$$

That is to say, the work to process n items is n times the work to process one item. This again justifies the statement that the work of sequential search is proportional to the length of the array.

Suppose that we try to analyze the running time of binary search in this same way. The binary search proceeds by doing one unit of work to look in the center location in the array. If that is not a hit, then the recursion says that the binary search must do the same process over a data set half as large. Of course if the array only has one item, it only takes one unit of work. We just verify that that item is, or is not, the target of the search. Suppose that we again let W_n represent the work done (time expended) for exactly n items.

Then an equation defining this work that corresponds to the first two sentences of this paragraph is

$$W_n = 1 + W_{n/2}, \text{ if } n > 1, \text{ and } W_1 = 1.$$

This can be solved if we substitute $n = 2^k$ into the equation and then do repeated substitutions on the righthand side using this definition itself.

$$W_{2^k} = 1 + W_{2^{k-1}}, \text{ if } n > 1, \text{ and } W_1 = 1.$$

$$= 1 + 1 + W_{2^{k-2}}$$

$$= 1 + 1 + 1 + W_{2^{k-3}}$$

$$\ldots$$

$$= k$$

Therefore, $W_n = k = \log_2(n)$, and we have a logarithmic algorithm. This is very good, since the log of a number is small in comparison to the number. This justifies our earlier claim that we can binary search an array with a million items with only about 20 repetitions.

Exercise. Normally the quicksort exhibits the following behavior. The partition step splits the array into two parts of about equal size. Therefore, the work done is the work done to do the partition, which is linear, plus the work done to quick sort the two halves. But sorting the two halves separately is just twice the work required to sort an array half as big. Of course, an array with only one element takes no work at all to sort, since it already is sorted. Use this idea to verify the claim that quick sort is $O(n \log_2(n))$.

Some algorithms work well on most data sets but perform badly on a few. Quick sort as presented here is such an algorithm. In an average case the quick sort is $O(n \log_2(n))$. However, the algorithm as presented has a very strange behavior if we give it a sorted array to start with. In this case, the partition doesn't divide the array into two parts of equal size, but into one part that is empty and the other which has just one less element. So, in this case, the running time is the time required to do the partition (linear) plus the time required to sort an array with one less item. Now the recurrence is

$$W_n = n + W_{n-1}, \text{ if } n > 1, \text{ and } W_1 = 0.$$

It is easy to show that the solution of this recurrence relation is a quadratic function of n. Therefore, quick sort is no better than insertion sort on a few cases. For quick sort we say that the average running time is $O(n \log_2(n))$, but the worst case running time is $O(n^2)$. As a shorthand, we will use $\lg(n)$ in place of $\log_2(n)$, as the log base 2 commonly occurs when measuring efficiency.

Exercise. Actually, if we use big O to measure efficiency, any log base is equivalent to any other and so the base doesn't matter. Why?

There is another measure of running time that is occasionally useful, though not for these algorithms. Suppose we want to build a class to implement arrays that can be expanded. A nice technique is to do the following. The class has a member variable that is an array of some convenient size at creation. If we later learn that the array was too small, we expand the array as follows. Allocate a new array, twice as long as the original, copy the elements from the old array into the new one, and then delete the old array, assigning the new one to the member variable. If we ask how much time it takes to insert an element into this "array class", the answer is that it depends. If it is not time to expand, the time is constant. If an expansion is required, the time is linear in the number of items currently stored, to account for the copying time. But if we average this out over all insertions, we find that the (average) time is still constant, actually about twice the time of one of the atomic instructions. Note that to make this work, you must double the size when you expand, not just increase it by a fixed amount. Such an algorithm is called *amortized constant*, since we amortize the cost of an expensive operation out over several cheap operations, with the average being constant.

2.8   Using Arrays with the STL

Most of the algorithms provided with the Standard Template Library work for arrays as well as those additional containers provided by the STL itself. This was one of the primary design decisions of the STL. They work because pointers into arrays satisfy the requirements of random access iterators. Since most of the algorithms work with such iterators, they work with arrays.

To use the algorithms you must include the header <algo.h> provided with the STL and probably provided with your C++ compiler. To sort an array, we need a pointer to the beginning of it and a pointer to the cell that would immediately follow the array (not a pointer to the last cell, a pointer to the following cell). Consider the following test example:

```
int testArray[] = { 3, 1, 4, 2, 5 };
int * first = testArray;
int * last = &testArray[5]; // Or testArray + 5;
sort(first, last);

for (int i =0; i< 5; ++i)
    cout << testArray[i]<<endl;
```

This produces

```
1
2
3
4
5
```

Notice that the sort function doesn't mention the array that it is sorting. It only needs pointers to the first cell and the "last" position. Technically, in the language of the STL, sort takes two iterators as arguments and sorts the section of the container between the two iterators, including the item at the location of the first iterator and not including the position of the second. Sort works for many (but not all) of the container classes, and most algorithms take one or more iterators as arguments.

There are two requirements for using the sort routine of the STL. The first is that the pointer must de-reference to a type that supports operator<. In other words, the component type must support this operator. The second is that the operator< of that type must have the property that if a < b, then it is not true also that a == b. If your type doesn't meet this specification, then you might get a compiler error that operator< is not defined, or if it is but the operator fails to satisfy its condition, then using sort may result in an infinite computation.

A somewhat less obvious requirement of the STL sort is automatically fulfilled by arrays and array pointers. Sort requires that the iterators (here pointers) passed in satisfy the requirements of random access iterators. Since array pointers have this property this is not a problem, but applying sort to some other data structures (e.g., linked lists) might not be possible.

The STL sort algorithm is a variation of quickSort. It is a bit more sophisticated than the one shown above, as it works efficiently for already sorted arrays, though it will be inefficient for some collections of data. The STL has other sort routines that are slower on average than sort, though they can be guaranteed to always be faster than quadratic algorithms like selection sort. See sort_heap in the index or in Chapter 6, for example.

Another STL algorithm that can be used in exactly the same way as sort is reverse, which reverses the elements of an array (or other container).

Note that when you apply one of the STL algorithms using an iterator, the value of that iterator may change. It may no longer point to the location to which it originally pointed. We say that an iteration "consumes its iterator."

2.9   Another Example. A Simple Database

One of the important problems in computer processing is how to efficiently and effectively store large amounts of information. The solution is called a database. We shall present an extremely simple solution here that is not really adequate for large amounts of data, but it introduces a few key concepts.

Data is stored so that it may later be retrieved. Usually the data is stored once, updated infrequently, but accessed frequently. Eventually the data will likely be removed. For example, when a new employee is hired, a new record is placed into the employee database, describing the relevant information about that person. The data is modified or updated only when some piece of information changes, such as name or address. The data is retrieved at least as frequently as the pay cycle, since it is needed to write a paycheck. Finally, when the person leaves employment the data is removed from the active part of the database, though the information may simply be moved to an archival region.

Since retrieval is done more frequently than creation/modification/removal, it is important to organize the database so that lookups are fast, even if this somewhat slows the speed of insertions. One of the chief ways that this is achieved is to choose from among all of the data to be stored, some portion that can be guaranteed to be uniquely associated with the data entity (here person), and that will not be the same for any other entity. This portion of the record is called the *key*, and the remainder of the data for that entity is called the *information*. Therefore, data is a collection of key-information pairs. social security numbers are often used in the United States as a key for employee records, since they are required to be maintained by employers (for taxing purposes) and they are also (supposed to be) unique. In general, however, the type of the key and the type of the information differ from one database to another, and even from one portion of the same database to another, so it is useful to abstract these types. We can do this with a class template.

```
template <class Key, class Information>
class DataRecord
{   public:

        DataRecord(Key k, Information v)
        :   key(k),
            information(v)
        {
        }

        Information getInformation() const
        {   return information;
        }

        Key getKey() const { return key; }

        bool match(const Key k) const
        {   return k == key;
        }

    private:
        Key key;
        Information information;
        DataRecord(){}
```

```
            // Needed to create arrays of
            // DataRecords.
        friend class Database<Key, Information>;
    };
```

We can now build a database using an array to hold DataRecords. This solution, as mentioned before, is overly simplified, as it requires that we know the maximum size of the database in advance, which is seldom the case.

```
template <class Key, class Information>
class Database
{  public:

        Database(int size)
        :  currentSize(0),
           storage
           (   new DataRecord<Key,
               Information> [size]
           )
        {
        }

        void store
        (   const Key k,
            const Information v
        )
        {   storage[currentSize++] =
               DataRecord<Key, Information> (k, v);
        }

        Information retrieve(const Key k) const
        {   for(int i = 0; i < currentSize; i++)
               if(storage[i].key == k)
                   return storage[i].information;
            return Information();
               // The default value of type
               // Information;
        }

    private:
        DataRecord<Key, Information> * storage;
           // Save the data in an array.
        int    currentSize;
    };
```

We can now store information into our database, where it is saved in the next available slot in the array. We can also retrieve the information associated with any key, though it takes a sequential search of the database to achieve it. Thus, though it works, it does not satisfy the efficiency requirements that specify that lookups should be fast. Here insertions are fast but retrievals are very slow.

To create a database, you need to specify the key and information types as well as the maximum size.

```
Database< int, char*> BonMot(100);
BonMot.store(22, "Have a nice day.");
BonMot.store(11, "Have an OK day.");
BonMot.store(33, "Have a wonderful day.");
BonMot.store( 5, "Have a day.");
cout << BonMot.retrieve(11) << endl;
cout << BonMot.retrieve(99) << endl; // Prints garbage.
```

Exercise. Speed up retrievals, even at the expense of insertions. One way to do this is to sort the database after each insertion. This requires that DataRecords have an operator<, which you will need to write. This operator should consider only the keys and ignore the information values.

Exercise. Devise a better mechanism for signaling that the data sought is not to be found. You can change retrieve into a bool function that returns its information value in a reference parameter, for example. Throwing an exception is another possibility.

2.10   Arrays That Contain Pointers

If we assign a value to some component of an array, then a copy of the value is made and stored at that component. Sometimes we want to avoid this copying because of its cost, or because the logic of the problem dictates that we not make copies of things. In this case we may store pointers to values rather than values themselves as the components of the arrays. This same technique may be applied to other containers as well, of course.

For example, in a database, it might be desirable to store the same objects in several places without copying. We try to keep only a single copy of data in a database to simplify the problem of updating values. If several copies of a piece of data are stored, then all must be updated at the same time. One way to achieve this is to avoid copies altogether, keep one copy of each piece of data, and use pointers as needed to simulate replication.

To do this our database will store pointers to data records rather than data records. Each cell of the array will contain just a pointer to some actual data record, or possibly be NULL.

Aside from the avoidance of copying, there is another major advantage of using pointers as the contents of our containers. This is the possibility of making the containers heterogeneous: of storing different types of things in the same container. This can't be done with complete freedom in C++, however, since pointers have a type that includes the type of the value that they point to. However, we may use the object-oriented features of C++ to achieve heterogeneity. We return again to derived classes.

Since we define a new class when we derive one class from another, we have different types. However, these types are partly compatible with each other. In particular, a pointer to a base type may hold a value that is a pointer to a derived class. This means that if we have a container, such as an array, defined to hold pointers to some class, then it may in fact hold pointers to any class derived from that class. For example, we may create an array of pointers to SpreadSheetCells and store pointers to NumericCells and FormulaCells as well.

```
SpreadsheetCell* lotsOfCells [100];
    // Array of cell pointers

lotsOfCells[0] = new FormulaCell(...);
lotsOfCells[1] = new NumericCell(...);
```

2.11   Another Use for Pointers—Lists

As a final brief note, we mention that pointers may be used to refer to other values than arrays. One of the most fruitful uses is to use pointers as links to chain data cells together. Each cell will now contain not only a value, such as an array cell does, but also the address of another cell. In this way the cells do not need to be stored contiguously, but can be anywhere in the free store. The advantage of this is that it is quite easy to insert a cell "between" two other cells and nothing needs to be moved. All that is required is that the addresses that impose the physical ordering on the cells be updated. In this way we can build sequential structures called linked lists. More generally, we can use more than one such address in a cell and build nonsequential structures such as trees and graphs. Lists will be taken up in detail in Chapter 7.

2.12   Summary

Make certain that you understand each of the following terms:

array
array section
alias
big O
binary search
cell
component

half open interval [a, b)
index
initialization
invariant
iterator
pointer
pointer duality law
quicksort
recurrence relation
searching
selection sort
sequential search
sorting
subscript

2.13 Exercises

1. Build a calendar generation program. Fill in a 6 by 7 array with numbers representing the days of a month. Consider columns to represent the days Sunday through Saturday. Input a date and build a calendar for the month containing that date. If a cell does not correspond to a day in that month, give it a zero or negative value. Provide a print routine to print nicely formatted monthly calendars.

2. The following sequence of exercises should be worked together. The following ordinary function will compare CountedInts:

```
bool cmpi
    (const CountedInt& a, const CountedInt& b)
{   return a.getValue() < b.getValue();
}
```

It returns true provided that the first parameter has a value less than the second. Such a function is very useful if CountedInts are to be placed in STL containers. For example, create an array of 20 CountedInts. They will be initialized automatically by the default constructor. Notice that the definition of the array itself will call the default CountedInt constructor on all elements. Verify this by scanning over the array and writing out the "order" of each element using getOrder.

```
CountedInt ci[20];
for(CountedInt* cip = ci; cip != ci+20; ++cip)
    cout << cip->getOrder()<<' ';
cout<<endl;
```

Now verify that all of the values stored are zeros.

3. Set some values into the CountedInts stored in the array of the last exercise. Then verify that you have your values by printing out the entire array again. Then shuffle the values around with the STL algorithm random_shuffle:

```
random_shuffle(ci, ci + 20);
```

Now verify that you have the same values by printing out the values. Also print out the orders, to show that you have the same objects as before in the same cells.

4. Now sort the array with

```
sort(ci, ci+10, cmpi);
```

Again verify that the values have been sorted. Note that we need the comparison operator as the last parameter of sort.

5. We would not need the last parameter of sort in exercise 4 if we had given CountedInt an operator<. In that case, sort would have used this operator if we had not supplied the third parameter. Try this.

6. Save 10 rolls of a ten-sided die in an array. Print out the array. Sort the array. Reverse the sorted array. Shuffle the array. Sort it again. Scan the array to find the number of rolls on which the value was even. Use iterators (pointers) for all of this. You should not use subscripts anywhere. Perform all of the above again using subscripts to get access to the cells. You should not use pointers (iterators) anywhere. Unless you have access to another library of algorithms, this last part is much harder. Why?

7. Build a database in which the keys are strings and the data values are also strings. Sometimes such databases are called property lists. The keys name some property, and the data value is the value of that property. Property lists are attached to various objects. For example, a window object could have a property named "HasVerticalScrollbar" with the value "true." The advantage of using strings for the keys is the flexibility to add additional properties without rebuilding the database system, as we are not using a fixed set of properties. To enable the next two exercises, first write a function that will write out a complete database. This could be a friend function with prototype

```
template <class Key, class Info>
ostream& operator<< (ostream & o, const Database<Key, Info>&
db)
```

Such a function should return the same ostream that it gets as a parameter after sending all elements of the database to the stream o, with appropriate formatting. Such friend functions are the standard way of giving objects print capabilities.

8. It is sometimes necessary to sort a database. If we store the DataRecords in an array, then this can be arranged with a few changes to the database system. One typical way is to add a sort member to the Database class. Implement this idea. The prototype should be

```
void sort();
```

9. A better way to permit sorting of a database is to provide a mechanism compatible with STL iterators. To do so requires only that we provide begin() and end() members to our Database class that return pointers to array cells. We can return variable storage for the value of begin() and &(storage[currentSize]) for the after then end value required by end(). With these functions provided, we can use the STL algorithm *sort*, which requires such iterators for its parameters. Note that sorting char* strings is a bit tricky since the ordinary operator< won't work. If you use this kind of string, then you need to provide a string comparison routine like

```
bool cmp(char* a, char* b)
{   return strcmp(a,b) < 0;
}
```

In this particular case we need to be able to compare DataRecords based on only their keys. The following function will do this.

```
bool    cmp
(   DataRecord<char*, char*> a,
    DataRecord<char*, char*> b
)
{   return cmp(a.getKey(), b.getKey());
}
```

This function could be passed to the generic sort routine of the STL as a third parameter, as in

```
sort(db.begin(), db.end(), cmp);
```

where db is the name of our database.

10. C++ does a pretty good job of handling strings. You can allocate a fixed amount of space for a string, just by using a string value

```
char * x = "These are the times."
```

You can allocate a large buffer in which to put a string as you read it when you don't know how big it will be:

```
char buf [256];
```

You can also allocate a string on the free store when you know its length:

```
char * ans = new char[18];
```

Only the last method gives you the flexibility to decide at run time how big the string will be. But there is another way, called a string buffer. It has the advantage of not requiring calls to the allocator new, which can take a lot of time if done frequently. Suppose we have an array in our program that is large enough to hold several strings:

```
char spellbuffer[4096];
```

We are going to pack strings into this buffer, one after the other. A string will then be referenced by knowing the index of its first character in the buffer, which we obtain when we insert it. We keep an integer variable, nextFree, initially 0 that is always the index of the next cell of the array that has not yet been filled. We can insert a string S into the array with two statements:

```
strcpy(spellbuffer + nextFree, S)
nextFree += strlen(S)+1;
```

The location of the spelling of S in the buffer is the original value of nextFree before we increment it.

Write functions insert and retrieve. The insert function takes a char* and inserts it into the buffer, returning the integer index at which it starts. Function retrieve takes an integer index and returns the string at that index.

Chapter 3
Overview of Container Mechanisms

3.1 Storage Mechanisms

In this chapter we are going to examine a number of ways that a programmer can store relatively large amounts of data for a program. We have already examined arrays, which use dense storage, and we saw that we can allocate such storage either automatically or on the free store. Two other methods of importance and frequent use are linked storage and hashed storage. Normally, linked storage is done only in the free store and hashed storage may be a combination of linked and dense storage and may involve either automatic or free store data or even a combination.

Dense storage is needed when we need to access elements in a random order and do so quickly. It is also useful if we can predict the total number of items to be stored in advance. Linked storage is needed when we need to be able to insert items between existing items frequently. Hashed storage is often used when we need to retrieve items quickly, do not need to rearrange them or retrieve them in a particular order. Hashed storage is also useful when you can't predict in advance the total number of items to be stored, though there are variations of hashed storage that require this knowledge in advance.

Linked storage is the most flexible of the methods considered here. With links it is possible to build sequential structures called Lists (Linked Lists), as well as non-sequential structures such as trees and graphs, with complete generality.

3.2 Dense Storage

Dense storage, as used in arrays, has many advantages and only a few disadvantages. The main advantage is that when we know where the structure is, we know automatically where every part of it is. Internally, when we use a subscript reference like A[i], the system multiplies i by the size of a cell and adds that to the address A to obtain the address of cell i. This multiplication and addition are very fast, so the access is very fast. When you use a struct or a class in C++, the system also uses dense storage for the value. In this case, each member of the struct or class is given a fixed offset from the beginning of the value. Then a member access like B.x is evaluated by adding the fixed offset of x to the beginning address of B to obtain the member's address.

The main disadvantage of dense storage is the difficulty of extending the size of fixed blocks, especially if they have large size. A running program has many items to be stored and a fixed amount of memory in which to store them. In order to make good use of memory, a compiler will pack data items together in memory without much wasted space. This means that our array or struct is surrounded by other data items. Therefore, it is usually impossible to expand the size of an array in place. If we underestimate the size of an array initially and want to expand it, then we will need to allocate a new, larger array on the free store, and copy the elements from the old to the new array. This is time-consuming, and if done frequently, can greatly slow an algorithm.

A secondary, though important, disadvantage of dense storage is the difficulty of making room for additional components in the middle of a block. The very nature of dense storage implies that the old values must be moved to make room for the new value. This moving of old values takes time that, generally speaking, is proportional to the number of elements to be moved.

3.3   An Extended Example Part 1: The Array Stack

A stack is a container object that keeps items in the order in which they were inserted. When we remove an item from a nonempty stack, it is always the item most recently inserted of those still remaining. The standard name for this protocol is LIFO, for Last-In, First-Out. A stack can be defined formally in terms of its state, which is modified by its operations. The operations on a stack are empty(), which tells us if the stack is empty; full(), which tells us if it is full and should not be inserted into; push(val), which is the insert operation; pop(), the removal operation, which removes the most recently inserted item and returns it to the caller; and top(), which returns the most recently inserted item without removing it. The rules defining a stack are as follows:

1. Immediately after creation, empty returns true.
2. Immediately after push, empty returns false.
3. If a stack is in a state in which empty returns true, then pop and top are errors.
4. If a stack is in a state in which full returns true, then push is an error.
5. (If a stack is in state S in which full returns false and we push an element E and then immediately pop, then the pop will return E to us and the stack will again be in state S.
6. Immediately after a (successful) push(E), top returns E without changing the state.

In actuality we have defined a bounded stack here, since it can hold a fixed number of items. If we remove this restriction, or otherwise guarantee that full always returns false, we have a stack proper.

One of the classic uses of a stack is to evaluate postfix expressions. Such expressions have each operator written after all of the operands of that operator. For example, the expression (a + b)*(c + d) would be written in postfix as a b + c d + *. The way to evaluate an expression written in postfix is to read the expression, one symbol at a time, from left to right. If we read an operand, then simply push it on a stack. If you see an operator, then pop the appropriate number of operands for that operator from the stack, apply the operator to the values popped, and then push the result back onto the stack. When you reach the end of the expression, you have the value on the top of the stack.

We can implement a Stack class in many ways. We will do so first with dense storage, employing an array as our internal storage mechanism. We will use a dynamic array so that we can decide when we create a stack how large it should be. It is possible to obtain a stack very easily from the STL. However, we will build one here ourselves to see what is involved. Even given the fact that we intend to use dense storage for the elements, there are still many decisions that need to be made to build our stack abstraction. The choices we shall make here will all be such as to illustrate what goes on in the STL containers, though it is certainly possible to implement things differently. We should emphasize, however, that what we shall build is quite a bit simpler than what occurs in the STL. We shall only be illustrating concepts here, not attempting to extend the Standard Template Library.

As a minimum, our class needs a constructor, a destructor, copy constructor, overloaded assignment operator, and the specific operations of a stack. In addition we shall define an associated iterator class and a means of generating certain iterators from any given stack. The name of our class is ArrayStack, which is not a particularly good name, but it does emphasize the implementation, which is our intention here.

The implementation of our stack will require three variables: _size is the physical size of the array that we allocate; _top is an index of the topmost element in the stack; and _elements is a dynamic array of size _size, initialized in the constructor. When we insert a new element, we first increase _top by one and then insert the new item in the slot referenced by _top.

We will intersperse the complete definition of the ArrayStack class with our comments.

```
template <class T>
class ArrayStack
{  public:
      typedef T value_type;
      typedef ArrayStackIterator<T> iterator;
```

These types are for convenience. They let other classes get access to the types that we are using by employing standard names such as iterator, rather than the proper names.

```
      ArrayStack(int size = 100)
      : _size(size),
        _top(-1),
        _elements(new T[size])
      {
      }
```

Here we allocate a new array according to the parameter, which, by the way, has a default value.

```
ArrayStack(const ArrayStack<T>& S)
:  _size(S._size),
   _top(S._top),
   _elements(new T[S._size])
{  for(int i = 0; i<= _top; i++)
      _elements[i] = S._elements[i];
}
```

The copy constructor is used when we create one stack from another. We must allocate a new array for the new stack. We don't want two stacks to share the implementation array. Otherwise, changing one stack would change the other as well. This would be a disaster in this situation. Why?

```
ArrayStack<T> operator=
(const ArrayStack<T>& S)
{  if(this != &S)
   {  delete [] _elements;
      _elements = new T[S._size];
      _size = S._size;
      _top = S._top;
      for(int i = 0; i<= _top; i++)
         _elements[i] = S._elements[i];
   }
   return *this;
}
```

This is the assignment operator. Note that it guarantees that we aren't trying to assign the same array to this one. Again, without this check we could have a disaster. What happens if we would delete the current _elements before copying the old values without this check? Note how much code is shared between the copy constructor and the assignment operator. This is typical of C++. It is convenient to factor out this common code into a private procedure so that it is easier to maintain.

```
~ArrayStack(){ delete [] _elements; }
```

The destructor must delete the array that the constructor created.

```
void push(const T& v)
{  _elements[++_top] = v;
}
```

To push onto a stack, we must first advance the _top member and then store the new element into the resulting component. Notice that we do not check for legal array limits here. It might be preferable to do so, though it would take time. The user has the ability to check for *overflow* using the function full() and must generally do so in any case. A test here would likely just repeat a test done elsewhere in a correct program.

```
T pop(){ return _elements[_top--]; }
```

A pop is the opposite of a push. We must return the element at the current _top and then reduce the _top value. Again there is no test for *underflow*. The user will likely (and should) use empty() before calling pop().

```
T top()const{ return _elements[_top]; }
```

Top is like pop except that we don't change the _top member.

```
bool empty()const{ return _top < 0; }
```

```
bool full()const{ return _top >= _size; }
```

In empty and full, we just return information about the state of the stack.

```
iterator begin()const
{   return
        ArrayStackIterator<T>(_elements, 0);
}
```

The begin() function returns an iterator, which is an ArrayStackIterator<T> according to the typedef seen above. We shall examine the iterator class in a moment.

```
iterator end()const
{   return
        ArrayStackIterator<T>
        (_elements, _top+1);
}
```

The end() function also returns an iterator. We initialize it with the index of the first empty slot after the active elements of the stack. Notice that this is not the slot after the array necessarily, but the slot after the active part of the array.

```
private:
    int _size;
    int _top;
    T* _elements;
```

These are the member variables that implement the structure. The order in which these are listed can be important. This is because constructor defined above initializes them in the initialization section rather than in the code block. The rule is that the initializations are done in the order in which the member variables are defined, not in the order in which the initializations occur in the constructor definition. They happen to be the same order here, but if, for example, we had defined _elements first (before _size) and then used _size rather than size as the initializing value in the constructor definition, then _elements would not be properly initialized. This can lead to subtle errors if you forget the rule.

```
    friend class ArrayStackIterator<T>;
};
```

Finally, we note that the ArrayStackIterator<T> is declared to be a friend class. This implies that the member functions of that class will have access to the member variables (all the private members, actually) of this one.

All of this seems pretty straightforward, except possibly the need for the begin and end functions. Why bother? The stack seems complete. What can be done with these two functions and the values they return? We shall return to these questions momentarily, but first a simple example of use.

```
void main()
{   ArrayStack<int> as;
    as.push(3);
    as.push(5);
    as.push(1);
    cout  << as.top() << ' '
          << as.pop() << as.pop() << endl;
    ArrayStack<char*> ss;
    ss.push("Hi.");
    ss.push("Bye.");
     . . .
}
```

The creator of every class has a dilemma to face and a problem to solve. If the class properly employs information hiding so that details of the implementation are hidden from users, then how does a user get necessary algorithms implemented? One way is to assure that the class has all necessary algorithms for use implemented as member functions (or combinations of member functions). This is a rather heavy requirement and requires a lot of foresight. Suppose that we discover after the fact that some required processing is missing. What do we do? One option is to modify the class itself to add the required functionality, and this is often done. Modifying existing code, however, is problematic, since it can introduce errors and make previously working code break. Another option is to build a derived class and to implement the new functionality there. This is also often done and in many cases is superior to the first solution. The STL takes a different approach to this problem, however.

In the Standard Template Library, very few of the algorithms needed to manipulate an abstraction are implemented in the class corresponding to that abstraction. Instead, the class defines functions that make certain information about the abstraction—here a stack—available in such a way that the user can implement any needed algorithm without modifying the structure itself. In fact, it is possible to build such algorithms in such a way that they work with other data abstractions as well as the one for which they were originally designed. This is the purpose of iterators.

Iterators are any types, built-in or user-defined, that have certain characteristics similar to those of pointers. In particular, we need to be able to de-reference an iterator to get access to the value that it references. We need to be able to advance an iterator using operator++, and we need to be able to test two iterators for equality. Specialized iterators have additional properties, as we shall see. What follows is a user-defined class that implements an iterator type corresponding to our ArrayStack type. It is much simplified from what is actually available in the STL, but again, it is intended primarily to introduce the concepts needed and not to be an extension of the STL. We shall see that it gives us enough power to be able to use a variation of our selectionSort algorithm of the previous chapter to sort stacks, although sorting a stack is a somewhat foreign concept.

In this implementation, an iterator (ArrayStackIterator) uses an integer representing an index and a pointer to an array. This array is actually the same array (not a copy) that represents the implementation of the ArrayStack that this iterator is *iterating over*.

```
template <class T>
class ArrayStackIterator
{   public:

        typedef T value_type;
```

The value_type is the type of data stored in the associated array.

```
        T& operator*()
        {   return _array->_elements[_where];
        }
```

This is the de-reference operator. It gives us access to the item the iterator references at the time. Note that by returning a T& rather than a T, we return the value itself, not a copy. This means that we can store into this value as well as retrieve the current value. This means we can modify the associated stack without pushing or popping, of course. This might be undesirable. We could prevent this by making the operation const and returning a const reference instead.

```
bool operator<(const ArrayStackIterator<T>& i)
{   return _where < i._where;
}
```

Here we compare two iterators using <. The implication is that the iterators are iterating over the same stack. Any other use will return garbage information. We just compare the _where member variables of the two iterators.

```
ArrayStackIterator<T> operator+(int i)
{   return
        ArrayStackIterator<T>(_array, _where + i);
}
```

Operator+ lets us add an integer to an iterator. This is the exact analogue of pointer arithmetic in which we add an integer to a pointer. We want the addition of i to point us up i slots in the stack.

```
T& operator++()
{ return _array->_elements[++_where];}

T& operator++(int)
{return _array->_elements[_where++];}
```

These are the two *auto increment* operators. The first is the preincrement version that moves the iterator along one cell and returns the value in the new position. We increment _where before we use it to retrieve an element (reference). The version with the unused int parameter is a C++ hack that defines the post-increment operator. Again, we use _where++ as the basis of the implementation. Note that we could turn this iterator class into something like a bidirectional iterator if we also implement the two operator-- versions.

```
private:
    ArrayStackIterator
    (   ArrayStack<T>* s, int where = 0
    )
    :   _where(where),
        _array(s)
    {
    }
```

The constructor just makes a copy of a pointer to an ordinary array and an index. These come from the array that creates the iterator. These iterators are created only by functions such as begin() and end() of the ArrayStack class. We guarantee that iterators are created only by ArrayStacks by making the constructor private. Note that we don't need a copy constructor here or an overloaded assignment or a destructor, since the supplied versions will suffice.

```
    int    _where;
    T* _array;
```

```
    friend class ArrayStack<T>;
```

This friendship relation gives the ArrayStack class access to the private constructor of this class.

```
};
```

Exercise. What we have done with ArrayStackIterators is a little backwards when you think of it. In reality, an iteration over a stack should start at the top and proceed to the bottom. Ours proceeds in the opposite order. Rebuild ArrayStack and ArrayStackIterator as necessary to implement this improved idea.

In order to see what we can do with this, lets reexamine the selection sort from Chapter 2. The last version we had of that function template was

```
template < class T >
void selectionSort(T* start, T* end)
{  for(T* where = start ; where < end ; where++)
    {   T* loc = where;
        T small = *loc;
        for
        (   T* inner = where + 1;
            inner < end;
            inner++
        )
            if(*inner < *loc)
            {   loc = inner;
                small = *loc;
            }
        *loc = *where;
        *where = small;
    }
}
```

This is close to what we want, but not exactly. Here we explicitly use pointers to T as parameters and as locals. We want to replace these pointers with iterators. To do so we are going to change the template parameter type to TI and let this refer to an iterator type, rather than the type of data collected in the array (or other container). We won't have a parameter for the collected type at all, which gives us a problem since the type of local variable small must be this collected type. This was the purpose for the typedef value_type defined in the iterator class. We replace T* in the above by our new template parameter TI and replace T by TI::value_type.

```
template < class TI>
void selectionSort(TI start, TI end)
```

```
{   for(TI where = start ; where < end ; where++)
    {   TI loc = where;
        TI::value_type small = *loc;
        for
        (   TI inner = where + 1;
            inner < end;
            inner++
        )
            if(*inner < *loc)
            {   loc = inner;
                small = *loc;
            }
        *loc = *where;
        *where = small;
    }
}
```

Note: The STL is a bit more sophisticated about providing this value_type for iterators. In the STL it is done indirectly through the use of generic functions, while we have done it directly. The STL solution is preferable, as it permits ordinary arrays and pointers to be used as well as other containers and iterators. Our selectionSort will not work with arrays and pointers since, being built-in rather than defined by classes, they can't provide this value_type. This topic will be taken up again in Chapter 5.

Notice what operations we apply to the variables of the template parameter type: variables start, end, where, and loc. We assign one iterator to another. We use operator<, operator++ (postfix), and operator*. All of these are implemented in our class (except the assignment, which the system provides). We can therefore pass this function ArrayStackIterators and expect that it will sort the region of our stack between these iterators.

```
void main()
{   ArrayStack<int> as;
    as.push(3);
    as.push(5);
    as.push(1);
    as.push(4);

    selectionSort(as.begin(), as.end());

    cout << as.pop() << endl;
    cout << as.pop() << endl;
    cout << as.pop() << endl;
    cout << as.pop() << endl;
}
```

Note that the selectionSort algorithm is not part of the ArrayStack class, which did not need to be modified in order to provide this new functionality. This gives us power in two ways. First, the same algorithm will be used with a LinkStack that we intend to build in the next section. Second, we can add algorithms to a program without modifying existing code. Of course this is only possible because the iterator mechanism is very general and very powerful.

We close by noting that in the STL the array, vector, and deque types all use variations of dense storage. We shall examine some of the details in future chapters.

Exercise. Transform the quickSort algorithm in the same way that we have translated the selectionSort. Test it by sorting ArrayStacks.

Exercise. Use the StopWatch class of Chapter 1 to verify in practice that selectionSort is $O(n^2)$ and quickSort on random data is $O(n \log(n))$. Create a rather large stack and sort it, timing the operation. Now do the same on stacks twice as large and four times as large. What did you learn?

3.4   Linked Storage

With dense storage, our data structure is compactly stored in one place in memory. With linked storage, on the other hand, it is distributed in small pieces that are linked together. Think of taking lots of bits of paper with values on them and lots of bits of string with their ends glued to the bits of paper. The strings represent the links. We could connect the paper bits into a single chain, or a ring, or lots of other geometries if we permit more than two bits of string to be glued to the same piece of paper. This is similar to linked storage but not exactly the same, as we shall see.

The main difference between the links, which are actually pointers, and the bits of string is that pointers can only be traversed in one direction by using the de-referencing operator. We need two pointers to be able to move in two directions between adjacent bits of paper (data). Suppose that you glue lots of bits of paper-string into a linear chain. Then it is pretty clear that you can pick up the entire chain by picking up any piece. This is not so if you have a chain of links (pointers) and use only single linking from some first piece to some last piece. In this case, to pick up the entire chain, you need to pick up its first link. Since you can't move backwards along pointers if you pick it up elsewhere, you won't have access to the items "before" the place you pick it up.

Pointers are very much like string in other ways, however. A similarity between strings and links is that if you cut a linear chain, you lose access to the part cut away unless you are careful to hold on to both pieces at the time the cut is made.

To build a linked implementation of a data structure, we normally use two structs or classes. One of these classes defines *nodes* and the other defines the data abstraction of interest: a stack, for example. The nodes are an implementation detail and are not, properly, part of the abstraction. They are just the stuff out of which we build our stack, or list, or whatever. A Node normally contains a data value of some type: the type that we collect in the container, or occasionally a pointer or a reference to such a type. The Node also has one or more link fields. These are just pointers to other Nodes. If we want a linear, sequential structure or a ring, we only need one pointer per Node. If we want bi-directional links, we need two pointers per Node. Trees and graphs may require more, even a variable number of pointer variables in each Node.

A standard form for Nodes of a singly linked structure would look like the following:

```
template <class T>
class Node
{   private:
        Node(T val, Node<T>* next = NULL)
        :   _value(val),
            _next(next)
        {
        }
        T _value;
        Node<T>* _next;
    friend class . . .
};
```

We have made everything in the class private and have indicated that some class will be a friend of this class. This is because this class defines an implementation detail only, so its features should be private to the class that uses it and not available to others. The constructor "links" in its parameter, which is a Node*, to this Node, in effect attaching it after the Node being constructed.

In the absence of the other class, and assuming that the constructor, at least, is public, we can construct a sequentially linked structure by repeatedly calling the constructor (carefully).

```
Node<int> * head = new Node<int>(5);
head = new Node<int> (4, head);
head = new Node<int> (3, head);
head = new Node<int> (2, head);
head = new Node<int> (1, head);
```

At this point, head points to a Node with a 1 in it. That Node is followed by a Node with a 2, then a 3, etc., until the last Node with the 5 in it has a _next field of NULL. Note that each time we set a new value into head, we first use the old value as the "tail" of the Node being created. The following sequence of pictures, Figure 3.1 through 3.3, should help.

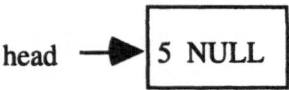

Figure 3.1. After: Node<int> * head = new Node<int>(5);

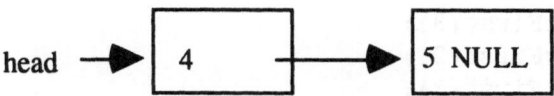

Figure 3.2. After: head = new Node<int> (4, head);

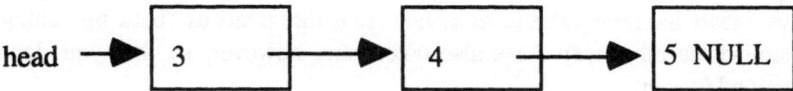

Figure 3.3. After: head = new Node<int> (3, head);

The boxes represent the Nodes, and the arrows from one box to another represent the _next field of each Node. Note that we have only one variable here. To get access to the Nodes after the first (head) we must use expressions, not simple variable names.

It is generally a mistake to build a linked list in this way, using just a pointer to refer to its head. Instead we normally define a second class that will encapsulate (and hide) this head pointer.

```
template <class T>
class List
{  public:

      List()
      :  _first(NULL)
      {
      }

      void insertFirst(T val)
      {  _first = new Node<T>(val, _first);
      }

   . . .
   private:
      Node<T>* _first;
   };
```

This class will be the friend class of the Node class.
We would now create the same list with the following code:

```
List<int> L;
L.insertFirst(5);
L.insertFirst(4);
```

```
L.insertFirst(3);
L.insertFirst(2);
L.insertFirst(1);
```

There are many variations on linked storage as indicated above. One of the easiest is to circularly link the list so that the last Node, rather than having a NULL pointer in its _next field, has a pointer to the first Node. Maintaining this circularity requires care when we insert and remove data. Its advantage is that it lets us "back up" along links by going around the other way. This also takes care, however, so that you don't go around and around forever.

Another variation is double linking. Put two Node* fields in each Node: _next and _previous. It is then very useful to put two Node* fields into the List class as well: _first and _last. In fact, even with single linking, it is often of use to maintain a pointer in the list class to both the first and last Nodes of the chain. This gives us access to both ends of the chain. Note that it is easy to do inserts at either end, easy to do deletions at the front, but difficult to delete at the rear, as we shall see in a moment.

If a list is singly linked, then we can effectively only provide forward iterators: those that can move from beginning to end in the direction of the linking. If we doubly link a list, then we can easily provide bidirectional iterators. This is the approach taken in STL lists.

To delete a Node at the front of a List we could use a member function like the following:

```
void deleteFirst()
{   Node<T>* temp = _first;
    _first = _first->_next;
    delete temp;
}
```

The difficulty of deleting elsewhere is illustrated by Figure 3.4, in which we suppose we want to delete the Node with the 5, but all we have is a pointer to that Node.

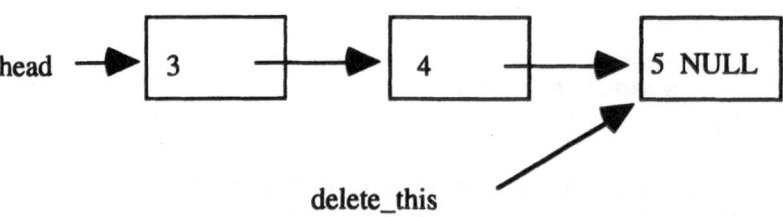

Figure 3.4. Problematic deletions.

The difficulty is not in deleting the Node itself, but in keeping the rest of the List legal. We always want the last link in a list to be in some specific state, usually NULL. The problem is that this new last link will be the link in the Node with the 4 after we delete the last Node. We can get access to this Node only with difficulty, since we don't have a direct link to it and we can't follow links backwards. The correct way to delete a Node in a singly linked list is to have a pointer to the Node that precedes it, not to the Node itself. See Figure 3.5. We are much better off if we have a pointer to the Node with the 4, since the _next field of this Node needs to be updated to keep the List intact.

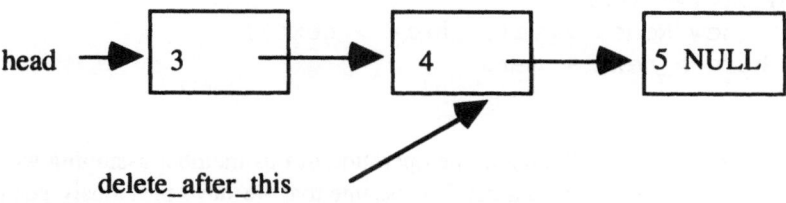

Figure 3.5. Correctly positioned for deleting Node 5.

Well, how do we get such a pointer? The answer again involves our iterator concept. Suppose we build the List class with a member function begin() that returns an iterator to the beginning. The implementation of this iterator class can be just a Node*, perhaps named _here, since it names a position within a list. Then we can continually advance the iterator, with operator++, until we refer to the Node preceding the one we seek. We can check where we are using the de-reference operator*. Then, from the iterator itself, we can execute the deleteAfter operation, which is a member of the iterator class, not the list class.

```
void deleteAfter()
{   Node<T>* temp = _here->_next;
       // The node to be deleted
    _here->_next = temp->_next;
       // Point around temp
    delete temp;
}
```

This function works correctly even if the Node to be deleted is not the last Node in the chain, since it doesn't set the _next of the current position to be NULL, but to the current value of the Node to be removed, which completes the chain. Of course, all depends on first getting our iterator to the right location.

Exercise. Draw a sequence of link pictures, similar to Figures 3.1 through 3.3, that illustrate the operation of the deleteAfter function step by step.

Using such an iterator we can also insert a new Node between two existing Nodes. To do so again requires having a pointer (iterator actually) to the first of the two Nodes. We need to create the new Node, make its _next refer to the second of the two Nodes we are inserting between, and then make the first Node refer to the new Node. Therefore, the following can be part of our ListIterator class. The first statement carries out the first two of the above three steps.

```
void insertAfter(T val)
{   Node<T>* temp =
        new Node<T>(val, _here->_next);
    _here->_next = temp;
}
```

Figures 3.6 through 3.8 detail the operation of this member assuming we are attempting to insert the value 7 into a list. We assume that we have previously positioned an iterator to the location of the insertion. Note again that this is not a list member, but a list iterator member.

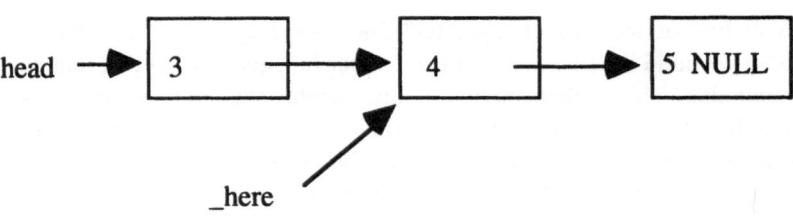

Figure 3.6. Before inserting between the 4 and the 5.

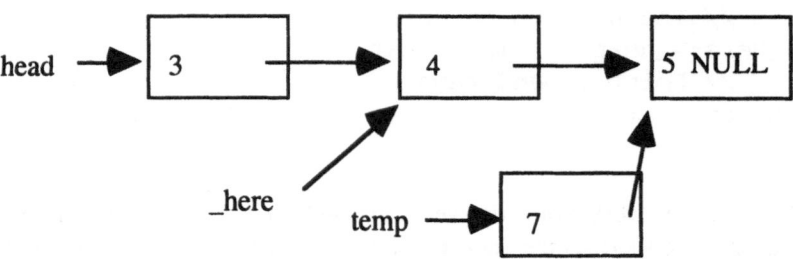

Figure 3.7. After the first statement, inserting a 7.

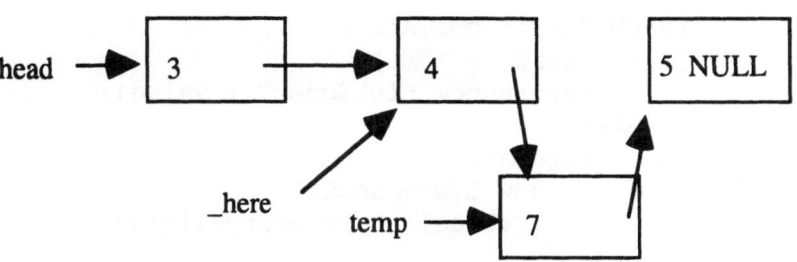

Figure 3.8. After the last statement, inserting a 7.

While we have described the deleteAfter and insertAfter members as being actions of an iterator rather than a list, there is an alternative way to implement them. We CAN put code like this into the list class if we pass an iterator as a parameter to each of these. We would then use _here member of this iterator to implement the above operations. This is the method chosen in the STL, since it puts fewer restrictions on the iterators themselves, leaving them more general.

Exercise. Look at Figure 3.8. Novices sometimes delete temp, as the last statement of insertAfter, thinking that they don't need the pointer anymore. Carefully explain the effect of this and why it is a disaster.

3.5   An Extended Example Part 2: The Linked Stack

In this section we will rebuild our Stack using a linked implementation. Notice that the interface of this LinkStack class has identical functions with identical parameter lists. In other words, a LinkStack is functionally equivalent to an ArrayStack. There will be one difference in efficiency, as we shall note near the end of the section. We shall also need to build an associated LinkStackIterator class. First, however, we need a Node class as indicated above. We call this class LinkNode. It is as advertised above, except that it declares both the LinkStack and LinkStackIterator classes as friends. It also has an additional (recursive) member function copyAll() that we shall discuss when we look at the Link-Stack class.

```
template <class T>
class LinkNode
{   private:
        LinkNode(T val, LinkNode<T>* next = NULL)
        :   _value(val),
            _next(next)
        {
        }
```

```
            LinkNode<T>* copyAll()
            {   if(_next == NULL)
                    return new LinkNode<T>(_value);
                else
                    return
                        new LinkNode<T>
                        (_value, _next->copyAll());
            }

            T _value;
            LinkNode<T>* _next;
        friend class LinkStack<T>;
        friend class LinkStackIterator<T>;
};
```

To push onto a LinkStack, we insert a new Node at the front. To pop we remove from the front. This means that single linking is sufficient, with no need for an additional pointer to the end.

```
template <class T>
class LinkStack
{   public:

        typedef LinkStackIterator<T> iterator;

        LinkStack()
        :   _first(NULL)
        {
        }
```

An empty LinkStack has its _first == NULL.

```
        LinkStack(const LinkStack<T>& S)
        {   copy(S);
        }

        ~LinkStack(){ free();}

        LinkStack<T>& operator=
        (const LinkStack<T>& S)
        {   if(this != &S)
            {   free();
                copy(S);
            }
            return *this;
        }
```

The copy constructor, destructor, and assignment operator have been factored into two auxiliary functions copy and free. Free deletes all of the Nodes in the current stack and copy sets the Nodes to be copies of the Nodes of its parameter. Copy is careful to preserve the order of the Nodes it copies. We will discuss these functions below.

```
void push(const T& v)
{ _first = new LinkNode<T>(v, _first);}
```

This is just an insert at the beginning of the list of Nodes as indicated above.

```
T pop()
{   T temp = _first->_value;
    LinkNode<T>* oldnode = _first;
    _first = oldnode->_next;
    delete oldnode;
    return temp;
}
```

Here we remove the Node at the beginning of the list of Nodes, but we also return the value stored in that Node. This will result in an error if the stack is empty when it is executed.

```
T top()const{ return _first->_value; }
```

We just return the first value. Again, it is an error if the stack is empty. We could also return a const reference here, const T&, rather than a copy. This would let us look at, but not change the value returned. We could also return a T& in fact, which would let us modify the top in place, without removing it from the stack.

Exercise. Explore the following three versions of top().

```
T top()const{ return _first->_value; }
T& top()const{ return _first->_value; }
const T& top()const
{   return _first->_value;
}
```

In each case, try to modify the returned value and then look at the stack as a whole.

```
bool empty()const
{   return _first == NULL;
}
```

```
bool full()const{ return false; }
```

These are straightforward. It is empty if its _first is NULL. The user of our LinkStack must be careful to use these functions or otherwise keep track of when the stack is empty. Such a stack is never full. Well, actually, it would be full if the allocator were unable to allocate a new Node. The allocator can in fact be used to return a sensible value for full in this case. We ignore this complication here.

```
iterator begin()const
{   return LinkStackIterator<T>(_first);
}
```

An iterator to the beginning of the stack contains a pointer to the first Node.

```
iterator end()const
{   return LinkStackIterator<T>(NULL);
}
```

An after-the-end iterator contains a pointer to the same spot as the last Node in the list. In this case that is the NULL pointer.

```
private:
    LinkNode<T>* _first;

    void free()
    {   while(_first != NULL)
        {   LinkNode<T>* temp = _first;
            _first = temp->_next;
            delete temp;
        }
    }
```

Free is used in the destructor and in the assignment operator. It deletes all of the Nodes in the list, leaving it empty. Note that it could as easily have called pop() repeatedly, though this is somewhat more efficient.

```
void copy(const LinkStack& S)
{   if(S._first == NULL)
        _first = NULL;
    else
        _first = S._first->copyAll();
}
```

This member function sets the current value to the same value as the parameter. It is used by the copy constructor and by the assignment operator. If the parameter is empty it sets itself (this) to be empty. Otherwise, it sets its _first to be the result of calling LinkNode::copyAll on the _first of the parameter. The effect of that is to recursively copy all of the Nodes that start with S._first, making a new chain. Function copyAll works by creating a new Node and installing as its next a copy of its own next. If its own next is NULL, then the copy is just NULL also, but otherwise, the copy may be made by calling copyAll recursively on its _next.

```
    friend class LinkStackIterator<T>;
};
```

What we have above is a new class that implements the same interface as the ArrayStack class. Except for the type name, they may be used interchangeably. Let us now turn to the associated iterator class, LinkStackIterator. Again we will comment the code as we go along. Note that this class implements the same interface as ArrayStackIterator, though we will see in a moment that it probably should not. An iterator here is implemented with a field _where, that is just a Node pointer.

```
template <class T>
class LinkStackIterator
{  public:

        typedef T value_type;

        LinkStackIterator(LinkNode<T>* where)
        :   _where(where)
        {
        }
```

We just remember the parameter in the _where field. No copy constructor, destructor, or assignment operator is needed here, since we are not managing memory in this class. The Node pointed to will not be destroyed, for example, until the stack that contains it is destroyed or the Node is popped.

```
        T& operator*()
        {   return _where->_value;
        }
```

The de-reference operator just de-references the current pointer. The pointer points to a Node, however, and we want the value, so we extract and return that.

Question. What happens if we de-reference an iterator that was created with LinkStackIterator(NULL)?

```
        bool operator<
        (const LinkStackIterator<T>& i)
        {   if(_where != NULL && i._where == NULL)
                return true;
```

```
            if (  _where == NULL
                || _where == i._where
               )
               return false;
            LinkNode<T>* temp = _where->_next;
            while(temp != NULL)
            {  if( temp == i._where) return true;
               temp = temp->_next;
            }
            return false;
         }
```

This is expensive to implement correctly. We require that the two iterators compared are "into" the same stack, of course. We are testing whether if we follow _next pointers from the current position we will eventually arrive at the position of i. This requires time that is linear in the number of elements in the stack. The bidirectional iterators of STL lists do not provide this operation because of its cost.

```
         LinkStackIterator<T> operator+(int i)
         {  LinkNode<T>* temp = _where;
            for(int x = 0; x < i; x++)
               temp = temp->_next;
            return LinkStackIterator<T>(temp);
         }
```

This is the *pointer arithmetic* operation again. Note that it cannot be done in constant time. It takes time proportional to the integer i because of the for loop. Perhaps it would be better to omit this function altogether for reasons of efficiency. Bidirectional iterators in the STL do not have such an operation.

```
         T& operator++()
         {  _where = _where->_next;
            return _where->_value;
         }
```

This is the prefix increment operator. Note that we move before we de-reference.

```
         T& operator++(int)
         {  LinkNode<T>* temp = _where;
            _where = _where->_next;
            return temp->_value;
         }
```

The postfix increment is a bit messier since we need to remember where we were as the basis of the returned value, but also move forward.

```
    private:
        LinkNode<T>* _where;
};
```

Well, there it is, with a few problems as indicated. However, since it does implement the same interface as the ArrayStackIterator, we can use these interchangeably. In particular, we can sort a LinkStack with our selectionSort algorithm.

```
void main()
{   LinkStack<int> as;
    as.push(3);
    as.push(5);
    as.push(1);
    as.push(4);

    selectionSort(as.begin(), as.end());

    cout << as.pop() << endl;
    cout << as.pop() << endl;
    cout << as.pop() << endl;
    cout << as.pop() << endl;
}
```

There will be a difference in performance, however, since the operator+ works more slowly here. For this reason the STL list class does not include the operator+ in its iterator. It is too expensive in general. This means that the generalized sort algorithm of the STL won't work with lists, because it requires this operator (random access iterators depend on it). Instead, the list class supplies its own specialized sort algorithm that works efficiently on lists but less efficiently elsewhere. We will examine that algorithm later.

One important lesson that you should learn from the above is that a linked list iterator behaves like a pointer, is implemented as a pointer, but is, in fact, an encapsulated object with a limited interface. It is not a "naked" pointer, but an object that contains and controls a pointer. This extra level of packaging provides safety, as it makes inappropriate pointer operations impossible.

Exercise. Just how inefficient is sorting lists with selectionSort and quickSort? Analyze these two algorithms, taking into account the fact that operator< and operator+ are linear time algorithms; the first is linear in the number of elements in the list and the second is linear in its parameter. The inefficiency of operator+ has little effect on selectionSort, since we only add one to any iterator there.

Exercise. Use a StopWatch object to verify your conclusions from the above exercise. Build a large ListStack and time its sort with the two sorts. Then double the size of the stack and repeat. Double again and repeat your measurements. Does this support your conclusions from above?

Exercise. Redo the selection sort algorithm so that it uses only operator++ and opera-
tor== in place of operator+ and operator<. What is the advantage of this change? Rebuild
the two stack iterator classes so that they also implement operator==.

3.6   Tree Storage

Trees are normally treated as a variation on linked storage, though it is possible to store
certain trees densely. The difference between the sequential linkages defined above and tree
storage is in the number of links in a node. The simplest kind of tree is a binary tree in
which each node has exactly two "next" nodes, called its children. See Figure 8.1 for example. A binary tree node might look like the following:

```
template <class T>
class BinaryTreeNode
{   private:
        Node
        (   T val,
            BinaryTreeNode<T>* left = NULL,
            BinaryTreeNode<T>* right = NULL
        )
        :   _value(val),
            _left(left),
            _right(right)
        {
        }
        T _value;
        BinaryTreeNode<T>* _left;
        BinaryTreeNode<T>* _right;
    friend class . . .
};
```

The analogue of double linking in a tree is to provide a pointer in each node to its parent: the node above it in the tree. The single node with no parent is called the root node,
and most often trees are drawn with the root at the top. If the BinaryTree class that uses
these node types needs to provide iterators, then parent links are very helpful.

```
template <class T>
class BinaryTreeNode
{   private:
        Node
        (   T val,
            BinaryTreeNode<T>* left = NULL,
            BinaryTreeNode<T>* right = NULL,
```

```
      BinaryTreeNode<T>* parent = NULL
   )
   : _value(val),
     _left(left),
     _right(right),
     _parent(parent)
   {
   }
   T _value;
   BinaryTreeNode<T>* _left;
   BinaryTreeNode<T>* _right;
   BinaryTreeNode<T>* _parent;
  friend class . . .
};
```

A node in a tree is called a leaf if it has no children. The root has no parent. In our implementation this means that both (all) children must be NULL. The height of a node is the number of links back to the root of the tree from that node. The height of the root is zero, that of its children is one, etc. The height of a tree is the maximum of the heights of all of its nodes. The height of a tree is important since we search for things in a tree starting at the root. If we arrange the tree appropriately we need only search a single path from root to leaf for an item. We would like these paths to be as short as possible.

A binary tree is called balanced when all of its leaf nodes are at approximately the same height. More specifically, a tree is balanced when the minimum and maximum leaf heights differ by only one. When a tree is balanced, the height of the tree is the logarithm of the number of nodes. Thus, we can store about a million values in a balanced binary tree of height twenty.

A *binary search tree* is a binary tree in which the elements inserted support the operator<, and the elements are kept in the tree in a special order. The rule is that the value in any node, A, is *less* than that of any node in the subtree whose root is the right child of A and the value in any node in the left subtree is *not greater* than the value in node A.

If we have a binary search tree and we list the values in the nodes in the order called *inorder*, then we shall list the values in increasing order according to operator<. Inorder listing of the nodes of a binary tree require that we list all of the nodes in the left subtree of any node before we list the value in the node, and that we list or otherwise process the values in the right subtree after listing the node. This can be easily arranged with a recursive function of the form

```
void inorder( BinaryTreeNode<T> * n)
{  if(n->_left != NULL) inorder(n->_left);
   process (n->_value);
   if(n->_right != NULL) inorder(n->_right);
}
```

In contrast, preorder processing of a tree requires that we process the root before its children. The form for this is as follows:

```
void preorder ( BinaryTreeNode<T> * n)
{   process (n->_value);
    if(n->_left != NULL) preorder (n->_left);
    if(n->_right != NULL) preorder (n->_right);
}
```

Finally, postorder requires that we process a node after both of its children.

One major advantage of a binary search tree is that it is easy to retrieve data stored in it. If we are looking for a certain value, then by examining the value at the root of the tree or any subtree, we always know whether to continue the search to the right or to the left if we haven't yet found the desired item.

The naive way to insert into a binary search tree always inserts at the bottom of the tree, inserting a new leaf. We compare the value to be inserted with the root node first and if the new value is less than the root, we move down to the left; otherwise, we move down to the right. We again compare and move down, until we reach a spot where the node that we are trying to move to is missing: a NULL pointer. We insert a new node at this point.

The problem with the above insert algorithm into binary search trees is that it might leave us with a tree that is not tree-like, but list-like. The ideal binary tree is balanced, meaning that each leaf node is at about the same depth. The reason for this is that a tree holds the maximum number of nodes for its height when it is balanced. This means that in a balanced binary search tree, we can search quickly for an item among a lot of data.

Question. What happens if we use the naive insert method in a binary search tree and then insert data into it that is already sorted?

Some algorithms for inserting into a balanced binary search tree require that the tree be rebalanced after each insertion. This balancing takes place along a path from leaf to root and only requires that a few pointers be adjusted, and so can be done in logarithmic time. The STL set class is based on a variation of a balanced binary tree. It does require that operator< be implemented on the values to be included in the set, however. Lookups in a balanced binary search tree are logarithmically related to the number of values in the tree and so it proceeds very quickly, since a logarithm of a number is small in comparison to the number.

A balanced binary tree can be stored efficiently in an array. We store the root in cell one (not zero, which is often kept free as a temporary location in the algorithms that process the tree). The left child of the node in cell n is stored in cell 2n and the right child is stored in cell 2n+1. Verify that this works and that it wastes relatively little space if the tree is balanced. The number of cells required in the array is $2^h + 1$, where h is the height of the tree. We can find the parent of a node in such a tree just by dividing the cell number of a value by 2.

3.7   Graph Storage

A graph is composed of nodes (or vertices), and links (or arcs). An arc connects a pair of the vertices. We can store data in the vertices, and in some graphs we also store data along the arcs. A graph with data on its arcs is sometimes called a network. Graphs are more complicated than trees, as you would suppose. One obvious way to build a graph is to keep in each node a list of the neighbors of that node. Another implementation is often more convenient. In this latter method, we keep a list of all the nodes in the graph. For each node we keep a list, not necessarily in the node itself, that gives the neighbors of the given node. Graphs can be directed or undirected. In a directed graph (digraph), the arcs are unidirectional like pointers. See Figure 5.4 for an example of a digraph. In an undirected graph, the arcs are just connections and have no direction. One can implement these with a pair of pointers.

Traversing all of the vertices of a graph may be easy or difficult. If we keep a list of the vertices it is easy, of course. If we do not, then it may be necessary to keep a "mark" value in each vertex. Before traversing the graph, we set all of the marks to false. Then when we process a vertex, we set its mark to true so that we don't process it again. Two common protocols for processing the vertices of a graph are *depth first* and *breadth first*. In breadth first, we process all of the near neighbors of a node before processing their neighbors: process the near neighbors before the far neighbors. In depth first protocol, when we process a neighbor of the first node we process its neighbors before returning to the next neighbor of the first. When we search a graph for an item starting at a given node, we might use breadth first if we expect that the target will be near the original node. If not, we might use depth first search.

The STL does not have a class representing graphs. However, using lists and arrays it is quite easy to build a graph abstraction.

3.8   Hashed Storage

Dense storage is a mechanism for achieving very fast lookup of stored items based on where the data is stored. To retrieve an item in constant time, you must know the subscript in which to look for the item. Hashed Storage, on the other hand, tries to achieve fast lookup based on what the data is. In other words, the value of the data, or some part of the data, is used to compute the storage location. Since it is not normally useful to look up data when we already have the value of the data, this sounds like a useless idea. However, it is commonly the case that we store a variety of information about a person or thing and we desire to look up the information while knowing the name or some other characteristic of the target. A telephone book is a simple example of this idea. We store names, addresses, and phone numbers in the directory. We use the name as a *key* to retrieve the rest of the information. The data itself consists of key-information pairs. We use the key to get access to the information. An individual in a phone book database might have a record like the following:

```
class cell
{  public:
       cell
       (  char* name,
          char* address,
          char* phone
       );
       unsigned int hash();
       . . .
   private:
       char* _name;
       char* _address;
       char* _phone;
}
```

In fact, a phone book stores the data in key order, making something like binary search possible. Hashed storage is quite different. In fact it is called "hash" because of the fact that the data, when viewed as a whole, appear to be mixed up in order, similar to the ingredients in the culinary delight (?) corned beef hash. This seemingly random mixing is only superficial, however, and there is a deeper structure.

In hashed storage, a computation is done on the value of the key. The value of this computation, called the hash, is used to indicate where in a storage structure the corresponding data will be stored. Depending on the specifics of the storage itself, the hash may result in a unique storage location in which the target may be found if it is stored at all, or simply indicate the place to start a search. This latter method is the most common and, while it may not result in constant retrieval time, it can greatly speed lookups by greatly reducing the number of items that must be examined to find the target or verify that it is not stored.

One common hash function on name data is to take the length of the name and its first character value, treated as a numeric ASCII code, and multiply these values together, resulting in an integer. Notice that this value is completely well determined and reproducible given the spelling of the name.

Suppose that our storage mechanism consists of an array of 100 linked lists. If we take the hash value of a given key, and take the remainder upon division by 100, we obtain a number between 0 and 99. This may be taken as a subscript into the array. If we wish to store data for this key, we store it on the list at this computed index. Then, if we wish to retrieve data for this key, we recompute the hash, reduce it to an index in the same way, and then search the corresponding linked list for the key. The expected time to find the item is the average length of the lists, which is about 1 percent of the total number of data items.

Of course, achieving fast lookup in practice involves two things. The first is having a hash function that distributes the keys to be stored uniformly over the resulting hash values and so uniformly over the lists, which, by the way, are called "hash buckets." The term bucket is used since it indicates a storage mechanism with little if any internal structure. The second essential feature of hash storage mechanism is correctly choosing the number of buckets so that the lists will all be short. This assumes that we may estimate the total number of items to be stored, though this need not be completely accurate.

When the keys consist of things like names or words in some human language, it turns out to be a bad idea to use all of the characters in the key as a basis for the hash function, especially if the hash function simply adds the character encodings. This is not just because it is time-consuming to do so. The problem, rather, involves the fact that some of the characters appear much more frequently than others, which skews the results. This can easily make some of your lists short and others very long. This can greatly lengthen the retrieval time, which is undesirable.

It is possible to build a self-organizing hash system in which the number of buckets expands or contracts dynamically as data is inserted and removed. To do so involves periodically examining the buckets for length, expanding or contracting the number of buckets as appropriate, and redistributing the stored data among the new buckets by recomputing the hash values. If the number of buckets is always a power of two, then this is particularly easy if remainders are the last step in the computation of the index. This is because if the remainder when we divide by 2^n is k, then when we divide by 2^{n+1}, it will be either k or $k+2^n$. This means that the new bucket for an item is either the same as the old one or possibly one other bucket.

When we can predict precisely how many items will be stored, it is possible to avoid the lists altogether. Suppose that we know that we will store exactly m values. Then we can allocate an array of m cells. If we know all of the keys in advance and work hard enough, we can find a hash function that will compute a different value for each of the keys. We store the data for this key in the cell computed by this hash function. Otherwise we use the computed value simply as a place to start a linear search for the data within the array. We must search "circularly," however, so that if we come to the end of the array before finding the item, we resume our search at the beginning. This method of hashing is called *circular hashing*, as opposed to the *separate chaining* which uses the array of lists described above.

When two keys result in the same hash value, we say we have a *collision*. A hash function with no collisions is called perfect. They are difficult to find, but possible, provided that we have a fixed, finite number of known keys.

One advantage of hashed storage over binary search trees is that we don't need a comparison like operator< for hashed storage. This makes hashed storage feasible in some situations in which binary search trees are not. Of course we require that the data provide either a hash function, or a means of devising one.

3.9   Indexed Storage

Indexed storage is somewhat like the index of a book. The words (keys) are arranged in a definite (usually alphabetical) order and are associated with some sort of pointing mechanism to the data records (pages) of interest. In a book index these are just page numbers, of course. The sorted order of the index makes it easy to search, and the pointers give us quick access to the desired information. Similarly, a phone book is like an index to people, represented by their phone numbers.

The main advantage of an index is that it lets us simulate having one file sorted on different criteria. For example, in an employee database, it might be advantageous to physically arrange the records according to an employee number. This would make it difficult to find a person based on their name or office, however. An index with key name and another with key office can be used to solve this problem.

To build a name index into the employee database, we would proceed as follows. First we scan the entire employee file, building a list of employee numbers (the primary key) and the associated names. When we are done we have a list that is in employee number order. We then sort this list by name. This sorted file is our index. Since it is sorted by name, it is easy to look up names. The associated employee numbers give us quick access to the full employee record, using the main file. A given file can have any number of indices.

The above described a record index. A related idea is called a block index. Suppose that the employee records are packed several to a block on a disk or similar device. Such blocks have block addresses, which we can think of as being numbers, though in reality they sometimes have a more complex structure. Given a block number, the disk device can quickly access the block. Suppose that we build an index by recording, for each record in the block, its first employee number and the disk block number. Recall that the file was sorted physically by employee number, so other employee records in the same block will have successive employee numbers. If we sort this index file by employee number, then we can get quick access to the block number for a given employee and hence, quick access to the rest of the data.

Part of the key to making the above work well is that the index is usually much smaller than the original file. We can take special advantage of this in the following way. Suppose we have a block index with employee number as the key and suppose that we store this index itself in disk blocks. Call this file the first level index. Suppose that we then build a (second level) block index to the first level index file. This file will be even smaller, since many indexing records will fit into a single block. We can, of course, continue this process to build higher level (and smaller) indexes to indexes at a lower level, until an index is small enough to hold it in computer memory. With such a multilevel indexing scheme, we can then get access to the records in the original file by finding the record in the highest level index that *covers* the record sought, tracing the associated block address to a single block of the next level index, searching it again for the record number desired, etc. Eventually we get to the lowest level index and then to the original file. This works in practice because we don't usually need many levels unless the original file is huge. Storing 20 to 100 index records in each block of an index is common. This means that for each level of the index, the number of available records expands by a factor of 20 to 100 for each level. This exponential growth implies that large files can be covered with indexes without much depth.

What we have described above, of course, is very similar to a tree structure, with the highest level index being the root, and the original file representing the leaves. It is complicated by the fact that we may need to insert and delete records. We wouldn't want to have to generate all of the index levels for each insert or deletion. The solution to this is to only partially fill the index blocks when the file is first created, leaving room for additional index records at each level. This complicates the algorithms that manipulate the index tree, but greatly speeds up the overall operation of the system. One variation on this idea is called a b-tree. This is not to be confused with binary tree, however. A b-tree is an n-way tree (up to n children at each level) where each leaf is at exactly the same height and where each internal node has between n/2 and n children.

At the other extreme is a simple two level structure, in which we maintain the data at one level and the index at another level. We shall see this technique used in a later chapter (Chapter 6).

3.10 Summary

Make certain that you understand each of the following terms:

binary search tree
` binary tree
circular hashing
collision
dense storage
graph
hashed storage
indexed storage
linked storage
multilevel indexing
perfect hash function
separate chaining
stack (including the defining rules)

3.11 Exercises

1. Add a size() function to each of our stack classes. It should return the number of elements stored in the stack. For the linked stack it may require linear time.

2. Rewrite LinkStack::size() so that it can be done in constant time. What other changes to the stack are required to make this possible? What does that do to the efficiency of the other member functions?

3. A queue is a structure similar in some ways to a stack. Stacks implement a LIFO, or last-in, first-out, protocol, whereas queues implement FIFO, or first-in, first-out. This means that the item removed from a queue is the one that has been in the queue for the longest amount of time rather than the shortest. Another way to think of it is that it is

sequential structure with inserts at one end and deletions at the other. The protocol for a Queue class template might be

```
template <class E>
class Queue
{ public:
    typedef E value_type;
    Queue();
    ~Queue();
    Queue(const Queue<E>&);
    Queue<E>& operator=(const Queue<E>&);

    bool empty() const;
    value_type& front();
    const value_type& front() const;
    void push(const value_type& x);
    void pop();
private:
    ... _front;
    ... _back;
};
```

Give a linked implementation of a queue. Private member variables _front and _back point to the first and last nodes of the implementing list. push() inserts the value at the location following _back. pop() removes the item pointed to by _front, and front() returns that item without removing it. An empty queue can be represented with both _front and _back NULL.

The formal rules for a queue are

1. Just after creation, empty returns true.
2. Just after push, empty returns false.
3. If empty would return true, then pop(); is an error; and t = front(); is an error.
4. If empty would return true, then push(x); pop() leaves the queue empty.
5. If empty would return true, then push(x); t = front(); returns x to variable t.
6. If empty would return false, then push(x); pop() is the same as pop(); push(x); also push(x); t = front(); is the same as t = front(); push(x);

4. It is somewhat difficult to define an iterator for the above implementation. It is made easier if we use a trailer node that does not contain data. An empty queue has a single node with both _front and _back pointing to it. This node is created when the queue is, and is never deleted until the queue is.

The iterator can be a separate class that maintains a pointer to a QueueNode as its main implementation variable.

Build an iterator class for the modified Queue class. The new Queue class needs public members begin() and end(). begin() returns an iterator to the first item. end() returns an iterator to the after-the-end location of the trailer node.

5. Test the stack implementations given in the text. Use a StopWatch object to time their operations over several thousand insertions and deletions.

Create An STL stack with a linked implementation. All this takes is the declaration

```
stack< list< int> > aStack;
```

You may now push and pop this stack. Be careful to put a space between the two ">'s" in the declaration, however, or the compiler may misinterpret what you have. How does the performance of this implementation compare with that of the linked stack implementation from the text?

Create an STL stack with a dense implementation with

```
stack< vector<int> > anotherStack;
```

How is the performance of this one?

6. Test your queue implementation against that of the STL queues in a similar way. You can create a linked queue with

```
queue< list< int> > aQueue;
```

and a dense queue with

```
queue< deque< int> > anotherQueue;
```

You can actually create a queue from a vector but the performance will be poor, since a vector has inefficient operations at the front. (Try it.)

7. Build a class DoubleLinkedDeque. It uses a doubly linked implementation and permits insertions and deletions at either end.

8. Build a hash table to implement a phone book. The key should be the name (a string) of the person and the data can have the phone number along with other information. Build a hashing function that works on the names. Note that it will not be possible with this implementation to list the names in alphabetical order without a separate sorting operation.

9. Build a Binary Search Tree phone book using the names as keys. Write a function that will compare the names using an operation like operator<.

10. Which of the two implementations of a phone book (See Exercises 6 and 7) give a better performance. Evaluate it theoretically as well as using a StopWatch object to time insertions and retrievals.

11. Build an index to a phone book so that we may look up people in the phone book by knowing their phone numbers and retrieve the names. You may use either the hash or the tree class for the basic phone book. The index, however, should have phone numbers for keys and provide access to an individual record in the phone book.

12. Postfix expressions are written with the operator symbol following all of its operands rather than between them (infix notation). For example, the ordinary expression (a+b) * c is written a b + c * in postfix. There are no parentheses in postfix notation, one of its advantages. Postfix expressions can be evaluated easily using a stack. The algorithm is quite simple. As you read the postfix expression left to right, if you see an operand (value), just push it onto a stack. If you see an operation, pop the correct number of operands for that operation from the stack, apply the operation to them, and push the result back onto the stack. You must be careful with noncommutative operations like subtraction, that you get the operands in the correct order: the first item popped becomes the rightmost operand. Implement this idea.

Chapter 4
Overview of the Standard Template Library

4.1. Components of the STL

The Standard Template Library has six different kinds of components. There are different subcategories of each of these component types. Here in one place is the complete listing of the library elements.

```
1. containers
   sequential containers
          array
          vector
          deque
          list
   sorted associative containers
          set
          multiset
          map
          multimap
   hashed associative containers
          (an extension)
2. iterators
       input iterators
       output iterators
       forward iterators
       bidirectional iterators
       random access iterators
3. generic algorithms
       nonmutating sequence algorithms
       mutating sequence algorithms
       sort related algorithms
       numeric algorithms
4. function objects
```

```
        arithmetic operations
        comparison operations
        logical operations
5. adaptors
        function adaptors
            negators
            binders
            pointer to function adaptors
        container adaptors
            stack
            queue
            priority queue
        iterator adaptors
            reverse adaptors
            insert adaptors
6. allocators
        default allocator
        custom allocators
```

We use the STL when we want to be able to store data in some structured way and to execute algorithms on the saved data. Depending on the nature of our problem and the type of algorithms we need to execute, some containers will be more suited to the task than others. Most of the algorithms work with most of the containers, but there are exceptions. It will become clear from the nature of the algorithms and the containers when there is a poor match. For example, the sort algorithms don't work on lists because of the difficulty of moving from one cell to a nonadjacent cell in a list. Instead, a specialized sort algorithm is provided for lists.

Each of the algorithms in the library is specified with its big O run-time bounds. This lets the user be sure about the performance of his or her programs. Most of the algorithms work with iterators. In fact, iterators are the interface between containers and algorithms that operate on them. This library was designed in this way so that the algorithms could be written in as general a way as possible so as not to have to duplicate the code for each container type. We create iterators by executing member functions of the container classes. For example, the member function `begin()` of each of the container classes returns an appropriate iterator for that container, initialized to point to the "first" element of the container. Similarly, function `end()` returns an iterator that points just after the "last" item. If we continually execute operator++ on the iterator returned by begin(), it will eventually reach the iterator returned by end(). If we pass these two iterators to an appropriate algorithm, the algorithm will be applied to our container.

There are different kinds of iterators, of course, and different kinds are associated with the different containers. For example, as we have seen, pointers behave like random access iterators. Likewise, vectors use random access iterators, so the begin() member of vector returns a random access iterator. On the other hand, list::begin() returns a bidirectional iterator. For this reason, the standard sort algorithm does not work with lists: sort requires a random access iterator. The reason for this is not that it is impossible to sort lists, just that the standard sorting mechanism (quicksort) is too inefficient on lists.

Adaptors are used so as to minimize the number of classes and functions in the library without reducing its power. For example, we can turn a vector or a list or a deque into a stack by using the stack adaptor. We don't need three kinds of stacks in the library, one for each way of using memory, because a single adaptor can provide these for us. Likewise, we can make any (bidirectional) iterator work backwards, from the last element to the first, by applying a reverse iterator adaptor.

4.2   A Motivating Example: A Spell Checker

Suppose that we want to build a rudimentary spell checker. One of the tools that we shall need is a dictionary of correct spellings that we can compare against. One way to generate such a file is to take a large text file, read it into some data structure, sort the words, remove adjacent duplicates, and then save the result. If we pick a large enough file, then we shall have a lot of words as the basis of our dictionary. Of course the original file needs to have correctly spelled words if this is to be useful, and it will be especially helpful if we can allow this file to grow over time by appending additional words to it.

Since we don't know in advance how large a word file we shall be processing, and since we want to sort the structure efficiently, we can choose to use a vector as the basis of our solution. Arrays aren't flexible enough in terms of size, and lists don't sort as efficiently. We could also use a deque, but the added flexibility of deques in being able to grow at either end, which we don't need, comes at the cost that the algorithms that we wish to use will operate more slowly (by a constant factor) than will be the case if we use a vector.

In order to see the results of our work, and as an aid in debugging, it will be helpful to have a function that writes vectors.

```
template <class T>
void writeVector(vector<T> v)
{   for
    (   vector<T>::iterator i = v.begin();
        i < v.end();
        ++i
    )
        cout << *i << ' ';
    cout << endl<<endl;
}
```

This function writes out a space-separated listing of the elements of a vector. We will be using strings (char*) as our template argument, and strings can contain spaces, though ours won't, so the above function might not be the best for strings. It is useful for most other types, however. We can get a special version of writeVector for just strings simply by writing it.

```
void writeVector(vector<char *> v)
{   for
    (   vector<char *>::iterator i = v.begin();
        i < v.end();
        ++i
    )
        cout << *i << endl;
    cout << endl;
}
```

One of the nice features of C++ is that the compiler will choose the most appropriate version of writeVector for us. If we write a vector<char*>, then this latter function will be used. If we write a vector<int>, then the template will be used to build us a writeVector for ints.

It is even easier to use an ostream iterator to output a vector.

```
ostream_iterator<int> out (cout);
    // creates the iterator
```

Once we have the iterator we can use the copy algorithm of the STL to copy the vector to the stream:

```
copy(v.begin(), v.end(), out);
```

The type char* is quite finicky, as you know. We need to be careful to allocate memory correctly for such strings. It is useful to read a string into a fixed length buffer, but for storage, it is most useful if the length of the storage block is tailored to the length of the string so that we don't waste space. The following function will read from an input file stream and store one word in each cell of a vector<char*>:

```
void readStrVec
(   ifstream & inp,
    vector<char*> &V
)
{   char* input;
    char buf[80];
    do
    {   inp >> buf;
        if (strncmp(buf,"",80) == 0) break ;
        int len = strlen(buf);
        input = new char [len+1];
        strcpy(input, buf);
```

```
        V.push_back( input );
    }
    while (true);
}
```

We could also use an istream iterator and the copy algorithm to read a vector. For example, to read a set of int values into a vector v from cin, we can say

```
istream_iterator<int> in(cin);
    // Iterator to the "beginning".
isteram_iterator<int> end;
    // Iterator to the "end" of the stream.
copy(in, end, v.begin());
```

This would be harder for char* values, since we want to allocate storage for them before storing them into the vector. This last assumes that the vector is big enough to hold all of the values to be input. Note that the copy algorithm is not part of the vector class. It can be used to copy many kinds of things, but those things need to be specified using iterators. We can even copy a vector v to a vector w using copy (if w is at least as big as v).

```
copy(v.begin(), v.end(), w.begin());
```

The vector class template defines a number of members for inserting, removing, and accessing values stored in the vector. Member function push_back inserts a new item at the right end of the vector. We can also compare two vectors for equality if the element type values can be compared for equality. The same is true of less than comparisons. One container is less than another if some prefix of each is the same (equal to) the corresponding prefix of the other, and at the first point of difference, the element of the first is less than the corresponding element of the other. This is called lexicographic ordering.

The main function that calls readStrVec might look something like the following:

```
void main()
{   ifstream inp("words.txt");
    vector<char *> V;
    readStrVec(inp,V);
    writeVector(V);
    . . .
}
```

Suppose that our file "words.txt" contains the following:

```
these are the
times that
try us
all the more
```

The input operator>> for strings breaks at spaces, so we shall get one word of this file in each cell of the vector V. The output of our main fragment will be

```
these
are
the
times
that
try
us
all
the
more
```

Our next task is to sort the results of reading the file of words. Unfortunately, if we do this naively, we won't get what we desire. The usual way to sort a container that has random access iterators is the following:

```
sort(V.begin(), V.end());
writeVector(V);
```

This won't work in this case, since what we are storing in the vector V are pointers. Sort works by applying operator< to the elements, and operator< for pointers simply compares pointer values (addresses), not the values that the pointers reference. When I ran the above on my computer, I got

```
more
the
all
us
try
that
times
the
are
these
```

We need to do better. In fact, we need the alternate form of algorithm sort, that uses a third parameter to specify how the comparison is to be made. This third parameter needs to be a function object.

A *function object* is an object (value of a class type) that supports `operator()`. Supporting this operator means that the object may be "called" as if it is a function. We need to build a class (or struct) in which operator() defines the string comparison <. This is very simple to do. We use a struct, rather than a class, simply to make everything public.

```
struct strless
{   bool operator()(char* x, char* y) const
    { return strcmp(x, y) < 0;
    }
};
```

This struct has only one member: operator(), which returns the "<" comparison for strings. This is just what we require. The correct code for sorting our vector<char*> then is

```
    sort(V.begin(), V.end(), strless());
    writeVector(V);
```

The third parameter passes in a new strless object. It looks like a function call, but it is a constructor call that initializes our strless object. Algorithm sort will use this object as a function to compare strings during the sort. In any case, the result of the above code fragment is

```
all
are
more
that
the
the
these
times
try
us
```

A function object that returns bool, or a type convertible to bool, is called a predicate. The above class strless defines a binary predicate, since operator() has two parameters. A unary predicate takes a single argument and returns bool. The STL uses these extensively.

We could, by the way, reverse the order of the sort, simply by changing the "<" to a ">" in the definition of strless::operator(). There is a better way to get this reverse sort done, however, given struct strless. That is to apply a function adaptor to it to reverse the sense of the comparison. To do this, we must first be a bit more sophisticated in our function objects. We built a simple class strless above, but we didn't put quite enough into it to make it work properly with the STL. The easiest way to complete it is to derive strless from the built-in less function object class that comes with the STL.

```
struct strless: public less<char*>
{   bool operator()(char* x, char* y) const
    { return strcmp(x, y) < 0;
    }
};
```

The major difference here is that we need to define certain types to the STL so that the various algorithms know what types we have for our parameters. This is similar to what we did with the `value_type` in our stack classes in Chapter 3. Having done this (and we should do it with strequal as well), we can now sort in reverse order with

```
sort(V.begin(), V.end(), not2(strless()));
writeVector(V);
```

The function adaptor `not2` takes a binary predicate (2 arguments) and transforms it into its negation. It actually constructs a new function object whose operator() returns the negation of that of the parameter. We apply `not2` to our function object `strless()` to get another function object that is used by sort. The result of this sort would be

```
us
try
times
these
the
the
that
more
are
all
```

Notice that we have some repeated words here and in the original sort, since we had duplicate words in the original file. We wish to remove such duplicates. This is a two step process with the STL. First we use algorithm unique, which simply rearranges the contents of the vector (or other container) so that its unique elements are at the beginning. It returns an iterator to us to tell us the end of the range of this initial interval of unique values. Again, we must not be naive in calling it, however. Usually we would write simply

```
vector<char*>::iterator tail
    = unique(V.begin(), V.end());
writeVector(V);
```

But again this won't work here. (Try it.) The problem again is that our vector saves pointers and unique uses operator== to determine what values are the same. This will be pointer comparison here, and since our values are held in strings with different addresses, none of them will look like duplicates. Again we need to use a function object to evaluate equality between strings.

```
struct strequal: equal<char *>
{  bool operator()(char* x, char* y) const
   { return strcmp(x, y) == 0;
```

```
    }
};
```

The correct call of unique is

```
vector<char*>::iterator tail
    = unique(V.begin(), V.end(), strequal());
writeVector(V);
```

The output of this is as follows (assuming we did an increasing sort). Note that the vector V has not changed its length, and it does not have the same contents.

```
all
are
more
that
the
these
times
try
us
us
```

What has happened here is that the unique elements were copied to the front and kept in the same relative order. This may result in some values getting overwritten. The second copy of "the" was overwritten by the "these." This leaves us with two copies of "us" at the end. The iterator that is returned from unique will reference the second copy of "us," which is the end of the unique range. We next need to delete the tail of extra values.

```
V.erase(tail, V.end());
writeVector(V);
```

This will leave us with the desired values: one each of the words in the original file, sorted alphabetically.

```
all
are
more
that
the
these
times
try
us
```

At this point the vector contains nine elements, as we can observe by evaluating V.size(). The size of a vector is its current size. Its size will grow as we execute member function push_back(T). This function pushes a value onto the back of the vector, so that it grows at the end. The original size was zero when we created it at the beginning of main(). The physical size doesn't grow with each push_back, however, as this is time-consuming (as we shall see in the next chapter). Instead, the vector is created with a certain capacity. The vector won't grow physically until we try to exceed this capacity. You can discover the capacity by evaluating V.capacity(). Here it is 1,024.

4.3   Containers

In this section we shall consider the design elements of container classes, focusing especially on those elements that are common to the various classes. In later chapters we will look at the differences and the specifics of each class. As indicated above, many of the most important algorithms for manipulating containers are not defined as members of the container classes, but externally as generic algorithms. However, it is necessary to have some support, especially for inserting, deleting, and accessing elements within the containers.

All container classes in the STL support a common functionality in addition to some specialized operations. They may differ in the efficiency with which they perform some of the common operations, however. Arrays are a special case. They have this functionality, but often use different syntax to achieve it. For example the accessor function begin() that returns an iterator to the beginning of a container corresponds to a pointer to the beginning of the array.

The common functionality falls into seven categories: types, constructors, destructor, accessing, comparison, assignment, and swap.

Types. All containers define at least nine types. These are defined by typedefs within the class declarations. The purpose of these is to make it easy for the algorithms to declare appropriate temporary data.

value_type is the type of data stored in the container. This is the same as the template parameter type. For example, the value_type of a vector<int> is vector<int>::value_type. It will be int, of course. While it seems silly to define this, recall that we must be able to recover this type from within a function template, where we do not have knowledge of what the template parameter will be.

reference is the type of references to values in the container. Usually this is just &T, where T is the parameter, but it can be otherwise.

const_reference is the type of const references to data stored.

iterator is the type of iterators appropriate to this container type.

const_iterator is the type of iterators over constant containers of this type.

reverse_iterator is the type of iterators that can iterate over the container in reverse of the usual direction.

`const_reverse_iterator` is the type of reverse iterators into const containers of this type.

`size_type` is a numeric type that can represent the size of containers of this type.

`difference_type` is a numeric type adequate to hold any generated value of the difference between two iterators.

All of the iterator types provided by containers are at least bidirectional. The vector and deque iterators, as well as the pointers used with arrays, are random access iterators. Note that, since arrays are not defined by a class but are the built-in arrays of C++, the above types are not formally defined for arrays.

Constructors. All containers have a default constructor and a copy constructor. The copy constructor requires linear time.

Destructor. All containers have a destructor. It applies the destructor to each element of the container. The destructor requires linear time in the number of elements stored. Be aware, however, that if destruction of the individual elements is slow, then so will be the destruction of the container.

Accessing. All containers support seven member functions for obtaining information about the container and its contents.

`begin()` returns an iterator to the first position in the container.

`end()` returns an iterator to a position just after the last position in the container. [begin(), end()) form a valid interval in the container that includes all elements stored. For an empty container, this interval will be empty.

`rbegin()` returns an iterator to the last position.

`rend()` returns an iterator to a position just before the first item.
[rbegin(), rend()) forms a valid interval that includes all elements stored. It provides for reverse iteration over the container.

`empty()` returns true if and only if there are no elements in the container.

`size()` returns the current size of the container. This is the number of values stored. The physical capacity may be higher.

`max_size()` returns the size of the largest possible container of this type.

All of the accessing operations require only constant time.

Comparison. All container classes support the usual comparison operators. The operator== and operator< are used to define the other four comparisons, so they behave as expected. They depend on the presence of operator== and operator< of the parameter type, which is the element type of the container. The comparison operations take linear time as they are applied to all (or many) corresponding elements of the containers.

Assignment. All container classes overload the assignment operator to make assignment of containers safe.

Swap. All containers support a swap operation that will swap the contents of two containers of the same type in constant time. For example, if a and b are vectors, then a.swap(b) will exchange their contents.

As a simple illustration of the generality of the design of the STL, the following function template will correctly write out the contents of any container in the library. This is because every container defines an iterator type, begin() and end() iterators. All iterators can be de-referenced, and all iterators produced from containers are bidirectional and support the operator!=. Note that not all support operator<, however, which is a property of random access iterators.

```
template<class container>
void writeContainer(container C)
{   for
    (   container::iterator i = C.begin();
        i != C.end();
        ++i
    )
        cout << *i<<' ';
    cout << endl;
}
```

Note that while we said that all iterator types may be de-referenced, it is not the case that all *values* of iterators may be safely de-referenced. For example, the vector::end() iterator does not refer to a valid slot in the vector and so should not be de-referenced. This is exactly similar to the situation with C++ pointer variables. They are a de-referencable type, but not all values of a pointer refer to a valid item. A pointer may be NULL, or it may be uninitialized. The same kind of thing is true of iterators (though they may not, in general, be NULL).

4.3.1   Sequence Containers

The sequence containers are vectors, deques, and lists. Vectors use dense storage, similar to arrays, though vectors may change in size as a computation proceeds. Deques use a simple tree of dense blocks. Lists use doubly linked storage.

In addition to the general requirements of containers, all sequence containers have additional members. These fall into three categories: constructors, insertion, and deletion.

Constructors. All sequence containers have a constructor that will place n copies of a value into the new container. They also have a constructor that will create a new container with the values defined by any valid iterator interval. Even one from a different kind of container.

Insertion. Sequence containers have three member functions named insert. They all have an iterator as first parameter. It gives the location at which we shall insert. The first version of insert will insert a given value at the location of the iterator. Note that it makes room available for the new item. It does not overwrite existing items, but inserts "before" the item to which the iterator refers. This version returns an iterator to the newly inserted position. The second version of insert inserts n copies of a value at the location of the iterator. The last inserts the contents of a valid range at the location of the first parameter.

Note that the insertion routines all change the size of the container. Also be aware that the iterator returned by last() is a valid point of insert.

Deletion. Sequence containers all have two member functions named erase. The first removes an item at the location of an iterator. The second removes all values in a given valid interval. They both change the size of the container.

Note that insertions and deletions may invalidate iterators into that container. For example, in a vector, if we insert into the middle of the container, all iterators after that location will become invalid. We should not write programs that depend on the stability of iterators while insertions are in progress.

Finally, we note that the individual sequence containers have additional members as appropriate. We also note that container adaptors may be used to turn sequence containers into more restricted types, such as stack, queue, and priority queue.

4.3.2 More on the Spell Checker

Suppose that we wish to remove the word "the" from our spelling dictionary. Since the vector is sorted, we can use binary search to find the location of this word in the vector. The generic algorithm binary_search simply returns a bool value telling us whether the target is present or not. We need more: the actual location of the target. For this we can use the lower_bound or upper_bound function. These give us the locations (as iterators) of the earliest and latest place in the container at which we could insert the target without destroying the sort. Since, in general, a sorted container can have duplicates, this just gives us the interval of values equal to the target if it is present. We don't need both values here, however, so we will just use lower_bound. This function requires a pair of iterators delineating the range over which it will search. It also requires the target of the search. Since we are using char* values, which require a special comparison function, we pass in the function object also. Note that we pass a strless object since that was the comparison used to sort the vector. Therefore, it is also used to binary search it.

```
vector<char*>::iterator where;
where = lower_bound
```

```
(V.begin(), V.end(), "the", strless());
```

Now that we know the position of the word "the," we can remove it with erase.

```
V.erase(where);
```

Now suppose that we wish to insert the word "souls" into the dictionary, but we want to insert it into its proper location. We can use lower_bound again to find this position.

```
where = lower_bound
    (V.begin(), V.end(), "souls", strless());
```

Now that we have an iterator to the proper location of insert, we may use insert to place the word into this location.

```
V.insert(where, "souls");
```

We don't want to do so here, but we could insert three copies of the word into the vector at this location with

```
V.insert(where, 3, "souls");
```

Finally, if we wanted a separate vector of all of the words that begin with "t", we can first find the interval in which they lie with

```
vector<char*>::iterator start, stop;
start = lower_bound
    (V.begin(), V.end(), "t", strless());
stop = lower_bound
    (V.begin(), V.end(), "u", strless());
```

We can now construct a new vector with just the "t" words using

```
vector<char*> t_words(start, stop);
```

The same strings are now in both vectors, V and t_words. We don't have copies of the strings in the two vectors, but they share pointers to the buffers containing the strings. This means that if we alter the spelling of one of the strings, it will show up as changed in both vectors. We also need to be careful about deleting a string held in a container, remembering that we hold a pointer to its buffer there. If we delete the string, then other pointers to it become invalid. For this reason we would be better off using a String class rather than char*, so that we could better control allocation, copying, and deallocation. The string class provided by the C++ standard would be a good choice.

We don't want to remove all of the "t" words from our dictionary, but we could do so with

```
start = lower_bound
    (V.begin(), V.end(), "t", strless());
stop = lower_bound
    (V.begin(), V.end(), "u", strless());
V.erase(start, stop)
```

Notice that we need to reset start and stop if they have been passed to some algorithm such as the constructor above. This is because the algorithms may modify the iterators. Again, we note that many of the algorithms "consume" their iterator parameters.

Algorithms such as lower_bound return iterators. These iterators may be used in many ways. The iterators returned by a vector are random access iterators, so we may do arithmetic with them, adding an integer to them, for example. We need to be careful with our operations on iterators, since it is possible to make the same kinds of errors with iterators as it is with pointers. In particular, it is possible to make an iterator point outside the container that generated it. If we try to de-reference where+10, for example, we are likely to get into trouble. The user needs to be aware that the STL was optimized for flexibility and efficiency, not for safety. Therefore, the user needs to take all care when manipulating iterators. In general, the same techniques you have learned for keeping out of trouble with pointers also work for iterators, because of the design that makes them so similar to pointers.

Exercise. In the Appendix, find the generic algorithms mentioned in this section and explain the template parameters and function parameters of each of them.

4.3.3 Sorted Associative Containers

There are four kinds of sorted associative containers in the STL: set, multiset, map, and multimap. Sets and maps have the property that an item may be present in the container only once if at all. Multisets and multimaps permit the "same" item to occur several times. The reason the word "same" is quoted in the last sentence is that the definition of sameness is up to a programmer and so needs to be interpreted in terms of what kinds of things are stored in the container. The values stored in maps and multimaps are pairs of items. The first element of a pair, its key, is used to retrieve items, and as the basis of "sameness." The second element of the pair, the information, may be of any kind. An example of a <key, information> value is a social security number as the key, with employee information as the information component. In sets and multisets the values stored are just the keys.

As implied by the name, sorted associative containers are sorted. This means that the contents need to be compared. Instead of doing this directly, with operator<, however, these containers use a function object to define the relationship. The default object, named Compare, is given as a template argument, but the user is free to substitute another. The STL provides a number of possible values of the template argument. One of these is less<T>() that uses the operator< as the basis of comparison. The comparison object must obey certain principles, however, if the algorithms are to work correctly.

As an aid in defining and using the sorted associative containers, the STL defines a struct template named pair that can be used to define ordered pairs of any types. These pairs are used as the values stored in maps and multimaps, and as the return type of function equal_range, defined below. This template is defined in <pair.h>. A pair has public member variables to set or retrieve the first and second elements of the pair.

The requirements of comparison objects are as follows:

To define a comparison object, you create a class and name it. We will suppose that the name "Comp" is to be used. Comp must define a binary operator(), returning a bool, that defines the ordering on the keys to be stored. If this operator returns true for a pair of values a, b, then we write a R b, (read "a is related to b"). Note that operator() may return true for a, b in that order, but false in the other order.

Transitivity. If a, b, and c are key values, and a R b, and also b R c, then a R c must also be true.

Trichotomy. If a and b are values, then exactly one of a R b, b R a, and "a is the same as b" is true.

When a function object obeys the above, we say that it a *strict total ordering* on the values. Notice that the law of trichotomy implies that a R b and b R a are never true simultaneously. This implies that operator<= will not serve as the basis of a comparison object.

Implied in the definition of a strict total ordering is the notion of "sameness" used in the first paragraph of this section. In particular, we say that two items, a and b, are the same if both a R b and b R a are false. This is not the same thing as saying a == b, of course. When a R b and b R a are both false, we say that a and b are *equivalent* to each other.

When we create a sorted associative container, we also give it a comparison object. If none is supplied, then the default object is used, which was defined by the template argument. We can also specify this operator using the constructor less<T>(), where T is the type of values to be stored. The STL also defines object greater<T>().

Note that operator< as defined on the built-in types of C++ acts as a strict total ordering.

In addition to the features shared by all containers, sorted associative containers have the following members.

constructors

Sorted associative containers have constructors that permit initialization with a comparison object. When present, this is the last argument of the constructor call. In general, you can construct a container from an arbitrary range, even a range from a different kind of container. This may not be fully implemented, given the current state of compilers, however.

access

`key_comp( )` returns the key comparison object.

`value_comp()` returns a constructed comparison object that works on values stored (keys for sets and multisets, pairs for maps and multimaps). In the case of maps and multimaps, the comparison object still works by comparing only the keys.

`insert()` (sets and maps only) inserts its argument only if it is not already present. The comparison object is used. The object will not be inserted if it is equivalent to an object already stored.

`insert()` (multisets and multimaps) inserts its argument into the sorted location. There are various forms of insert, including insertion of a range. This is properly defined using a template member function, which may not be fully implemented in your compiler. If this is the case, then you may be restricted to ranges defined by ordinary pointers only.

`erase(k)` deletes the object whose key is k if present. It returns the number of items erased. It erases all copies in a multiset or multimap.

`erase(i)` deletes the object to which the iterator i refers. There is also a version that will erase a range given by two iterators.

`find(k)` returns an iterator referring to the object with key k, if present, or end() otherwise.

`count(k)` returns the number of items whose key is k.

`lower_bound(k)` returns an iterator pointing to the first location whose key is not less than k according to the comparison object.

`upper_bound(k)` returns an iterator pointing to the first location whose key is greater than k.

`equal_range(k)` returns a pair of iterators consisting of the pair (lower_bound(), upper_bound)

4.3.4 Rebuilding the Spelling Dictionary as a Set

The spelling dictionary problem is easier if we use sets, since we don't need to sort them or remove duplicates. This is already implied by the use of sets. We do need to pass comparison objects, but we have been doing this already because of the special needs of char* values. Notice that our function object strless satisfies the requirements of a strict total ordering. We will want a different function to read a file into a set, since sets don't support push_back, but rather just `insert`. We first define a type called stringSet.

```
typedef set<char*, strless > stringSet;

void readStrSet(ifstream& inp, stringSet& V)
{   int i = 0;
    char * input;
    char buf[80];
    do
    {   inp >> buf;
        if (strncmp(buf,"",80) == 0) break ;
        int len = strlen(buf);
```

```
        input = new char [len+1];
        strcpy(input, buf);
        i++;
        V.insert( input );
    }
    while (true);
}
```

Now the result of

```
void main()
{   ifstream inp("words.txt");
    stringSet V;
    readstringSet(inp, V);
    writeContainer(V);
    . . .
}
```

is

```
all are more that the these times try us
```

As we see, the container is already sorted, and the second "the" was not inserted, since one was already present. If we don't want even the one copy of "the," we can remove it with

```
V.erase("the");
```

and if we wish to insert the word "souls," the following will do:

```
char* temp = new char[6];
strcpy(temp, "souls");
V.insert(temp);
writeContainer(V);
```

Now the result is

```
all are more souls that these times try us
```

Notice that we allocated a new buffer to hold the new word. While either of the next two calls to insert are legal, both will result in eventual problems.

```
V.insert("souls");
    // points to a static value
```

or

```
char temp [6] = "souls";
V.insert(temp);
      // points to an automatic value
```

This is not a problem with containers or the insert member. The problem lies in the nature of pointers. In the last example above, if we change the value of the temp buffer, we will change what is in the set. The first of these would be useful only in a set of constant strings.

Again supposing that we wish to have a listing of just the "t" words in a separate set, the following will work:

```
stringSet::const_iterator start
   = V.lower_bound( "t");
stringSet::const_iterator stop
   = V.lower_bound( "u");

stringSet t_words(start, stop);
writeContainer(t_words);
```

Assuming we did remove "the," this will produce

```
that these times try
```

4.4   Iterators

We have used iterators in many ways already, but have only scratched the surface of their capabilities and complexity. The STL defines many kinds of iterators, as we have already noted. Chief among these are random-access, bidirectional, and forward iterators. There are also two generalizations of forward iterators called input iterators and output iterators. These, in turn, have special versions called istream iterators and ostream iterators, respectively. We will explore some of the differences between these in this section.

The reason for having different iterator categories is dual. On the one hand, certain container types can only provide certain kinds of iterators efficiently. We want all iterator operations to be doable in constant time, so that the iterator operations don't slow down the operation of algorithms in which they are used. Thus, a list cannot efficiently provide random access iterators, but since they are doubly linked, they can provide bidirectional iterators efficiently. When we specify a container, we specify the strongest iterator type that it can (efficiently) provide. The second aspect of the need for different iterator categories has to do with the needs of the algorithms. Sorting algorithms, for example, may need to compare items at widely separated locations in the containers they sort. To do so may require more power in the iterator than would be required in a searching algorithm. When we specify an algorithm, we specify the weakest iterator type that can be used with it.

Most of the iterator types are not defined by classes in the STL. Instead they are informally defined by what services they provide—especially, which operators they overload. Thus, there is no class for forward iterators. The collection of requirements for an object like a forward iterator are informally called a *concept*. Any class or built-in type (pointers) that has the forward iterator operations defined (chiefly operator++) conforms to the concept and can therefore serve as a forward iterator. This is because the iterator classifications are used as template parameters, not as actual types. The categories of iterators are defined as an aid in documentation to aid the user of an algorithm understand what is required of the iterators that are passed. For example, the specification of the copy algorithm that will copy a range into a container is

```
template <class InputIterator, class OutputIterator>
OutputIterator copy
(   InputIterator first,
    InputIterator last,
    OutputIterator result
);
```

This is a way of saying that the template parameters have certain requirements, which if satisfied, we can guarantee the correct operation of the algorithm.

In addition to the presence of certain operators, the STL requires that the operators obey certain laws if the algorithms are to work correctly. We have already seen one simple example of this in our specification of an interval or range [a,b), where we assume that repeatedly executing a++ will eventually get us to b.

We will detail each of the iterator categories below. There are two varieties of each of these iterators, however. Since it is possible to build const containers that cannot be modified, we also need const iterators, so that we don't try to modify a const container by de-referencing an iterator. We therefore classify iterators as either const or mutable. A mutable iterator returns a reference from operator*, so that we can assign to such a de-reference. A const iterator returns a const reference (or possibly a value). The container classes all define a type called iterator and another named const_iterator. The first of these is generally mutable. The category of these iterators depends on the container. For example, vector<T>::iterator is a mutable random access iterator and vector<T>::const_iterator is a const random access iterator.

A given value of an iterator may be de-referencable or not. An iterator A is de-referenceable if it refers to a location within a container, and so *A is a value of the contained type. If a container C is nonempty, then C.begin() will return a de-referencable iterator. C.end() will return an iterator also, but it is not de-referencable. Instead, it refers to a past-the-end value. This location is a valid place for inserts in most containers, but not for retrievals.

There may also be a *singular* value for an iterator. This is a legal value of the iterator that does not refer to any location or any container. For example, NULL is the singular value of ordinary pointers. Some constructions of iterators result in a singular value as indicated. The algorithms are not guaranteed to work if passed singular values when they require iterators.

Iterator categories, then, are defined by the operators they provide. Somewhat more is required, however. It is not enough just to have an operator present for an iterator to work correctly. Since it is possible for the programmer to overload operators, he or she can give any desired meaning to any operator. The operators have to be consistent with each other for the iterators to work correctly with the algorithms. For example, a random access iterator must provide for the difference between iterators, b - a, as an integer n. The type must also provide an operator ++. However, these two operators must also be consistent with each other for things to work. This means that if b - a == n, then exactly n iterations of a++ will take us to b. If this is not the case, then our program may compile correctly, but is unlikely to operate correctly. It may work with poor efficiency, or it may fail altogether.

Iterators are used to define ranges. Most of the algorithms take a pair of iterators and define a range or interval that includes the first position and includes everything up to but not including the second. This is expressed as

```
[a, b)
```

where a and b are iterators. In order for this to be a valid range, b must be *reachable* from a. This means that repeatedly applying a++ will eventually have a == b. If this is not the case, the algorithm will fail, perhaps as an infinite iteration. It is up to the user to guarantee this, although the containers are helpful in returning iterators with begin() and end() that guarantee that end() is reachable from begin().

4.4.1   Forward Iterators

Forward iterators mark a location in a container and can be moved forward with operator++. A newly created forward iterator might be a singular value. If it is de-referencable, then it must support both prefix and postfix operator++ as well as operator== and operator!=. There is an additional requirement that may sound like it could not possibly be false. We require that if two mutable forward iterators obey a == b, then it must also be true that *a == *b, and ++a == ++b. We will show how this can be false when we look at input iterators.

4.4.2   Bidirectional Iterators

Bidirectional iterators have all of the properties of forward iterators. In addition, they may be moved backwards with operator--. Both pre and posfix forms of this operator are required. Furthermore, if --r == --s for de-referencable iterators, then r == s.

4.4.3   Random Access Iterators

Random access iterators have all of the properties of bidirectional iterators. In addition, they support *iterator arithmetic* with such operators as operator+ and operator-. They also support operator<. In particular, we need an operator+ and an operator+= that lets us add an integer to a random access iterator. We also need operator- and operator-=. We need two forms of operator+, actually, so that we can add an iterator and an integer in either order. We also need to be able to take the difference between two random access iterators into the same container. The value n that is returned should be consistent with the operator+, as well, so that if a - b returns n, then a + n should be b. Also, exactly n iterations of a++ should take you to b.

Random access iterators can also be indexed using operator[]. This should behave consistently with iterator arithmetic, as in the pointer duality law.

Finally, we need to be able to compare iterators with operator<, operator>, operator<=, and operator>=. Furthermore, operator< and operator> must be total ordering relations (as well as defining "opposite" orderings). This means that they obey the following two laws:

Trichotomy. For any two values, a and b, exactly one of a < b, a == b, and b < a is true.

Transitivity. If a < b, and also b < c, then a < c.

Actually, this is a bit more than is required. Operator == doesn't have such a special place here. In fact, we can define a relation a E b to be true whenever a < b and b < a are both false. What is required is that this relation E be an equivalence relation. This means that E satisfies the following three laws:

Reflexivity. For any a, a E a.

Symmetry. If a E b, then also b E a.

Transitivity. If a E b, and b E c, then a E c.

If this is the case, then E partitions all of the values into disjoint sets called equivalence classes. Any two elements a and b in one equivalence class satisfy a E b, and if c and d come from different equivalence classes, then c E d is false. As an example in which a perfectly reasonable ordering relation does not satisfy the above requirement, consider binary trees. Let an operation < be defined on the vertices of such a tree by a < b if a is an ancestor of b, but not the same as b. Then the induced relation E satisfies a E b if a is neither an ancestor or a descendant of b. It is possible to show that E does not satisfy the law of transitivity. (Four vertices on three levels will do.) Therefore, this operator< would not be a suitable candidate for a random access iterator operator<.

Note that the operator< defined on the built-in types of C++ satisfies the law, as the induced relation E is just operator== on those types (even for pointers).

4.4.4   Input Iterators

Input iterators are a generalization of forward iterators. This means that every forward iterator satisfies the requirements of an input operator, and more. Another way to think of
this is that input iterators drop some of the requirements of forward iterators.

Input iterators need to implement operators == and != for comparison. They need prefix and postfix versions of operator++ for advancing, and they need to be de-referencable.
They do not provide operator=, however, so that we may not be able to assign one iterator
to another. More importantly, the template argument is not required to be mutable. We
may not be able to use a de-reference of an iterator to change the container. This is because such iterators are used only for retrieving information from a container, not for putting information into it.

The final quirk of input operators is that, for two iterator values a and b, a == b does-
n't necessarily imply that ++a == ++b. This is because an input iterator is permitted to
change the global state of its container, for example, by advancing a read buffer. It is possible to associate an input iterator with an input stream in such a way that operator++
reads from the stream. If two iterators into the stream are positioned at the same location
and we use operator++ with one of them, the other will be "advanced" as well. Because of
this restriction on use, all algorithms that use input (or output) iterators are required to be
single pass algorithms. The iterator is consumed by its use and can't be reused.

4.4.5   Output Iterators

Output iterators are another generalization of forward iterators and are intended for putting
information into a container, but not for retrieving information. As such, they may be associated with output streams in which operator++ writes to the stream. Output operators
do not need operators == or !=. Operator++ (prefix and postfix) are used to advance. And
we need to be able to assign a value to a de-reference of such an iterator. We are not required to be able to read from such a de-reference, however. Therefore, if a is an output iterator that points into a container of ints, then

```
*a = 5;
```

would be legal, but

```
int x = *a;
```

would not be.

Input and output iterators are often used together. For example, in copying one container to another, an input iterator may be used on the source, and an output iterator on
the destination.

4.4.6   Istream and Ostream Iterators

The STL defines two classes to easily associate streams with input and output iterators. This makes it easy to treat streams as containers like the other containers in the library. Thus, we may apply some algorithms directly to streams without providing intermediate storage to hold the contents. Input streams provide input iterators and output streams provide output iterators.

We specify an istream_iterator by supplying (at least) the type of data to be read from the stream as a template argument. We construct an istream iterator by specifying a particular input stream. The end_of_stream iterator of a stream is constructed without parameters. Then, each execution of operator++ on the iterator is translated into an execution of operator>> on the stream. The value read is stored within the iterator, and will be returned by de-referencing the iterator.

```
istream_iterator<int> start(cin);
    // iterate over cin
istream_iterator<int> finish;
    // end_of_stream.
vector<int> vec(start, finish);
ostream_iterator<int> dump(cout);
copy(vec.begin(), vec.end(), dump);
```

Important Note: This example requires two features from C++ that may not yet be implemented, and hence this may not work with your version of the STL. In particular, istream_iterator actually has two template parameters, the second of which is the difference type between pointers to the first parameter. In this case the type is ptrdiff_t, defined by C++. We could have stated it here, but chose instead to use the new feature of default template arguments. In fact, ptrdiff_t is the default value of the second parameter. If these are not available, you need to specify the second argument, as in

```
istream_iterator<int, ptrdiff_t> start(cin);
    // iterate over cin
```

The second advanced feature that this example depends on is template members. In earlier versions of C++, individual member functions could not be templates: only classes and free functions. The latest standard provides for template members. The constructor we have used for vec is such a template member, in which the template argument is an input iterator. Hopefully by the time you read this, compilers will have caught up with the standard. This requirement is not so easily bypassed. Early versions of STL use various ways to compensate (partially) for this, usually by adding additional members to cover important cases that would be covered by a templated member.

4.5   Generic Algorithms

While containers are the most visible feature of the STL and iterators are its backbone, it is the algorithms that form its purpose. As indicated earlier, most of the algorithms are not provided within container classes, but interface to the containers through iterators. This permits many algorithms to be written only once and to operate correctly with many container types. One version of the STL that I use has 106 generic algorithms. There are a few places where a generalized algorithm won't work efficiently with some container type but a specialized algorithm will. If the algorithm is important enough, it may be included within the class of that container. This is exactly the case when sorting a list. Therefore, the list template provides a sort member, while vectors and deques use the general template algorithm.

Some of the algorithms work "in place," modifying the container on which they operate. Sort is like this. Other algorithms work on and return a copy of the input container. Some algorithms have both an in place and a copying version. For example, replace will replace old values with new in a range. This is an in place version. replace_copy will replace old values with new, but does not modify its input. Instead it puts a modified copy of the input into another container. The copying algorithms all have a _copy suffix. For example,

```
replace(start, done, oldValue, newValue)
```

will replace all copies of oldValue by newValue over the range, but

```
replace_copy
    (start, done, toWhere, oldValue, newValue)
```

will write the range [start, done) starting at iterator toWhere, replacing oldValue by newValue as it copies.

Some of the algorithms require that we pass in a unary or binary predicate as a function object. These algorithms only operate on elements or pairs of elements that satisfy the predicate: i.e., only if it returns true. These algorithms all end in _if. For example, replace_if will process a range replacing values that satisfy a unary predicate with a new value. There is also a copying version called replace_copy_if. Predicates are assumed not to modify their arguments. That is, they are supposed to merely return a value of true or false, without changing anything. Note that the predicates are called by these algorithms by applying them to the result of de-referencing iterators. Therefore, if we call replace_if with

```
replace_if(start, done, big, newValue);
```

where start and done are iterators, big is a unary predicate and newValue is the replacement value, then somewhere within the execution of replace_if will appear big(*i), where i is some iterator, perhaps iterator start. If this predicate execution returns true, then *i = newValue will be carried out.

Also, many of the algorithms have two versions depending on whether a predicate is passed or a standard predicate is assumed. For example,

```
sort(start, done);
```

will sort a range using the operator< on the elements of the range, while

```
sort(start, done, strless)
```

will sort using the binary predicate strless. These versions are not suffixed _if, since the predicate is not used to determine **if** the value should be included, but **how** the algorithms should operate.

If we don't count multiple versions and variations, there are about 56 fully generic algorithms in the STL. There are also a few public support algorithms and a very large number of support functions. The public generic algorithms can be organized loosely into ten categories.

The remainder of this section is intended to serve as a reference to the generic algorithms. As such, it need not be read completely through. The prototypes of all of the algorithms may be found in the Appendix. We will introduce each of the algorithms with a sample call, somewhat stylized, to indicate what kinds of parameters are required. Reference parameters in which values are returned will be shown in italics.

4.5.1. Minimum and Maximum Algorithms

The STL includes simple min/max comparisons written as templates so that other types won't need to provide these. It is not our intention to show many of the algorithms of the STL, but these are particularly simple.

value = <u>min</u>(valueA, valueB);
value = <u>min</u>(valueA, valueB, binaryPred);
value = <u>max</u>(valueA, valueB);
value = <u>max</u>(valueA, valueB, binaryPred);

The two versions of min might look like the following. Note that the first version uses operator< for the comparison, while the second uses a comparison object. Note that the class of the comparison object is a template argument, leaving maximum flexibility. Any class providing a binary predicate operator() may be used for this argument. Ordinary functions may also be used.

```
template <class T>
inline const T& min(const T& a, const T& b)
{  return b < a ? b : a;
}
```

```
template <class T, class Compare>
inline const T& min
(   const T& a,
    const T& b,
    Compare comp
)
{   return comp(b, a) ? b : a;
}
```

ForwardIter = <u>min_element</u>(ForwardIter1, ForwardIter2);

ForwardIter = <u>min_element</u>(ForwardIter1, ForwardIter2, binaryPred);

ForwardIter = <u>max_element</u>(ForwardIter1, ForwardIter2);

ForwardIter = <u>max_element</u>(ForwardIter1, ForwardIter2, binaryPred);

There are also two algorithms that return the minimum value in a range: one using operator< and the other using the comparison object. As is generally true of the algorithms that process a range, the input range is defined by the first two parameters. These algorithms are linear.

```
template <class ForwardIterator, class Compare>
ForwardIterator min_element
(   ForwardIterator first,
    ForwardIterator last,
    Compare comp
)
```

4.5.2. Generalized Numeric Algorithms

Each of these algorithms performs some arithmetic operation on a range or on a pair of ranges. Each has an alternate version in which the user can specify a particular binary operation to be used in place of the standard version. When present, this binary operation is defined by a function object, and that parameter is last.

total = <u>accumulate</u>(first, last, init);

total = <u>accumulate</u>(first, last, init, binaryOp);

Algorithm accumulate will add (using operator+) all elements of the range [first, last) to init and return the result. This is a single pass, linear algorithm, so all that is required is an input iterator. The type of init is a template parameter, and this type is also the return type. The alternate version repeatedly applies binaryOperation(init, *first++) and returns the result.

value = <u>inner_product</u>(InputIter1, InputIter2, OutputIter, val);

value = **inner_product**
        (InputIter1, InputIter2, OutputIter, val, binOp1, binOp2);

An inner product is the sum of the products of corresponding elements of two containers. Two ranges are required for input, but this is done with only three iterators, since the length of the second range must be the same as the length of the first. A fourth parameter gives the initial value of the total. The final value is returned. The second form passes two binary operations as the last two parameters, with the first replacing the sum and the other replacing the product. For example, we can get the product of sums of two int vectors of the same length with something like

```
inner_product
(   v1.begin(),
    v1.end(),
    v2.begin(),
    1,
    times<int>(),
    plus<int>()
);
```

Note that the function objects plus and times are provided with the STL.

OutputIter = **partial_sum**(InputIter1, InputIter2, OutputIter1);
OutputIter = **partial_sum**(InputIter1, InputIter2, OutputIter1,
binaryOp);

The partial_sum algorithm efficiently computes a sequence of running totals of an input range. For example, if a set contains 1, 2, 3, 4, 5, then the partial sums would be 1, 3, 6, 10, 15. This result is placed into a second range that may be the same as the first. A second version replaces operator+ with any binary operator.

```
partial_sum
(   set1.begin(),
    set1.end(),
    vec2.begin(),
    times<int> ()
);
```

This assumes that the vector vec2 has a size large enough to hold the resulting sequence of values.

OutputIter = **adjacent_difference**(inputIter1, InputIter2, OutputIter1);
OutputIter = **adjacent_difference**
        (inputIter1, InputIter2, OutputIter1, binaryOp);

The adjacent_difference algorithm is similar. It puts adjacent differences between values into a second range. The first "adjacent difference" is just the first value from the first range. Adjacent_difference and partial_sum perform inverse computations.

4.5.3   Nonmutating Sequence Operations

These algorithms operate on sequences, but they do not change them. While they work on sequences, they are not restricted to sequential containers since they use iterators to define their operations, and iterators return sequences of values even from nonsequential containers.

IterPair = **mismatch**(InputIter1, InputIter2, InputIter3);
IterPair = **mismatch**(InputIter1, InputIter2, InputIter3, binaryPred);

Algorithm mismatch compares corresponding values in two ranges (again defined by three iterators) and returns a pair of iterators indicating the first location in each range at which the corresponding values fail to be the same using operator==. The two iterators returned are equidistant from the beginnings of the input ranges. A second version, as expected, replaces operator== with a binary predicate of the user's choice.

boolVal = **equal**(inputIter1, InputIter2, InputIter3);
boolVal = **equal**(inputIter1, InputIter2, InputIter3, binaryPred);

Algorithm equal (again two versions) compares two ranges and determines if they are the same up to the end.

funObj = **for_each**(inputIter1, InputIter2, InputIter3, funObj);

One of the most powerful and general operations in the STL is algorithm for_each, which applies a user-supplied function to each element of a range. Any result produced by the supplied function is ignored. The function can, however, set global variables or even modify the elements of the collection. It should not, however, attempt to modify the collection itself. For example, suppose we consider the CountedValue template that we created in Chapter 1. We can write a function object to set the value in any given CountedValue<int> to zero.

```
struct setzero
{   void operator()(CountedValue<int>& c)
    {   c.setValue(0);
    }
};
```

If we have a vector vec4 of CountedValue<int> objects, we can set all of their values to zero with

```
for_each(vec4.begin(), vec4.end(), setzero());
```

> InputIter = **find**(InputIter1, InputIter2, value);
> InputIter = **find_if**(InputIter1, InputIter2, unaryPred);

Algorithm find and find_if search for a value in a range and return an iterator to the location of the value if found and the end of the range otherwise. Algorithm find has a parameter to specify the value sought and uses == to determine a "hit." On the other hand, find_if uses a supplied unary predicate, but no value. It returns the first location in the range for which the predicate returns true.

> ForwardIter = **adjacent_find**(ForwardIter1, ForwardIter2);
> ForwardIter = **adjacent_find**(ForwardIter1, ForwardIter2, binaryPred);

Algorithm adjacent_find looks for two adjacent values in a range that are the same with operator==. An alternate version uses a supplied binary predicate instead of the operator. Both return an iterator to the first location satisfying the goal, or the end of the range if there are no matches.

> **count**(InputIter1, InputIter2, value, *init*);
> **count_if**(InputIter1, InputIter2, unaryPred, *init*);

Algorithm count counts values that match a given value. Interestingly, the count is returned as a reference parameter, rather than as a function result, so that the user may specify the type of the count itself using a template argument.

```
template <class InputIterator, class T, class Size>
void count
(   InputIterator first,
    InputIterator last,
    const T& value,
    Size& n
);
```

Since n is incremented once for each "hit" with operator++, any type that implements this function may be used as the last parameter, including user-defined classes. The alternate version, count_if, replaces the value with a unary predicate. Each value of the range for which this function returns true causes the count to be incremented. This algorithm is a very good example of the total generality of the STL approach. Most libraries would just return an int or a long from such an operation, as this is the most common case. Here, we get to choose the type of the value to be incremented with complete freedom. We could even pass in an object from a class that changes the appearance of a dial each time its operator++ is executed.

```
ForwardIter = search
    (ForwardIter1, ForwardIter2, ForwardIter3, ForwardIter4);
ForwardIter = search
    (       ForwardIter1, ForwardIter2,
            ForwardIter3, ForwardIter4,
            binaryPred
    );
```

Algorithm search is passed two ranges, using four iterators this time. It determines whether the second range is a subrange of the first. If so it returns an iterator to the starting point of the subrange. The standard version uses operator== and the other uses a binary predicate passed by the caller. This algorithm is quadratic in the worst case, but behaves better in most actual uses.

4.5.4 Mutating Sequence Operations

These algorithms also act on sequences, but they modify some range as they operate. This is the largest category of operations, with about thirty algorithms. Notice that if the destination is a vector, for example, then the algorithms do not in general extend the length when they reach the end. The user is responsible for guaranteeing that the destination has sufficient size.

```
OutputIter = copy(InputIter1, InputIter2, OutputIter);
```

Algorithm copy copies one range to another. Be careful that the second container has sufficient room to hold the values. The two ranges can actually overlap as long as the first range (source) does not contain the first location of the second range(destination). It returns an iterator to the last item inserted into the destination.

```
BidirectIter = copy_backward
    (BidirectIterIter1, BidirectIterIter2, BidirectIterIter1);
```

Algorithm copy_backward, which needs bidirectional iterators, copies one range to another, but using last element first. The source range must not contain the last location in the destination range, but otherwise overlap is possible. Note that this doesn't reverse the order of the elements, just the order in which they are copied. It does copy into the destination working to the "left" of the initial point, however. This also returns an iterator to the last item inserted.

```
OutputIter = fill_n(OutputIter, count, value);
```

Algorithm fill_n inserts n copies of a value into a container.

```
template
```

```
<   class OutputIterator,
    class Size,
    class T
>
OutputIterator fill_n
(  OutputIterator first,
   Size n,
   const T& value
);
```

The return value points to the last item inserted.

swap(*value1*, *value2*);
ForwardIter swap_ranges(ForwardIter1, ForwardIter2, ForwardIter3);

Swap exchanges two values. Algorithm swap_ranges swaps two intervals of equal length, returning an iterator just after the last item in the second range.

OutputIter = transform(InputIter1, InputIter2, OutputIter1, unaryOp);

This function applies the unary operator to each element of the first range, writing results to the second range. It returns an iterator after the last item inserted. The output range may be the same as the input range.

OutputIter = transform
        (InputIter1, InputIter2, InputIter3, OutputIter1, binaryOp);

This version of transform applies a binary operator to corresponding elements of the two input ranges, writing results to the output range. It returns a past-the-end value of the second range. The output range may be the same as either input range.

replace(ForwardIter1, ForwardIter2, oldValue, newValue);
replace_if(ForwardIter1, ForwardIter2, unaryPred, newValue);
OutputIter = replace_copy
            (InputIter1, InputIter2, OutputIter1, oldVal, newVal);
OutputIter = replace_copy_if
            (InputIter1, InputIter2, OutputIter1, unaryPred, newVal);

Replace replaces all copies of oldValue in the input range with newValue. Replace_if replaces all values for which the predicate is true with newValue. The copy versions are similar, except that they place the results into an output range instead of modifying the input range.

generate(ForwardIter1, ForwardIter2, GenFunc);

OutputIter = generate_n(OutputIter1, count, GenFunc);

These algorithms fill a range by repeatedly calling a generating function and saving the results.

ForwardIter = remove(ForwardIter1, ForwardIter2, value);
ForwardIter = remove_if(ForwardIter1, ForwardIter2, unaryPred);
OutputIter = remove_copy(InputIter1, InputIter2, OutputIter1, value);
OutputIter = remove_copy_if
                    (InputIter1, InputIter2, OutputIter1, unaryPred);

These algorithms remove values from a range. The first removes all copies of the value. The second removes all values for which the predicate is true. The other versions are similar, except that they write the results to an output range instead of modifying the input range. If two elements of the input range are not removed, then their relative position after execution is the same as before. Therefore, the algorithm is called *stable*.

ForwardIter = unique(ForwardIter1, ForwardIter2);
ForwardIter = unique(ForwardIter1, ForwardIter2, binaryPred);
OutputIter = unique_copy(InputIter1, InputIter2, OutputIter1);
OutputIter = unique_copy
                    (InputIter1,
                             InputIter2,
                             OutputIter1,
                             binaryPred
                    );

Algorithm unique removes successive equal values from a range. The first version uses operator== to determine equality of pairs of values. The second version uses the binary predicate instead. The copy versions write results to an output range.

reverse(BidirectIter1, BidirectIter2);
OutputIter = reverse_copy(BidirectIter1, BidirectIter2, OutputIter1);

These algorithms reverse the order of the values in a range. The first modifies the input range and the second produces an output range.

rotate(ForwardIter1, ForwardIter2, ForwardIter3);
OutputIter = rotate_copy
                    (ForwardIter1, ForwardIter2, ForwardIter3, OutputIter);

The input to a rotation is defined by three iterators: the beginning, the middle, and the end. The rotate algorithms shift values leftward in the range so that the middle of the input becomes the beginning of the output and values shifted out are copied to the back. Therefore, the old beginning comes just after the old end in the output.

<u>random shuffle</u>(RandomAcIter1, RandomAcIter2);
<u>random shuffle</u>(RandomAcIter1, RandomAcIter2, randomGenFunc);

The random_shuffle algorithms permute the input range randomly. The first uses a built-in uniform random number generator, so that all orderings of the input are about equally likely. The second version allows the user to supply a random number generator, which should return values in the interval [0, 1).

BidirectIter = <u>partition</u>(BidirectIter1, BidirectIter2, unaryPred);
ForwardIter = <u>stable partition</u>(ForwardIter1, ForwardIter2, unaryPred);

These algorithms rearrange the values in a range so that all values that satisfy the supplied predicate come before those that do not. They return an iterator just after the last true value. The stable version does not reorder items from the same part of the result. If one item for which the predicate is true came before another for which it is also true prior to the execution, then it will remain before that other value after. The same is true for the false range.

4.5.5   Sorting Related Operations

The sorting related operations either sort a range, merge two sorted ranges into a sorted output, or partially sort a range. They all have an optional compare function that can be used to replace the standard operator<. If this object is used, then it must define a strict total order in the sense defined above in Section 4.4.3. That is to say, two elements, a and b, are considered equivalent under a compare function, comp, if both comp(a,b) and comp(b,a) are false. It is required that the function never return true for both comp(a,b) and comp(b,a), and also that the induced definition of equivalence is an equivalence relation in the mathematical sense. That is, it must be reflexive, symmetric, and transitive.

<u>sort</u>(RandomAcIter1, RandomAcIter2);
<u>sort</u>(RandomAcIter1, RandomAcIter2, compareFunc);

The sort algorithms sort a range using operator< or a supplied compare function. The compare function must define a strict total order. Sort is typically O(Nlg(N)), but can be quadratic in a few cases. It won't be quadratic on a sorted range, however.

<u>stable sort</u>(RandomAcIter1, RandomAcIter2);
<u>stable sort</u>(RandomAcIter1, RandomAcIter2, compareFunc);

Stable sort is like sort, except that "equal" values are not rearranged. In the second version "equality" is the equivalence relation induced by the compare function, NOT operator==. Stable sort is O(Nlg(N)) if there is enough workspace available to hold N/2 elements, where N is the size of the range. Otherwise, stable_sort is O(Nlg(N)^2).

partial_sort(RandomAcIter1, RandomAcIter2, RandomAcIter3);
partial_sort
(RandomAcIter1,
**   RandomAcIter2,**
**   RandomAcIter3,**
**   compareFunc**
);

A partial sort is defined by three iterators. The second should point into the range defined by the other two. The input range is rearranged, but only the portion between the first and middle positions is sorted and they are the same elements that would appear there if the entire range were sorted. In the above example, the range [RandomAcIter1, RandomAcIter2) will be sorted.

RandomAcIter = partial_sort_copy
**   (InputIter1, InputIter2, RandomAcIter1, RandomAcIter2);**
RandomAcIter = partial_sort_copy
**   (InputIter1, InputIter2,**
**   RandomAcIter1, RandomAcIter2,**
**   compareFunc**
);

The copying partial sort is defined by an input range and an output range that may be of a different length. If the output range is shorter than the input range, then it is filled with the sorted "smallest" values of the input range. If the output range is larger, then the sorted input range is placed into the initial portion of the output range, with the remainder left unchanged. The copying partial sort is O(Nlg(K)), where N is the length of the input and K is the smaller of the lengths of the two ranges.

nth_element(RandomAcIter1, RandomAcIter2, RandomAcIter3);
nth_element
(RandomAcIter1,
**   RandomAcIter2,**
**   RandomAcIter3,**
**   compareFunc**
);

The nth_element algorithm is defined by three iterators. The first and third define a range and the second a position within that range. The elements in the range will be rearranged so that the element pointed to by the second iterator will be in its correct location as if the range were sorted. Furthermore, all items "smaller" than that item will be to its left, and the larger items to the right. For the first version, smaller is defined by operator< and in the second, by the compare function. This is a linear algorithm in the average, but could be quadratic in a few cases.

```
ForwardIter = lower_bound(ForwardIter1, ForwardIter2, value);
ForwardIter = lower_bound
            (ForwardIter1, ForwardIter2, value, compareFunc);

ForwardIter = upper_bound(ForwardIter1, ForwardIter2, value);
ForwardIter = upper_bound
            (ForwardIter1, ForwardIter2, value, compareFunc);
```

Algorithm lower_bound returns the first location in a range at which the value can be inserted, assuming that the range is sorted. The range doesn't need to be sorted, however. The returned iterator points to the first location that is "not less" than the item. upper_bound returns the first location that is "greater" than the value. In a sorted list, lower_bound and upper_bound return, respectively, the first and last positions into which value may be inserted while maintaining the sorted order. These algorithms are linear in general, but logarithmic if the iterators are random access.

```
IterPair = equal_range(ForwardIter1, ForwardIter2, value);
IterPair
    = equal_range(ForwardIter1, ForwardIter2, value, compareFunc);
```

The equal_range algorithms return a pair of forward iterators that would be returned individually by lower_bound and upper_bound. These algorithms are linear in general, but logarithmic if the iterators are random access.

```
boolVal = binary_search(ForwardIter1, ForwardIter2, value);
boolVal = binary_search
    (       ForwardIter1,
            ForwardIter2,
            value,
            compareFunc
    );
```

These algorithms carry out a binary search on the indicated range and return whether or not they were able to find the value. They do not return where the value may be found, however. These algorithms are linear in general, but logarithmic if the iterators are random access.

```
OutputIter = merge
```

```
                 (InputIter1, InputIter2, InputIter3, InputIter4, OutputIter1);
OutputIter = merge
        (       InputIter1, InputIter2,
                InputIter3, InputIter4,
                OutputIter1,
                compareFunc
        );
```

These algorithms merge two sorted input ranges into a sorted output range. The merge is stable, so that items with equivalent values from one of the input ranges will maintain their relative positions in the output. They are both linear algorithms.

```
inplace_merge(BidirectIterator1, BidirectIterator2, BidirectIterator3);
inplace_merge
        (       BidirectIterator1,
                BidirectIterator2,
                BidirectIterator3,
                compareFunc
        );
```

These algorithms merge two halves of a range in place. It is assumed that each half of the range, namely [BidirectIterator1, BidirectIterator2) and [BidirectIterator2, BidirectIterator3) is sorted. The result will be sorted. These algorithms are linear if there is room for a copy of the entire range, and $O(N\lg(N))$ otherwise.

4.5.6   Set Operations on Sorted Structures

These algorithms all assume that the input ranges are sorted. This will automatically be the case for sorted associative containers, of course. The union, intersection, and difference algorithms work by merging ranges, so they work on multiset and multimap structures as well. The union of multisets contains the maximum of the number in the two inputs (not the total). The intersection of two multisets contains the minimum of the two. The algorithms are all linear. If an output range is used (all but algorithm includes), then it must not overlap with the input range.

```
boolVal = includes(InputIter1, InputIter2, InputIter3, InputIter4);
boolVal = includes
        (InputIter1, InputIter2, InputIter3, InputIter4, compareFunc);
```

Returns true if everything in the second range is contained in the first range.

```
OutputIter = set_union
        (       InputIter1, InputIter2,
                InputIter3, InputIter4,
```

```
                    OutputIter1
    );
OutputIter = set_union
        (       InputIter1,  InputIter2,
                InputIter3,  InputIter4,
                OutputIter1,
                compareFunc
    );
```

Produces those elements that are in either range.

```
OutputIter = set_intersection
        (       InputIter1,  InputIter2,
                InputIter3,  InputIter4,
                OutputIter1
    );
OutputIter = set_intersection
        (       InputIter1,  InputIter2,
                InputIter3,  InputIter4,
                OutputIter1,
                compareFunc
    );
```

Produces only those elements that are in both ranges.

```
OutputIter = set_difference
        (       InputIter1,  InputIter2,
                InputIter3,  InputIter4,
                OutputIter1
    );
OutputIter = set_difference
        (       InputIter1,  InputIter2,
                InputIter3,  InputIter4,
                OutputIter1,
                compareFunc
    );
```

Produces those elements in the first range that are not in the second.

```
OutputIter = set_symmetric_difference
        (       InputIter1,  InputIter2,
                InputIter3,  InputIter4,
                OutputIter1
    );
```

OutputIter = <u>**set_symmetric_difference**</u>
    (InputIter1, InputIter2,
           InputIter3, InputIter4,
           OutputIter1,
           compareFunc
    );

Produces those elements that are in either range but absent from the other.

4.5.7 Heap Operations

These operations all produce or manipulate a data structure called a heap. Heaps require random access iterators, so are ideally suited for vectors. Logically a heap is like a binary tree in which each node is larger than either of its children, putting the largest value at the root. A heap may be stored in an array-like structure, with the children of the node in cell n stored in cells 2n and 2n+1. This permits insertions and removals to be done in logarithmic time, while maintaining the heap property. Since the largest item is easy to find and remove, heaps are often used to implement priority queues. We shall return to heaps in Chapter 6.

A heap is defined with respect to a comparison operator, which is operator< by default. Note, however, that it is the "largest" value that is at the root of the heap.

    <u>**push_heap**</u>(RandomAcIter1, RandomAcIter2);
    <u>**push_heap**</u>(RandomAcIter1, RandomAcIter2, compareFunc);

Insert an item into the heap and maintain the heap property. The item inserted is originally just before location RandomAcIter2, and [RandomAcIter1, RandomAcIter2 - 1) is originally assumed to be a heap. The full range will be a heap on completion.

    <u>**pop_heap**</u>(RandomAcIter1, RandomAcIter2);
    <u>**pop_heap**</u>(RandomAcIter1, RandomAcIter2, compareFunc);

Remove the largest item from the heap [RandomAcIter1, RandomAcIter2) and restore the heap property. When done, only [RandomAcIter1, RandomAcIter2 - 1) forms a heap. The item "popped" can be found in the last location of the range (RandomAcIter1 - 1).

    <u>**make_heap**</u>(RandomAcIter1, RandomAcIter2);
    <u>**make_heap**</u>(RandomAcIter1, RandomAcIter2, compareFunc);

Rearrange the range so that it satisfies the heap property. It requires linear time.

    <u>**sort_heap**</u>(RandomAcIter1, RandomAcIter2);
    <u>**sort_heap**</u>(RandomAcIter1, RandomAcIter2, compareFunc);

Assuming that the range is originally a heap, this will sort the range. The time complexity is O(Nlg(N)).

4.5.8   Lexicographical Compare Operations

These algorithms compare two ranges. They compare corresponding elements and as long as the elements are equivalent, the process continues. At the first difference, if the first is less than the second, then true is returned, otherwise false. If the comparisons continue until the end of one and the first is shorter, then return true. In all other cases return false, including when the ranges are identical.

```
boolVal = lexicographical_compare
    (       InputIter1, InputIter2,
            InputIter3, InputIter4,
    );
boolVal = lexicographical_compare
    (       InputIter1, InputIter2,
            InputIter3, InputIter4,
            compareFunc
    );
```

4.5.9   Permutation Generation Operations

These algorithms generate all permutations of a sequence. next_permutation generates the lexicographically next reordering and prev_permutation gives the previous one. These are linear algorithms.

```
boolVal = next_permutation(BidirectIter1, BidirectIter2);
boolVal
    = next_permutation(BidirectIter1, BidirectIter2, compareFunc);

boolVal = prev_permutation(BidirectIter1, BidirectIter2);
boolVal
    = prev_permutation(BidirectIter1, BidirectIter2, compareFunc);
```

4.5.10 Miscellaneous Additional Operations

```
distance(InputIter1, InputIter2, distVal);
```

Distance computes and returns the distance between two iterators that form a valid range. It is done in constant time for a random access iterator and in linear time otherwise.

Actually, it increments the value of the third argument by the distance between the first two.

advance(InputIter, distVal);

This advances an iterator a fixed number of times. It is done in constant time for a random access iterator and in linear time otherwise.

4.6   Function Objects

As we have seen, function objects are used in place of ordinary functions to pass procedural information to an algorithm. The advantage of this is that it permits the template mechanism to choose an appropriate function based on how the template is used, without the programmer needing to provide several different versions of an algorithm. The function object categories that are the most used are the following:

```
unary predicates
binary predicates
compare functions
binary operators
unary operators
```

Because several particular function objects are often used, they are provided by the STL itself. The classes are all derived from either the binary_function class or the unary_function class. Both of these export typedefs that define the argument types and the result types of the function. In this way a function using the template can get access to the actual template arguments. For example, here is the definition of binary_function:

```
template <class Arg1, class Arg2, class Result>
struct binary_function
{   typedef Arg1 first_argument_type;
  typedef Arg2 second_argument_type;
  typedef Result result_type;
};
```

So a binary function has two arguments, possibly of different types, as well as a result type. There is a corresponding class unary_function<Arg1, Result> that defines operators of a single parameter. Note that, generally speaking, an ordinary function of two arguments can be used in place of a binary function object when necessary. One advantage of an object, however, is the ability to store variables in it, which will retain their values between uses.

4.6.1 Arithmetic Operations

The STL provides six function object classes to define the most common arithmetic operations. Typical is the plus class, shown here in its entirety.

```
template <class T>
struct plus : binary_function<T, T, T>
{   T operator()(const T& x, const T& y) const
    {   return x + y;
    }
};
```

Note that we don't require that the arguments be built-in types, just that type T supports an operator+.

Also provided are classes **minus<T>**, **times<T>**, **divides<T>**, **modulus<T>**, and **negate<T>**. The last of these is a unary function, while all of the others are binary.

4.6.2 Comparison Operations

Similar to the arithmetic operations are the comparison operations. Note that the return type is bool, but the argument types may be any type supporting the individual operator used.

```
template <class T>
struct equal_to : binary_function<T, T, bool>
{   bool operator()(const T& x, const T& y) const
    {   return x == y;
    }
};
```

The others are **not_equal_to<T>**, **greater<T>**, **less<T>**, **greater_equal<T>**, and **less_equal<T>**. These are all binary functions. Note that less<T> and greater<T>, may be used as compare functions in the sort algorithms, but the others may not, due to the restrictions on compare functions.

4.6.3 Logical Operations

The STL also provides two binary functions and one unary function for performing the common logical operations. These are **logical_and<T>**, **logical_or<T>**, and **logical_not<T>**. Again, these just apply the corresponding operator and return boolean results.

4.7   Adaptors

Adaptors take some object in the STL and transform it into something similar. There are adaptors for functions, containers, and iterators. We shall look at each of these in turn.

4.7.1. Function Adaptors

There are three kinds of function adaptors: negators, binders, and pointer-to-function adaptors. All function adaptors are functions that return a modified object from a given object. The negator adaptor **not1** takes a unary predicate and returns another unary predicate that negates the first one. Similarly, not2 negates binary predicates. Thus `not2(less<int>())` returns a binary predicate equivalent to `greater_equal<int>()`.

The binder adaptors take a binary function object and a value and produce a unary function object that uses that value as one of the parameters of the original binary function. Thus, **bind1st**(less<int>(), 5) produces a unary function that evaluates 5 < x for an argument of x. We say we bind 5 to the first parameter. Likewise, **bind2nd** will bind a value to the second parameter. Therefore, bind2nd(divides<int> (), 5) produces a function that divides its argument by 5.

The pointer-to-function adaptors take a pointer to an ordinary function and transform it into a function object so that it may be used with the library. There is both a **pointer_to_unary_function** adaptor and a **pointer_to_binary_function** adaptor. The first takes a pointer to a function of one argument and creates and returns a corresponding function object of one argument. In this way, ordinary C++ functions may be used wherever the STL requires function objects.

4.7.2 Container Adaptors

The STL defines three container adaptors: **stack**, **queue**, and **priority_queue**. These transform a container of another type into one of these. For example, the stack container adaptor can transform a vector, list, or deque into a stack. It does this simply by providing a restricted interface for the user. The container adaptors are defined as class templates. Thus stack< list<int> > provides a stack implemented as a list. The template argument for a container adaptor is a container of some type. Each adaptor works with only certain container types.

4.7.2.1 Stack Adaptor

A stack adaptor may be applied to any vector, list, or deque. The stack adaptor provides the following operations

```
bool empty(); const
size_type size(); const // number of elements
void push(const value_type&);
```

```
void pop();
value_type& top();
const value_type & top() const;
template <class T>
bool operator==( const stack<T>&, const stack<T>&)
    // Determines if two stacks have the same
    // elements.
template <class T>
bool operator<
(   const stack<T>&,
    const stack<T>&
)   // Compares the contents lexicographically.
```

4.7.2.2 Queue Adaptor

A queue adaptor may be applied to any list or deque. It won't work with vectors because of the difficulty of working at the front of a vector, which is required for a queue. The queue adaptor provides the following operations.

```
bool empty(); const
size_type size(); const // number of elements
void push(const value_type&); // Insert at rear
void pop(); // Remove at front.
value_type& front(); // Element at front.
const value_type & front() const;
value_type& back();   // Element at rear.
const value_type & back() const;

template <class T>
bool operator==
(   const queue<T>&,
    const queue<T>&
)   // Determines if two queues have the same
    // elements.

template <class T>
bool operator<
(   const queue<T>&,
    const queue<T>&
)   // Compares the contents lexicographically.
```

4.7.2.3 Priority Queue Adaptor

A priority queue adaptor may be applied to any vector or deque. It also requires that a comparison object be supplied. For example,

```
priority_queue< vector< float>, greater<float> >
```

will provide a vector-based priority queue of floats in which greater is used as the comparison object. Since priority queues remove the "highest priority" element on a pop and since greater's "highest priority" element is the smallest, this reverses the usual sense of a priority queue.

The priority_queue adaptor provides the following operations:

```
bool empty(); const
size_type size(); const // number of elements
void push(const value_type&); // Insert
void pop(); // Remove highest priority item.
value_type& top();
    // Element of highest priority.
const value_type & top() const;
```

4.7.3   Iterator Adaptors

There are two kinds of iterator adaptors: reverse iterators, and insert iterators. An iterator adaptor transforms an iterator so that it behaves differently when executing its operators, especially operator++ and operator=.

4.7.3.1 Reverse Iterators

A reverse iterator adaptor transforms a bidirectional iterator into one in which the directions of travel are reversed. Thus, operator++ will be transformed into operator--, and vice versa. Each of the STL container types produces two reverse iterators rbegin() and rend() that perform the reverse iteration. There are special versions of the reverse iterator adaptor for bidirectional and for random access iterators.

The constructor **reverse_bidirectional_iterator**(BidirectIter x) will produce a reverse iterator equivalent to x. If x is a random access iterator, then use **reverse_iterator**(RandomAcIter x) instead, and the result will also be a random access iterator, but it will operate in the opposite direction from x.

4.7.3.2 Insert Iterators

Normally iterators apply operator= to de-references to modify existing positions in a container. When using an insert iterator, these applications are translated into insertions instead.

Suppose, for example, that we want to compute the partial sums of an existing set<int> and put the results into a new vector. The following will produce an error:

```
vector<int> V; // New vector
partial_sum
(  set1.begin(),
```

```
    set1.end(),
    V.begin()
);
```

The problem, of course, is that the vector has no room for the data: it has size zero. We could initialize V with the size of the set, of course, but there is another solution. Instead of using V.begin() (or V.end(), which is just as bad), we can use a **back_insert_iterator** instead.

```
vector<int> V; // New vector
partial_sum
(   set1.begin(),
    set1.end(),
    back_insert_iterator< vector<int> >(V)
);
```

This iterator will take the *V = ... operations done within partial_sum and translate them into push_back(*V) operations instead. Thus, the vector will be properly extended when necessary. A back insert iterator can be generated from the function **back_inserter** by simply passing a container as the parameter. The container must support push_back, of course. The result is a back_insert_iterator over that container. Note that the parameters here are containers, not iterators.

There is also a **front_insert_iterator** that can be produced from any collection that has a push_front operation. These can be conveniently constructed using the function **front_inserter**.

Finally, there is an **insert_iterator** adaptor that can be produced from any container that has an insert operation. This version requires that we pass both the container and an iterator into that container.

For example, if we have a list L, and an iterator I into that list, then insert_iterator (L,I) will produce an iterator that will do insertions at the point of I.

4.8   Allocators

In STL an allocator is an encapsulation of a memory model. Some computers, such as Intel-based PCs have many different systems for organizing memory, and an allocator can be used to separate the details of the memory model so that other parts of the library need not be written to depend on a certain model. For example, in some memory models a pointer need only be 16 bits long. In others it is required to be 32 bits. The new operator of C++ depends on a certain memory model, but can be tailored to any such model. An allocator exports a number of types such as *pointer* and *reference*, that other classes can use. In particular, the *reference* type exported by a container class is defined in terms of a particular allocator's *reference* type. An allocator also defines an allocation function that can be used to obtain blocks from the free store. It is not our purpose to discuss allocators. Additional material can be found in the *STL Tutorial and Reference Guide*. [3]

4.9   Summary

Make certain that you understand each of the following terms:

> adaptor
> allocator
> bidirectional iterator
> concept
> container
> forward iterator
> function object
> generic algorithm
> input iterator
> istream iterator
> iterator
> ostream iterator
> output iterator
> past-the-end values
> random access iterator
> reflexivity
> symmetry
> transitivity
> sequence container
> sorted associative container
> singular values
> strict total ordering

4.10   Exercises

1. Find a long piece of text to process. Read it into a vector using an istream iterator with one word per cell. Then sort the vector and remove duplicate values with unique. How long does this take? Now read the same text into a set. Note that it is already sorted with duplicates removed. How long does this take?

2. Use binary search to find a large number of values (1000 or more) in the vector-based spelling table of Exercise 1. How long does it take to find all of the values? Compare this with the time required for the set-based spell table. Compare these times with the times required to find twice as many values. Be careful to not always search for one (or only a few) value.

3. How long does it take to print out a long vector that was previously sorted? How long does it take to print out a set with the same values?

4. An alternate method of maintaining a sorted container is to use a vector, but insert each item into its sorted location rather than sorting after inserting all items. How long does it take to do this, compared to the operations asked for in Exercises 1 and 2?

5. Repeat Exercise 1 using a list instead. You can sort it with the sort member of list, rather than the generic sort algorithm. How long does this take?

6. Repeat Exercise 1 using a deque. What can you say about the relative efficiency of a deque and a vector on these operations?

7. Compare stable_sort with sort for its time requirements on a large vector.

8. Merge two spelling tables with set_union. How much difference in time is there for set and vector implementations?

9. Build a spelling table by reading into a multiset and then removing duplicates with unique. How long does this take compared to set operations?

10. Use count to determine how many items are in your spelling table. Use count_if to find the words with an even number of characters.

11. Use an appropriate STL generic algorithm to find the longest word in your spelling table.

12. Use an appropriate STL generic algorithm to put quote marks around each word in the spelling table. Don't change the original table, but produce a new one instead.

Chapter 5
Vector Programming

5.1. Vectors—Expandable Arrays

Suppose that you have a problem in which you need an array, but the size of the array can't be known at the time at which you create it. An example is when you need to read in data from a file of unknown size and process it. You need to create the array in which you wish to put the data before you begin to read the file, but you won't know until the end of the file how much data there is. Vectors are ideal for this kind of problem, provided that the problem only requires the array to grow at one end. If it must grow at both ends, then a deque is better suited to the task. Here we are assuming, of course, that the other processing required of the data requires an array-like structure. If we don't require random access iterators in our processing, then a list will probably be a better choice in which to hold the data.

The basic strategy for an expandable array is to initially allocate an array whose size is a good guess at the size of the data. If this is difficult to do, then make a guess that is adequate for a relatively small data set. Then begin to fill the array, keeping track of how much data you have inserted relative to the size of the array allocated. If you reach the end of the array, then simply allocate a larger array, copy the original array into the new one, and then continue with the new, larger, array after deleting the original one. This sounds like it might be slow, and it is. However, if the right strategy is chosen for allocating the new array, then the time expended won't be so bad—on the average. This is because for most allocations the insertion time is a small constant. It is only when we reach the boundary that we absorb a large cost.

If an array can expand, then it can also shrink. If we discover that a large part of the array is unused, and likely to remain unused, then we could also allocate a new, smaller array, copy the old to the new, and continue with the new array. This might free up memory on the free store for use elsewhere in the program.

5.2   The Indexing Problem

One problem that occurs frequently in applications is that of building an index to a file. Suppose that we have a file that consists of records with two fields. The first field is the *key* that is used to retrieve records. The purpose of retrieving a record is to get access to the second field, the *value*. If the file is large, then it is useful to keep the file sorted by key. There are many problems, however, in which it is not desirable to sort the records by key, since they may need to be often processed in some other order, so that processing requires that the ordering not be by key. In this case an index file will be very helpful. Figure 5.1 shows an example of a simple file and Figure 5.2 shows its index.

Smith, John	123 Main St	Anytown
Jones, Mary	234 Oak Ave	Gotham City
Kumar, Sue	345 Jefferson Ln	Oak Island
Woo, Mark	456 Maple Ln	Village Home
Kahn, J. P.	567 Front Street	Uptown

Figure 5.1. A sample file.

Jones, Mary	1
Kahn, J. P.	4
Kumar, Sue	2
Smith, John	0
Woo, Mark	3

Figure 5.2. An index file.

If we store the original records in a vector, so that we may easily extend its length, then records may be accessed by subscript, assuming that we know which subscript to use to obtain a given value. An index is a file of records, also with two fields. The first field consists of the keys of the original file and the second field is just integer subscripts into the first file. The subscript stored with a key in the index file is the location in the first file at which a record with that key can be found. We suppose that we store the index file in a vector also. Then, we can sort the index file by key, leaving the original file (vector) in its original order. To get access to a record we first search the index vector, perhaps using binary search. This give us a subscript into the original file's vector.

As an overly simplified example, suppose that we have a file consisting of standard C++ string objects for keys and float values. We store this file in a vector< pair< string, float> >. To get access to the string class you should include <string> (not <string.h>) into your file. The index is stored in a vector<pair< string, int> >. We can create the index when we read in the data file. The following function will read both the file and create the index. Note that strings are normally read a word at a time from an input stream. This is because the stream will break at any whitespace character.

```
void readStrVec
( ifstream & inp,
  vector<pair<string, float> > &V,
  vector<pair<string, int> >&I
)
{ int i = 0;
  string input;
  float val;
  while( inp >> input)
  { inp >> val;
    V.push_back
         ( pair<string, float> (input, val) );
    pair<string, int> p(input, i++);
    I.push_back(p);
  }
}
```

After reading the file and creating the index, we sort the index with

```
sort(Index.begin(), Index.end());
```

This requires that we provide a special operator< so that pairs will be compared using strcmp on the keys.

```
inline bool operator<
( const pair<string, int>& x,
  const pair<string, int>& y
)
{ return x.first < y.first;
    // compare 2 string objects.
}
```

We can now search the index to obtain subscripts into the original file. The subscript gives us the desired original pair with the desired key.

```
vector<pair<string , int> > :: const_iterator where;
where = lower_bound
      ( Index.begin(),
        Index.end(),
        pair<string , int>("times",0)
      );
float val = Data[where->second].second;
```

Note that only the index file was sorted. This can be a big advantage when the original file may not be sorted and also when it contains very large value fields, which are expensive to move and hence expensive to sort. Note also that in this particular case, we have not even copied the keys into the index file. We simply have pointers to the original key strings. Therefore, the index file itself may be small in comparison to the original file. If the size of the file is known in advance, we may use an array instead of a vector, of course. Indexed files on disk use a variation of this technique in which the integers in the value fields of the index are replaced by disk block addresses.

5.3   How We Can Implement Vectors

In this section we will explore the implementation of a class that is much like the STL vector class, though a little less sophisticated. It will give us a chance to see some implementation tradeoffs as well as become more familiar with the philosophy and requirements of the STL. We will call the class template ExpandableArray. The template parameter is the type of data to be held in the structure. A minimally useful implementation is presented below and discussed immediately after.

```
template <class T>
class ExpandableArray
{   public:
        typedef T& reference;
        typedef T value_type;
        typedef T* iterator;
          // Use ordinary pointers.

        ExpandableArray()
        :   _values(new T[100]),
            _size(0),
            _capacity(100)
        {
        }

        ExpandableArray
            (long n, const T& val = T() )
        :   _values(new T[2*n]),
            _size(n),
            _capacity(2*n)
        {   if(val != T())
            for(long i = 0; i < n; ++i)
                _values[i] = val;
        }
```

```
ExpandableArray
    (const ExpandableArray<T>& A);

ExpandableArray<T>& operator=
    (const ExpandableArray<T>& A);

~ExpandableArray();

long size(){ return _size;}

long capacity(){ return _capacity;}

reference operator[]( long w )
{  return _values[w];
}

iterator begin(){ return &_values[0]; }

iterator end(){ return &_values[_size]; }

void push_back(const T & t)
{  if( _capacity == _size )
    {  reserve(2*_capacity);
    }
    _values[_size++] = t;
}

void reserve(long n)
    // make capacity at least n
{  if(_capacity < n)
    {  T* new_values = new T[n];
        _capacity = n;
        for(int i = 0; i < _size; ++i)
            new_values[i] = _values[i];
        delete [] _values;
        _values = new_values;
    }
}

private:
    T * _values;
    long _size;
    long _capacity;
```

```
            void copy(const ExpandableArray<T>& A);
            void free();
};
```

We emphasize that this class merely has the flavor of the STL vector class. It is much less sophisticated. Notice the following STL-like features, however. First, we export several types, so that a user can recover the value_type, for example. Second we define iterators to the beginning and the end of the active part of the structure. The iterators in this case are just pointers. They could have been much more sophisticated, actually. They are, however, random access iterators, so we can use all of the generic algorithms with them. Third, we provide operator[] so that we can use the structure like an array. Finally, we provide a means to extend the size of the structure in the member push_back. These are all similar to the STL vector class.

Notice, importantly, that operator[] does not check the legality of its parameter. This is in keeping with usual C++ practice that puts the responsibility for such checking on the programmer who uses the structure, rather than on the one that builds it. An alternative implementation that does do checking is outlined next. Notice that the legal subscripts are those between 0 and _size-1, not between 0 and _capacity-1. The cells between _size and _capacity-1 are not logically part of the ExpandableArray. They are there to permit push_back operations to extend the logical size of the structure without having to extend its physical size.

```
template <class T>
reference ExpandableArray<T>::operator[]
(   long w
)
{   if( w >= 0 && w < _size ) return _values[w];
    else exit(1);
} // Range checking version.
```

Here we cause the program to exit if the user gives an illegal subscript. There are better solutions available in C++ for this, including the throwing of an exception.

What is missing? The STL vector class provides more types and more member functions, including the capability of shrinking the size of the structure as well as growing it. The STL vector also provides members to insert an item between two existing items, making room for the new item by moving all of the following items. Some of these operations will be discussed below, and some will be exercises. We will study the STL vector class later in this chapter.

Our ExpandableArray class has three constructors. The default constructor creates an empty structure with a nonempty capacity. The capacity of an ExpandableArray is the *maximum number of items* that it can hold before it needs to be grown. It is the physical, as opposed to the logical, size of the structure. The second constructor lets us set the size and initialize all cells to a given value. If the value is not given, we use the default value of the value_type. In this case we set a larger capacity than the size; in fact, it is twice as large. The idea is that vectors are intended to be expanded, so we expect them to grow, and hence allocate space to make this easy.

Exercise. Discuss the tradeoffs in overallocating space at the beginning. Do you think this is a good idea or a bad idea? What factors should be considered in determining this? Is 100 cells in the default constructor too much or too little? Is doubling the size on reallocation too much or too little? Modify the definition of ExpandableArray to suit your own concept of what is appropriate.

Expansion in capacity of the structure is controlled by the push_back function. When we reach capacity we call *reserve*, asking for a capacity twice that of the current structure. This is achieved by allocating an array of the desired size and copying all elements into the new array. We then keep this new array and delete the original. This copying is an expensive operation as it must be done with a loop, giving us linear time. Therefore, we don't want to do it very often. Expanding the array by a fixed factor, rather than a fixed amount, is an important means of achieving good performance in the push_back operation. Notice that push_back is very fast most of the time and slow only occasionally. If we look at the average effort, however, we find that it is actually constant. The extra time for the expansion averages out to a constant amount over the other insertions.

To see this, consider that if we start with a single cell and double the capacity each time, then just after a capacity expansion to 2*n, we have n active cells in the structure. We have reorganized about lg(n) times at a total cost of copying of about 2*n. This is in addition to the n simple insertions. Therefore, the total insertion cost is about 3 * n for n items or about 3 per item. This is called amortized constant time. It is not actually constant, but on the average it is constant.

This will not be the case if we expand the structure by a fixed amount, say 100 cells, each time we need to expand capacity. In that case the reorganization step will be done much more often and so the cost will be much larger on the average. In that case we will have reorganized about k = n / 100 times at a total cost of copying of about k*(k+1) * 50. Since this inserts n items, we see that the copying cost alone is about 50*(k+1) per item. This is a linear function so the costs would be amortized linear, rather than amortized constant.

Notice that we are clearly trading space for time with the above solution. Doubling the capacity when we need more does take up a lot of space. However, it also saves a lot of time. In modern computers, space is generally much cheaper than time, so this is a good tradeoff. Space is cheaper than time since it is cheaper to buy twice as much memory as it is to buy a processor twice as fast. There are situations, however, in which memory is at a premium and cannot be expanded. In such a case, another solution would be preferable.

5.4   Memory Management

The definitions of five of the members of ExpandableArray were not shown above. These
are the destructor, the copy constructor, the overloaded assignment operator=, and the two
private functions used to implement these three members: copy and free. All classes that
manage memory need a destructor, a copy constructor, and an overloaded assignment. This
means most classes that have any pointer or reference members. The reason that we need
to write these members is that the compiler-supplied versions of them will not do the
right thing in most circumstances. This is because they only provide for memberwise operations. Thus, if we assign one ExpandableArray object to another ExpandableArray variable, we could wind up with two ExpandableArrays that share internal representation as in
Figure 5.3. That is to say, the _values pointer of each of two ExpandableArrays could
point to the same memory location. Then, modifying one of the ExpandableArrays would
automatically modify the other as well.

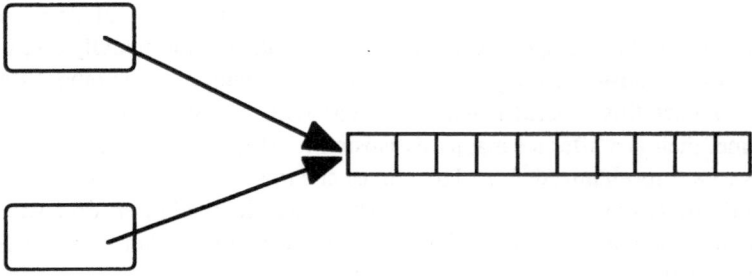

Figure 5.3. Two objects sharing an implementation.

The copy constructor, destructor, and overloaded assignment operator are designed to
solve this problem. The copy constructor and overloaded assignment are very similar, but
are quite different in purpose. They are both used for making copies of one object for insertion into another. The copy constructor is used when you pass an object by value to a
function and when you create one object from another directly using initialization syntax.
In each of the following three cases a copy constructor will be called.

```
afunction(anObject);
    // Function call
AClass aNewObject(oldObject);
    // Create a new object from old.
AClass aNewObject = oldObject;
    // Initialization.
```

An assignment operator is used when you assign to a variable of class type.

```
aVariable = anObject;
```

An initialization looks like an assignment, but it is not the same, and different members are used in the two cases. The difference is that in an initialization, the left side variable doesn't hold a value yet, while in an assignment we must deal with the current value of member variables before giving them new values from the righthand side object.

The three necessary operations can be provided in terms of two helper functions, copy and free. Copy copies one object's member variables to another, and free cleans up any allocated memory that should not be shared with other objects. Given these, we can easily provide a destructor, a copy constructor, and an overloaded assignment.

```
template <class T>
ExpandableArray<T>:: ~ExpandableArray ()
{  free();
}


template <class T>
ExpandableArray<T>:: ExpandableArray
(  const ExpandableArray<T>& A
)
{  copy(A);
}


template <class T>
ExpandableArray<T>& ExpandableArray<T>:: operator=
(  const ExpandableArray<T>& A
)
{  if(this != &A)
   {  free();
      copy(A);
   }
   return *this;
}
```

In other classes, these three members nearly always look exactly like this. You need a good reason to deviate from the above pattern. Notice that the assignment operator guards against assignments in which the value held in the left side variable is exactly the same object as that held in the right side expression. We need to do this since we are destroying the contents of the left side object. If they are the same, this would be a disaster.

Member free is used to deallocate memory. Here we have the _values field that was previously allocated and holds the contents of the ExpandableArray.

```
template <class T>
void ExpandableArray<T>:: free()
{  delete [] _values;
}
```

The purpose of copy is to copy the internals of the parameter into the object *this*. We assume that *this* has previously been cleared.

```
template <class T>
void ExpandableArray<T>:: copy
(   const ExpandableArray<T>& A
)
{   _size = A._size;
    _capacity = A._capacity;
    _values = new T [ _capacity ];
    for(long i = 0; i < _size; ++i)
        _values[i] = A._values[i];
}
```

There are a few classes in which we deviate from the above. These are classes in which two or more objects may safely share an implementation. This could be the case if we built objects out of pointers, but the objects could not be modified after they were created. It would then be safe to share implementation as long as we can be sure when it is safe to delete the implementation. This would happen when we delete the last object sharing that implementation. This can be done by keeping a count in the shared data that keeps track of how many objects share the implementation. This count would be updated in constructors and destructors. This is an important technique, though it is used fairly rarely. We won't discuss if further in this book, but you can study it further in [1]

5.5   Adding to the Functionality of ExpandableArrays

In this section we shall discuss several operations that should be added to the ExpandableArray template to extend its usefulness. Rather than present template preambles with each of them, we shall assume that they are added inline in the definition of the template itself.

Since iterators are fundamental to the STL and operator[] is fundamental to array like structures, it is useful to have members that translate between subscripts and iterators. Member index translates an iterator into an equivalent index into the array. It works because an iterator into an Expandable array is a random access iterator so that we may do arithmetic on it.

```
long index(iterator i) {return i - _values;}
```

This is equivalent to i- begin(), of course.

To translate in the other direction, we use member location:

```
iterator location(long i){return _values + i;}
```

which is equivalent to begin() + i.

In both of these we have assumed that the subscript type is long. This is not necessarily the case, however. STL container templates export a difference_type that is some integer type sufficient to hold the difference between any two iterators into the container. It might, indeed, be long for most implementations, but it might be otherwise. Declaring and uniformly using difference_type adds to the efficiency and portability of the STL. Likewise, the size and capacity functions return values of type size_type.

Next, we have an operator[] defined in ExpandableArray, but if we want to insert const objects into our structure, we need another version that returns const references.

```
const reference operator[]( long w )const
{   return _values[w];
}
```

This member will be employed rather than the other whenever the container has const objects in it. Note that the body of the function is the same; only the returned value is different. This member is also, itself, marked const, since it cannot be used to modify the container itself. In spite of the fact that the function bodies are the same, the effect is different, as the compiler enforces const operations. If we write code that implies modifying a const object by applying a nonconst operation, the compiler will inform us of the error.

Occasionally it is necessary to insert an object into the middle of an expandable array. Here we don't mean just changing a value at some iterator position, but actually making room between two existing elements. This is not an especially efficient operation on array-like structures, though it can be done. We must increase the size of the structure and then move all elements "to the right" of the desired insertion position one cell to the right. We then have an empty cell into which to insert the desired item. This operation is linear in the size of the structure, though if the location of the insertion is near the back of the structure, it goes quite quickly.

```
void insert(iterator i, const value_type& v)
{   if(_size == _capacity) reserve(2*_capacity);
    for(iterator j = end(); j != i; --j)
       *j = *(j-1);
    *i = v;
    _size++;
}
```

If we can insert new items at the back of an ExpandableArray, making its size larger, then we ought to be able to remove them there as well. This operation will be left to an exercise. We can also erase an item in the middle of an expandable array by closing up the space to the right of the removed item. The insert and erase operations can also be used to provide push_front and pop_front operations on expandable arrays.

5.6   Programming with Expandable Arrays

In Chapter 2 we took subscript-based searching and sorting algorithms and turned them into pointer-based versions using the pointer duality law. In Chapter 3 we went a bit farther and modified these into iterator-based functions. These operations, as discussed in Chapter 3, had the following prototypes, in which the iterator template parameter needs to be a random access iterator.

```
template < class iterator >
void selectionSort
(   iterator start,
    iterator end
)

template<class iterator>
iterator BinarySearch
(   const iterator:: value_type& t,
    iterator first,
    iterator after
)       // Searching for t between first, after.
```

As defined above, these cannot be applied to expandable arrays. This is because iterators over ExpandableArrays are ordinary pointers that, when treated as iterators, cannot define the value_type that is required. In this section we will see how to solve this problem, though the solution is quite subtle and involved. It does show the power of templates, however.

Our goal is to be able to sort and search any expandable array or any subsection of such a structure. For example,

```
ExpandableArray<float> costs(20, 0.0);
. . .
selectionSort(costs.begin(), costs.end());
```

The solution for BinarySearch is actually easier. All we need to do is to provide an additional template parameter for the value type of the iterator. This works because a value of this type appears as a function parameter and it is function parameters that are used for template function selection.

```
template<class iterator, class T>
    // random access iterator with
    // value type T with operator< and operator==
iterator BinarySearch
(   const T& t,     // Searching for t between
                    // first, after.
```

```
    iterator first,
    iterator after
)
{  if(first >= after) return first;
   iterator mid = first + (after - first)/2;
       // Middle of range.
   if(t == *mid) return mid;
   if(*mid < t )
       return BinarySearch(t, mid + 1, after);
   else
       return BinarySearch(t, first, mid);
}
```

Note that the new template parameter is used not only as the type of a function parameter, but also to define a temporary variable within the function.

We can't apply this solution to selection sort because we will pass only iterators to this function. But suppose that we do write a version that has an extra template parameter for the value type. It might look as follows.

```
template < class iterator, class T >
void selectionSort_aux
(   iterator start,
    iterator end,
    T*
)
{  for
   (   iterator where = start ;
       where < end ;
       where++
   )
   {  iterator loc = where;
      T small = *loc;
      for
      (   iterator inner = where + 1;
          inner < end;
          inner++
      )
          if(*inner < *loc)
          {  loc = inner;
             small = *loc;
          }
      *loc = *where;
      *where = small;
   }
}
```

Note that we haven't named the extra function parameter of type T* since we don't intend to actually use the value passed for this parameter. It can be used for template selection nevertheless. We have named this function selectionSort_aux, because we intend to use it as an auxiliary function to define the iterator-based selectionSort function. We can let this function do the work of selectionSort simply by calling it and passing some dummy value of the required type for this extra parameter.

```
template < class iterator >
void selectionSort
(   iterator start,
    iterator end
)
{   selectionSort_aux
    (start, end, someValueOfType_T_star);
} // the _aux function does the work.
```

The problem is coming up with the right value to pass. In this particular case we could de-reference the start iterator and then take the address of the result, letting someValueOfType_T_star be &(*start). There is a small problem with this solution, however, since in the case that start is not properly initialized, the address will not be valid. Therefore, the solution in the STL is a bit more sophisticated.

The STL defines a collection of function templates for the value type of any iterator or pointer. The definition for the pointer version is

```
template <class T>
inline T* value_type(const T*)
{   return (T*)(0);
}
```

This function returns a default object pointer for any pointer type passed to it. Notice that the syntax (T*)(0) is actually a cast of NULL to type T*. The important thing is not the value, but the fact that it is typed. It therefore produces the dummy value we need for template selection. A similar function is also defined for each iterator type. Given this family of functions, we can write the final version of selectionSort.

```
template < class iterator >
void selectionSort
(   iterator start,
    iterator end
)
{   selectionSort_aux
    (start, end, value_type(start));
} // the _aux function does the work.
```

5.7   Building a Stack Adaptor

Adaptors are one of the major components of the STL. They also demonstrate a particularly good use of template programming. In this section we shall create a stack adaptor template called StackAdaptor. It is similar to the stack template of the STL itself, though somewhat less sophisticated. This template uses a template variable that doesn't represent the element type of the items to be included, but rather some container type, such as one built from our ExpandableArray template. It is important to note, however, that any container type could be used, provided that it has the functionality that the StackAdaptor template demands.

As discussed in Chapter 3, a Stack is a FIFO mechanism that is very useful in processing when we may need to delay handling some item while we handle some other item and then want to return to previous items. This is especially true when we handle composite items made up of simpler parts. We may want to begin handling the whole object, then discover that it contains some part that we need to handle before we can continue processing the whole. Languages (including computer languages) are like this, where large constructs are composed of smaller ones with their own structure. To handle such situations it is often useful to push information about the larger object onto a stack while we handle the part of interest. We can then return to handling the larger object by popping the previously saved information.

The StackAdaptor template builds a Stack from some other container type. In particular, we could build a stack with

```
StackAdaptor< ExpandableArray< int> > aStack;
```

Here the implementation of the stack would be an expandable array of ints. We would thus be able to stack ints. Furthermore, the operations we would perform would not be ExpandableArray operations, but stack operations such as push and pop instead.

```
template <class container>
class StackAdaptor
{   public:
        typedef container::value_type value_type;
        typedef container::iterator iterator;

        StackAdaptor():_elements(){}
        void push(const value_type& v)
        {   _elements.push_back(v);
        }
        void pop(){_elements.pop_back();}
        value_type& top()
        {   return _elements[_elements.size() - 1];
        }
        const value_type& top()const
```

```
      {  return _elements[_elements.size() - 1];
      }
      iterator begin()
      {  return _elements.begin();
      }
      iterator end() {return _elements.end();}
      bool empty()const
      {  return _elements.empty();
      };
      long size()const{return _elements.size();}

   private:
      container _elements;
};
```

The constructor simply constructs a default object of type container as its _element field and passes most operations to this internal representation object. We provide two versions of top since a stack might contain const objects or mutable objects. We can obtain a reference in either case. Note that the pop operation returns nothing. It simply removes the top item from the stack. If you also need a reference to the object that pop would remove, you should use top first. Some people prefer a pop that also returns a reference to the object removed. This is not provided here, nor in the STL itself.

It is very instructive to examine what is really needed from the container object. The template makes use of only the following: a default constructor, push_back, pop_back, size, begin, end, empty, iterator, value_type and operator[]. Therefore, any container type that implements these would be acceptable as a template parameter for this adaptor. It should be clear why this type of template is called an adaptor. It adapts the interface of its representation object so that it seems to provide different operations than the underlying class provides.

Notice how the definitions of types in classes like ExpandableArray help us here. We can define an Iterator for the stack adaptor to be the same type as that of the container parameter without actually knowing what that type is when we write the stack adaptor template. The template mechanism fills in the appropriate types for us when we instantiate the template.

The use of operator[] in the above class is troubling, since few container types can efficiently implement it. In fact, all we use it for is obtaining access to the last element in the representation object. This operation is much simpler to provide than a general operator[], so we can improve StackAdaptor by modifying it to use a required member back instead of operator[].

```
template <class container>
class StackAdaptor
{  public:
      typedef container::value_type value_type;
      typedef container::iterator iterator;
```

```
StackAdaptor():_elements(){}
void push(const value_type& v)
{   _elements.push_back(v);
}
void pop(){_elements.pop_back();}
value_type& top()
{   return _elements.back();
}
const value_type& top()const
{   return _elements.back();
}
iterator begin()
{   return _elements.begin();
}
iterator end() {return _elements.end();}
bool empty()const
{   return _elements.empty();
}
long size()const{return _elements.size();}

private:
    container _elements;
};
```

As defined above, our expandable array class can't meet the requirements of this adaptor. It will be an exercise to provide it with the necessary members.

5.8   The STL vector Template

Now let's look at the actual vector class template from the STL. We will examine only the interface of this class, leaving out almost all details of the implementation. We will intersperse the interface with some commentary on the various members. Note that this implementation was written before C++ fully supported the STL. In particular, future versions of C++ will support default template parameters, in which case the allocator will be a template parameter rather than assumed to be imported from class Allocator<T>, as here.

```
// Copyright (c) 1994
// Hewlett-Packard Company
template <class T>
class vector {
public:
```

```
typedef Allocator<T> vector_allocator;
typedef T value_type;
typedef vector_allocator::pointer pointer;
typedef vector_allocator::pointer iterator;
typedef vector_allocator::const_pointer
    const_iterator;
typedef vector_allocator::reference
    reference;
typedef vector_allocator::const_reference
    const_reference;
typedef vector_allocator::size_type
    size_type;
typedef vector_allocator::difference_type
    difference_type;
typedef reverse_iterator
    <   const_iterator,
        value_type,
        const_reference,
        difference_type
    > const_reverse_iterator;

typedef reverse_iterator
    <   iterator,
        value_type,
        reference,
        difference_type
    > reverse_iterator;
```

Class vector exports several types including pointer, reference, and iterator types. This permits algorithms to declare these items as needed. In this case we just use the types defined by the default allocator.

```
protected:
  static Allocator<T> static_allocator;
  iterator start;
  iterator finish;
  iterator end_of_storage;
```

These are the implementing member variables. The allocator obtains a block of storage and start points to the beginning of it, end_of_storage to the end, and finish to the end of the active part of the vector.

```
void insert_aux
    (   iterator position,
        const T& x
    );
```

From an interface perspective this function is unimportant, as it is protected. It is used to implement insert.

```
public:
    iterator begin();
    const_iterator begin() const;
    iterator end();
    const_iterator end() const;
    reverse_iterator rbegin();
    const_reverse_iterator rbegin() const;
    reverse_iterator rend();
    const_reverse_iterator rend() const;
```

The above functions generate the standard iterators that we have seen many times. The reverse_iterator functions return iterators that iterate backwards over the vector: from last element to first.

```
    size_type size() const;
```

This function tells us the current size of the vector: the number of elements currently stored.

```
    size_type max_size() const;
```

The max_size is the limit that the system puts on a vector of this type. It is the maximum capacity that the vector can have.

```
    size_type capacity() const;
```

The capacity is the maximum number of elements that can be stored without reallocating storage for the array. It is always at least as big as size, and never bigger than max_size.

```
    void resize(size_type sz, T c = T());
```

Member resize either truncates the vector on the right to size sz, or pads it with value c on the right to reach size sz.

```
    bool empty() const;
```

This tells us the current state of the vector. Is it currently empty?

```
    reference operator[](size_type n);
    const_reference operator[](size_type n)
        const;
```

These two members let vectors behave like arrays. We can index from 0 through size-1.

```
vector();
vector(size_type n, const T& value = T());
vector(const vector<T>& x);
vector
(   const_iterator first,
    const_iterator last
);
```

The first constructor creates an empty vector. The second creates a vector with n copies of value. The next is the copy constructor, and the last copies any iterator range into a new vector. The definition of the STL does not require that the source container be a vector, though with the above declaration it would. The standard specifies that this last constructor should be defined as

```
template<class InputIterator>
vector
(   InputIterator first,
    InputIterator second
);
```

This is an example of a template member function. Vector itself is a template, and some of its member functions have additional template arguments. Not all compilers implement this yet, so compromises are often made. See the STL home page for a complete implementation of STL [11]. It may not be usable with your compiler, however.

```
~vector();
```

The destructor releases storage for the vector as usual.

```
vector<T>& operator=(const vector<T>& x);
```

The overloaded assignment operator creates new storage for the copy as necessary. It also releases the old storage associated with the variable on the righthand side of the assignment.

```
void reserve(size_type n);
```

Member reserve guarantees that the capacity is at least n elements.

```
reference front();
const_reference front() const;
reference back();
const_reference back() const;
```

Members front and back give us access to the elements stored in the vector. They are not iterators, but the data themselves. Since they return references we can operate directly on the values themselves, not copies.

```
void push_back(const T& x);
```

This is the primary insert operation. It inserts x efficiently at the rear of the vector.

```
void swap(vector<T>& x);
```

This member exchanges the contents of two vectors of the same type.

```
iterator insert
(   iterator position,
    const T& x
);
```

This member inserts x at location position, moving all elements down to the right to make room for the new value. The new item will be before the item originally referred to by position. The reason that it is before and not after is to make it possible to use this to insert before the first location in the vector. It requires time that is linear in the number of elements to be moved. It returns an iterator to the item inserted.

```
void insert
(   iterator position,
    const_iterator first,
    const_iterator last
);
```

This second version of insert inserts a range of values before position. The source range does not need to be a vector. In more recent versions of the STL this is a member template function with the actual iterator type as the template parameter. Earlier versions of C++ did not support classes in which the members were themselves template functions.

```
void insert
(   iterator position,
    size_type n,
    const T& x
);
```

Member insert inserts n copies of x at location position.

```
void pop_back();
```

This member removes the last element in the vector, decreasing the size. It may decrease the capacity as well.

```
void erase(iterator position);
void erase(iterator first, iterator last);
```

The erase members remove values from the vector, closing up space as required. The first removes a single item at location position. The second removes a range of values. They both decrease the size and, perhaps, the capacity.

```
};
```

5.9   A Graph Implemented with STL vectors

In this section we are going to use STL vectors in two different ways to build a variety of graphs known as directed graphs (digraphs). A directed graph is composed of vertices, also called nodes, and arcs which connect the vertices. The arcs are directed in the sense that they go from one vertex to another. It is possible for the beginning and the end of an arc to be the same vertex also. Figure 5.4 shows an example of a digraph with eight nodes and nine arcs. We have numbered the nodes for convenience. If we want an ordinary (undirected) graph, the arcs can simply be doubled: For each arc in the digraph, provide another in the opposite direction.

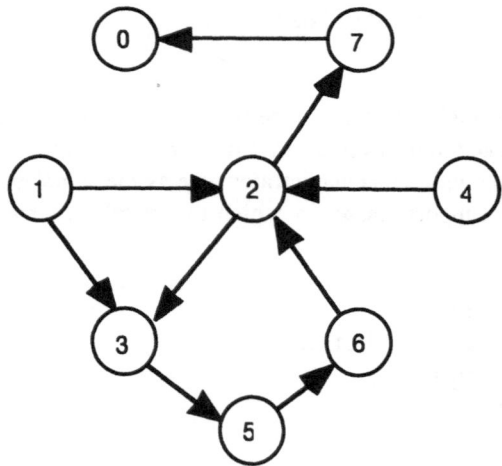

Figure 5.4. An Example of a digraph.

A digraph can have any number of nodes and any number of arcs. Our implementation of digraphs will need to be very flexible. It is also possible to store arbitrary data in the nodes. For some problems it is also necessary to associate data with the arcs, though we won't do that here. When a digraph has data along the arcs, it is sometimes called a network.

Because the data stored in a node can have arbitrary type, we shall build a DiGraph class template with parameter T representing the type of stored data. Because the DiGraph is a container, it needs an associated iterator. We shall see that vector iterators will serve here. Finally, we shall also build a class template for the nodes out of which the digraph is composed. We won't need a class for the arcs, however, though it might be useful to have one if we were building networks.

Because the nodes are considered to be internal to a graph, we won't permit the user to create any nodes, except via the DiGraph of which they are to be a part. To create the nodes of the above digraph, we can use the following:

```
DiGraph<int> G;
GraphNode<int>& gn0 = G.newGraphNode(0);
GraphNode<int>& gn1 = G.newGraphNode(1);
GraphNode<int>& gn2 = G.newGraphNode(2);
GraphNode<int>& gn3 = G.newGraphNode(3);
GraphNode<int>& gn4 = G.newGraphNode(4);
GraphNode<int>& gn5 = G.newGraphNode(5);
GraphNode<int>& gn6 = G.newGraphNode(6);
GraphNode<int>& gn7 = G.newGraphNode(7);
```

This creates the eight nodes and inserts them into the graph. It also gives us names by which we can manipulate the nodes as needed. It doesn't create any arcs, however. To do this, we can write

```
G.arc(gn1, gn2);
G.arc(gn2, gn3);
G.arc(gn1, gn3);
G.arc(gn4, gn2);
G.arc(gn3, gn5);
G.arc(gn5, gn6);
G.arc(gn2, gn7);
G.arc(gn7, gn0);
G.arc(gn6, gn2);
```

Our implementation of DiGraph will use a vector to store the nodes of the graph. The constructor creates an empty vector and each invocation of newGraphNode() creates and returns a reference to new GraphNode, while also inserting the node into this vector. Note that newGraphNode returns a reference only. The actual node is kept within the DiGraph itself: in the vector.

The next issue to deal with is the storage of the arc information. There are a number of ways to do this, of course. We could store arc information in the DiGraph itself. This would provide a centralized depository of arc data that might be advantageous in some problems. It is also possible to distribute the arc information among the nodes, however, with each node containing information about those arcs that point out from it. This is the trick that we shall employ here. Each node will have a vector that contains references to those nodes that can be reached by following one arc from that node. For example, the vector within node 1 of our example graph will contain references to nodes 2 and 3.

It isn't quite as simple as detailed in the previous paragraph, however. Recall that we also need iterators for our digraphs. We want to be able to iterate over the nodes of a given graph, often to obtain access to the data stored within those nodes. Therefore, an iterator will be a sort of reference to a node. Thus, the _neighbors vector in a given node will actually store iterators into the graph, not C++ references. But since the nodes of the graph are stored in a vector, a vector (of graph nodes) iterator can be used as a graph iterator.

We shall build two class templates:

```
template <class T> class GraphNode;
template <class T> class DiGraph;
```

The graph node class is quite simple. When we construct a new graph node, we also create an empty vector of graph iterators. Note that the value of a node is a public member, so it may be set directly. We can use operator* to get a copy of the stored value. Internally, a graph node has two additional private member variables. Member _mark is used in a number of graph traversal algorithms in which it is necessary to *visit* each node once. To prevent visiting nodes multiple times (and perhaps trying to execute infinite loops), we unmark each node in a graph before we begin the algorithm and mark a node when we visit it. The algorithm is careful, then, to visit only unmarked nodes. All nodes are created *unmarked*. We provide private member functions to mark and unmark a node. These can only be called by members of DiGraph<T>.

```
template <class T>
class GraphNode
{ public:  // No public constructor.
    T value;
    T operator*(){ return value; }

  private:
    int _index;
    bool _mark;
    vector< vector< GraphNode<T> >::iterator >
        _neighbors;

    void mark(){_mark = true;}
    void unmark(){_mark = false;}
```

```
    bool marked(){return _mark;}

    GraphNode(const T& t = T())
    :  value(t), _index(-1),
       _mark(false),
       _neighbors()
    {}
    GraphNode(const T& t, int index)
    :  value(t),
       _index(index),
       _mark(false),
       _neighbors()
    {}

  friend class DiGraph<T>;
    // Lets DiGraphs construct nodes.
  friend class vector< GraphNode<T> >;
    // Lets us keep the default constructor private.
};
```

The _index member of a node saves the index in the graph's vector at which this node can be found. It is used primarily in creating arcs between the nodes and gives us an efficient way to discover the physical location of a node from the node itself, without searching for it. Thus, the sixth node created in a graph will be saved in the sixth slot of the vector of that graph and will have an _index of five (since all counting is from zero). The default node constructor sets an illegal value for this variable.

Note that nodes are relatively inactive. They don't have member functions for inserting values into the _neighbors vector, for example. Nodes are acted upon rather than themselves being active. It is members of DiGraph<T> that will act on them. There isn't even a public constructor in the node class.

```
template <class T>
class DiGraph // Directed graphs.
{  public:
     typedef T value_type;
     typedef GraphNode<T> node;
     typedef vector<node>::iterator iterator;
     typedef vector<node>::const_iterator
        const_iterator;
```

As usual, we export a few types. The node type provides a convenient shorthand. It also allows the user to use Digraph<...>::node for the node type.

```
     DiGraph():_vertices(){}
```

The constructor creates an empty vector to hold the vertices.

```
// Create GraphNodes using the following member.
node& newGraphNode(const T& t)
{   _vertices.push_back
    (node(t, _vertices.size()));
    return _vertices.back();
}
```

This is how we create new nodes. Note the constructor call of class node as an argument to the vector push_back call. By passing the _vertices.size() value to the node constructor, we initialize the node's _index member.

```
// Connect two nodes created with the
// above member. The arc is directed.
void arc(node& from, node& to)
{   from._neighbors.push_back(iterator(&to));
}
```

We create an arc by naming first the tail and then the head of the arc. The _index variable in a node correctly finds the slot of the _vertices vector in which that node resides.
We push an iterator to the "to" node onto the _neighbors vector of the "from" node.

```
iterator begin()const
{   return iterator(_vertices.begin());
}
iterator end ()const
{ return iterator(_vertices.end());
}
```

These are the standard container iterator generators. We just pass back vector iterators
as expected. Notice, then, that iteration over a vector is in node creation order. This might
not always be desirable. In fact, another standard ordering of the nodes of a graph is called
depth first ordering.

In depth first ordering, we start at some convenient node and list it. We then recursively list the reachable neighbors of that node, but, by the nature of the recursion, when
we list the first neighbor of the first node we then list its neighbors before returning to
list the remaining neighbors of the first node. In this way we search deeply into the graph
relative to the first node. If not all nodes are reachable from the first, then we may repeat
the process from other nodes until all are listed. We provide a member function here that
will list the nodes reachable from a given node, which may not include all nodes in the
graph. It is also important that each node be listed only once. This is the purpose of the
_mark fields in the nodes. We begin the process by unmarking all of the nodes in the
graph. DiGraph provides a member to do this for us.

```
// Returns a depth first listing of the
// nodes of the graph
// that are reachable from node gn.
vector< iterator > depthFirst(node& gn)
{   vector< iterator > result;
    unmark();
    depthFirst_aux(iterator(&gn), result);
    return result;
}
```

Member depthFirst returns a vector of iterators in which each node in the graph is represented by one iterator and these iterators are arranged in depth first order. The real work is done by a private member function depthFirst_aux, shown later.

```
private:
    vector< node > _vertices;
```

This is, of course, the implementation.

```
void unmark()
{   for
    (   iterator i = begin();
        i != end();
        ++i
    )
        (*i).unmark();
}
```

Here we just send the unmark message to all of the nodes, using the begin and end iterators in the usual way.

The following private member function is the helper for depthFirst. It takes an iterator indicating the current location, and if this location is not marked, inserts it into the second parameter, a vector, and then recurses on each of its neighbor locations. Note that (*gi) is a node and so has a _neighbors field. This field is a vector and so has begin and end iterators. Therefore, a vector<iterator>:: iterator makes perfect sense. A value i of type vector<iterator>:: iterator refers to an iterator so (*i) is an iterator: a DiGraph::iterator.

```
void depthFirst_aux
(   iterator gi,
    vector< iterator >& A
)
{   if(! (*gi).marked())
    {   (*gi).mark();
        A.push_back(gi);
        for
```

```
    (   vector<iterator>::iterator i
            = gi->_neighbors.begin();
        i != gi->_neighbors.end();
        ++i
    )
        depthFirst_aux(*i,A);
    }
  }
};
```

We also provide a function template to make it easy to write out a DiGraph. Note how it is defined in terms of the DiGraph::iterator. This can only be used, however, if type T, which is the type of the value of a node, also supports operator<<.

```
template <class T>
ostream& operator<<(ostream& os, const DiGraph<T>& g)
{   for
    (   DiGraph<T>::iterator i = g.begin();
        i!= g.end();
        ++i
    )
        os<< (*i).value<<" ";
    return os;
}
```

Let's note a few things about this implementation. One of the most important is that once a node is inserted into a graph, its physical location in the vector never changes. This gives us complete freedom in referring to it either by its index in the vector or by a pointer to the node. Also, the _index field in a node always refers to the index within the node's graph at which the node can be found. This is an important *class invariant* of the node class. A class invariant is a Boolean statement that is always true when the class is viewed from without. Class invariants may be false, briefly, while member functions are executing, but before any public function terminates, all class invariants must be restored so that a client may never see an invariant that is not true. It is worth documenting class invariants with comments. For example, just after the declaration of the _index variable, we might write

```
// Invariant. The value of _index is always the
// location of the node within its graph's
// implementing structure.
```

Next, we should note that it will be difficult to use this design in a flexible way. In particular, it will be hard or impossible to implement many graph algorithms without actually modifying the template itself. This is because the interface reveals very little about the nodes and arcs of a graph that most algorithms will need to access. The marks maintained by the nodes are completely private, for example. It is a very flexible design from within, but one that is limiting from without.

5.10   Summary

Make certain that you understand each of the following terms:

adaptor
copy constructor
destructor
digraph
invariant
memory management
network
overloaded assignment operator=
vector

5.11   Exercises

1. Add the necessary elements to the ExpandableArray class to meet the requirements of the StackAdaptor class.

2. Build a QueueAdaptor class. What requirements does it have for its container template argument?

3. Add the following member functions to the ExpandableArray class. Some of them are discussed in Section 5.5.

a) void insert(iterator, const value_type&); insert the value at the location of the iterator, making room as necessary.

b) void pop_back (); remove the last element.

c) operator< ; One expandable array is less than another if they are identical up to some point at which the first has a value less than the second. If one is shorter but contains the same elements in the same order up to the end, then the shorter is less.

d) operator==; two expandable arrays are == if they have the same length and identical elements.

e) const value_type &back()const and value_type& back(); return a reference to the last element of ExpandableArray. Why do we want both of these?

f) void erase(iterator) and value_type erase(iterator); remove and perhaps return the element at the location of the iterator, closing up the space as necessary.

g) void pop_front(); remove the first element, closing up space.

h) void push_front(const value_type&); insert value at the beginning, making room as necessary.

4. Modify the ExpandableArray class so that it also shrinks as the size grows smaller. For example, when it is only half full we could reallocate a smaller array to hold the elements.

5. Build an undirected graph class. The implementation can be like our directed graph, but with two iterators to represent each arc.

6. Build a network class. A network is like a graph except that the arcs may contain data of some kind. You will need an arc class template as well as a node template.

7. Write a function depthFirstOrder() that creates and returns a list of all the nodes in a graph in some depth first ordering.

8. Graph iterators are challenging. One way is to take a *snapshot* of the graph when the iterator is created. This can be done by calling depthFirstOrder from Exercise 7. The iterator can then be a list iterator into the resulting list. Note that such iterators can't be used to insert and delete items, because you will be changing the graph after its snapshot, so the iterator is invalid. They are useful for many purposes, however. If you do it carefully, you can even use the iterators to modify values stored in the graph. Just be careful about what you store in the list returned by depthFirstOrder().

9. Test the stack adaptor shown in the text against the STL stack adaptor. For StackAdaptor (from the text), use ExpandableArray as the argument. For stack (from the STL), use vector as the argument. What performance differences do you observe?

10. Assume you start with an empty vector and it doubles each time that it needs additional space. Suppose you insert into it and do not remove any items. If it has 10,000 items, how many times have you reorganized? How many times has each item been moved from one implementing array to another because of reorganizations? Counting an insertion and a move each as one step, how many steps have been executed? How many per item? How many times have you had to call the allocator?

11. Another way to represent a graph is to use an adjacency matrix. Such a matrix is a two-dimensional array with one row and one column for each node in the graph. The intersection of a row and a column contains a one to indicate an arc from the row entry node to the column entry node. There are zeros in the table where there are no arcs in the graph. Or the table could contain data to be stored along the arcs, with a *nodata* object stored if

there is no arc. Implement such a graph representation. You will also need to store the nodes in some (STL) container.

12. See Exercise 11. Implement a way to transform DiGraphs as implemented in the text into adjacency matrix representations and back again.

Chapter 6
Dequeue Programming

6.1   Queues and Double-Ended Queues

A queue is a structure into which we can insert items at one end and remove them from the other. It has the property that the next item removed is the one that has been in the container for the longest amount of time. This is called first-in first-out (FIFO) storage. Queues are used internally in computer operating systems to manage many resources, such as current users. Since there is only a single CPU on most systems, only one user process can be active at a time. When the currently executing process gets interrupted, it is put into the user queue (an *enqueue* operation) and another process is removed (dequeued) and allowed to run. This guarantees that each process gets its turn to execute.

A double-ended queue, or dequeue (or deque) is somewhat more general since we are allowed to insert and remove from either end. A siding on a railroad is like a dequeue. See Figure 6.1. We can insert railroad cars at either end of the siding and also remove them there. If we restrict ourselves to inserting and removing at the same end, a dequeue behaves like a stack. If we always remove from one end and always insert at the other, it behaves like a queue. A deck of cards is also like a dequeue since we can insert or remove cards easily from either end: i.e., the top or bottom.

A Dequeue

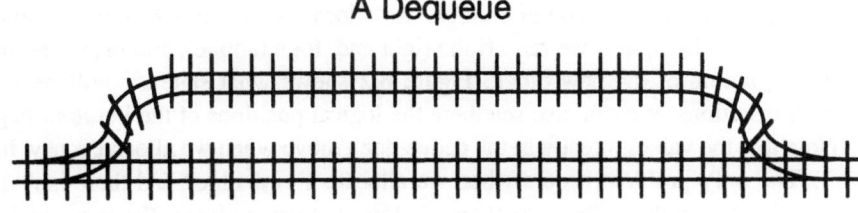

Figure 6.1. A railroad siding is like a double ended queue.

When implementing a dequeue in a computer program, we need to be especially careful to make the insert and remove operations at the ends as efficient as possible, since these are the most common operations.

6.2   Implementing a Dequeue

One simple implementation trick is not too bad in practice. We could use a scheme similar to what was done with vectors, except instead of starting to insert the first item entered in the first cell of our implementing array, we could insert it into the middle cell. Then it is easy to insert an item to the left or to the right, until we fill one end of the array. We will need to keep track of where the left and right ends of the active section are, of course. When we do reach the end of the array, we can allocate a new array, twice as large as the original and copy the current elements to the new array, leaving about as much space at each end in the new array.

There are a few difficulties with this plan, however. When the user is making the dequeue behave like a stack, we are reorganizing more often than necessary. The situation is even worse when making a dequeue behave like a queue. In this case you might require a reorganization when only one or two elements were stored in a structure with thousands of open slots. More fundamental, however, is the problem of iterators. When we reorganize such a structure, each element moves its location in the implementing array. If it were at subscript 341 before, it may wind up at subscript 243 afterwards. This doesn't happen with vectors, since each element retains its location relative to the beginning of the structure after a reorganization. Thus, each reorganization will invalidate all indexes into the array and perhaps all iterators as well, since these are often relative to the beginning of the physical structure.

The STL deque class template uses a somewhat more sophisticated arrangement that is partially based on the above simple plan. The implementation of the STL deque uses a two-level storage structure consisting of an array called the map and a collection of blocks. The actual data stored in the deque are stored in the blocks. The map contains pointers to the blocks. Both the map and the blocks can be quite large, and in fact, the map grows with use of the deque. See Figure 6.2. When we first insert an element into a deque (with either push_front or push_back), we allocate a map and one block. We insert a pointer to the block in the middle of the map. We insert the new item in the middle of the block. If we do additional push_front and push_back operations the values are stored in this same block, either to the left or to the right of the currently filled portion. The map doesn't need to be modified.

When we reach one end of a block, we allocate a new block, insert a pointer to it in the map (to the right if we ran off the right end, for example), and insert the new value at the beginning of the new block. Figure 6.2 shows what state we will be in after many such insertions. We can also see there the logical positions of the iterators begin and end. Note that the values already in the deque don't move when we allocate a new block.

The only problem occurs when we allocate a new block and there isn't room in the map for the pointer at the correct end. In this case we reallocate the map, making it twice as large. We insert the existing pointers into the new map, centering them in the new storage. We then have room to insert the new pointer to the new block. Again, the values in the deque don't move, just the block pointers do.

Notice that in this scheme, all blocks except one or two will be completely filled. We need to keep track of where we are in these two blocks, as well as where we are in the map.

An iterator into such a structure is not a simple pointer into one of the blocks. This is because we want to be able to execute operator++ on the iterator and, in fact, do pointer arithmetic on the iterators, since we want deques to support random access iterators. We can implement such an iterator by using three pointers into a block and one into the map. If an iterator, i, refers to an object, then pointer *i.first* points to the first cell of the block of our object, pointer *i.last* points just after the last cell, pointer *i.current* points to the object itself, and pointer *i.node* points to the cell in the map that holds the pointer to the block of the object. We can then advance the iterator until *current* reaches *last*. At this point we advance *node* and set *first* and *last* to refer to the beginning and end of the new block. This is made somewhat easier because the sizes of the blocks are all the same and they never change. Only the map changes size. Knowing the block size, we can even do pointer arithmetic on iterators.

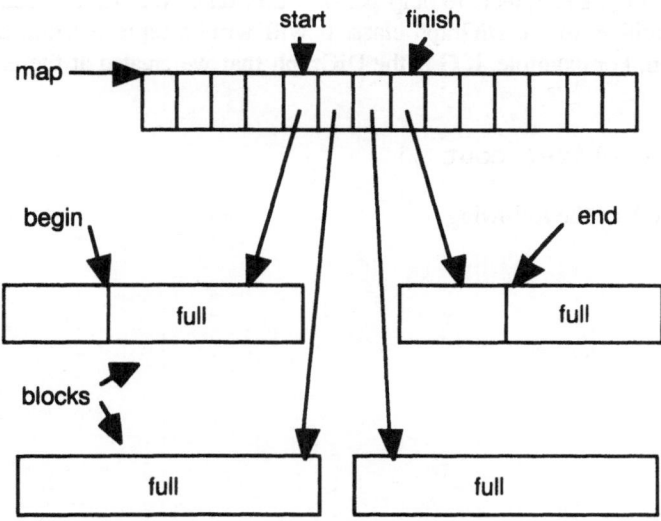

Figure 6.2. Storage for a deque.

The storage method discussed above makes insertions at the beginning and end of a deque very efficient. Reorganization is very infrequent if the block sizes are reasonably large. Note, however, that reorganization invalidates all iterators into the deque. Therefore, we need to be careful when using a deque (as well as a vector, by the way) not to do insertions when iterator validity must be maintained. The advantage of this method over the simpler one discussed at the beginning of this section lies in the less frequent reorganizations that occur.

We note in passing that one common mechanism for organizing very large disk files uses a variation on this method, but it uses multiple levels of maps. Pointers in each level map point to the map below, with the bottom map level pointers pointing to disk blocks. Some additional information is usually required in the maps in addition to the pointers. This is called b-tree storage. This topic is beyond the range of this book. It is commonly discussed in books on database programming.

6.3   A Simple deque Example

Sometimes we need to output a complex structure to a file and later restore it. For example, we might like to save a DiGraph in a disk file and then later read it into another program. For the DiGraph case, it would be useful to save the graph by first saving all of the node data, and then all of the arc data. This is because when we restore, it is most convenient to create all of the nodes first, before we attempt to create any arcs. Otherwise, we might try to create an arc between nodes that hadn't been recreated yet. We can use a deque, acting like a queue, to help perform this task. We want to add a new member function, archive, to the DiGraph class. It will write a representation of any DiGraph on an ostream. For example, if G is the DiGraph that we created at the end of the last chapter, then

```
G.archive( cout );
```

will produce the following.

```
0
1
2
3
4
5
6
7
(1,2)
(1,3)
(2,3)
(2,7)
(3,5)
(4,2)
(5,6)
(6,2)
(7,0)
```

We first write out a list of the data in the nodes (the values), and then we write a list of all of the arcs using index numbers.

The function proceeds by first iterating over its own DiGraph. For each step of the iteration it outputs the value of the current node, and inserts the arcs pointing out from this node into a deque. We use push_back for this. To get access to all of the neighbors of a given node (which are stored in a vector), we use another iterator over the neighbors. Then, after all of the nodes have been output, we next empty the dequeue, outputting the required arc data as we remove it. Each arc datum is saved in the deque as a pair of node pointers. To write an arc, we write out the indices of the corresponding nodes.

```
void archive(ostream& out)
{   typedef pair<node *, node * > pr;
    typedef deque< pr > deq;
    deq arcs;

    for
    (   const_iterator i = begin();
        i != end();
        ++i
    )
    {   out<< i->value<<endl; // Output this node.
        for // Save its arcs in the deque.
        (   vector<node*>::const_iterator j
                = i->_neighbors.begin();
            j != i->_neighbors.end();
            ++j
        )
            arcs.push_back(pr( i, *j ) );
    }
    while(! arcs.empty()) // Output the arcs.
    {   pr p = arcs.front(); arcs.pop_front();
        out << '(' << p.first->_index << ','
            << p.second->_index<< ')' << endl;
    }
}
```

6.4   The deque Interface

Externally, a deque looks like a vector with a few exceptions. First is the push_front and pop_front operations that are not part of the vector interface as they are for deques. Deques don't have a capacity or reserve member since reorganization involves only the internal map and not the elements themselves. This is somewhat problematic since we sometimes use those vector members to determine whether we can guarantee the preservation of iterators during insertions and removals. These tools are not available to us with deques. This means that the user should always assume that all iterators into a deque are invalid after any insertion or deletion. This is true even of the operations at the ends. Technically, references into a deque may be invalidated by insertions and deletions as well as iterators, though not all implementations do this. Be careful taking advantage of special features of an implementation, however, since that can drastically affect portability of the code.

Deques provide random access iterators, so all of the STL algorithms work with deques. There is also an operator[] so that deques can be made to look like arrays when necessary. Be cautious with this, however. A push_front operation changes the relative subscripts of all elements and an insertion in the middle affects all subscripts either before or after that point, whichever is closer. As with vectors, an insertion at the location of an iterator inserts the new item before the iterator's location. The space for the new item could be created at either end, but the algorithm will choose the closer end for efficiency.

6.5   Efficiency of deques

The implementation of the deque optimizes the push_front operation. It is a constant time operation, while for a vector, insertion at the beginning is linear time. The tradeoff is that all operations are slowed down slightly compared to vector operations. So push_back on a vector is faster than push_back on a deque, though only by a small constant multiple. Insertions in the middle of a deque take time proportional to the distance to the nearest end. Therefore, insertions near the ends are quite fast. Inserting a block of values at the same point in the middle is much faster than inserting the same elements individually, since space needs to be made available only once for all of the elements.

If insertions and deletions are to occur largely at one end, a vector may be a better choice than a deque. If insertions are to occur frequently in the middle, then a list is likely preferable to a deque. For a structure in which insertions and deletions are to occur at the ends, however, the deque is ideal. While a list also provides these operations efficiently, a queue is slightly faster at the ends.

6.6   More on Container Adaptors—The queue Adaptor

When you need a structure that behaves like a queue and you want to restrict the interface so that non queue-like operations are not possible, a queue adaptor can be used. You can apply this adaptor to either a list or a queue. Actually, you can apply it to any container that provides the required interface: namely empty, size, front, back, push_back, and pop_front. Both deques and lists from the STL provide the necessary operations.

A complete implementation of the queue container adaptor (from the Hewlett-Packard library) follows. It is extremely simple. All it does is pass operations on to the container with which it is created. Its only purpose is to provide a restricted interface. Since all of the members are inline, the efficiency of a queue will be the same as that of the underlying container that it adapts.

```
template <class Container>
class queue
{   friend bool operator==
        (   const queue<Container>& x,
            const queue<Container>& y
        );
    friend bool operator<bool operator<
        (   const queue<Container>& x,
            const queue<Container>& y
        );
public:
    typedef Container::value_type value_type;
    typedef Container::size_type size_type;
protected:
    Container c;
public:
    bool empty() const { return c.empty(); }
    size_type size() const { return c.size(); }
    value_type& front() { return c.front(); }
    const value_type& front() const
    {   return c.front();
    }
    value_type& back() { return c.back(); }
    const value_type& back() const
    {   return c.back();
    }
    void push(const value_type& x)
    {   c.push_back(x);
    }
    void pop()
    {   c.pop_front();
    }
};

template <class Container>
bool operator==
(   const queue<Container>& x,
    const queue<Container>& y
)
{   return x.c == y.c;
}

template <class Container>
bool operator<
(   const queue<Container>& x,
```

```
        const queue<Container>& y
)
{   return x.c < y.c;
}
```

If the Container parameter also provides operator== or operator<, then so will the resulting queue. Note that we could have used a queue adaptor in our DiGraph archiving
function, since we treated the deque like a queue there.

6.7   Priority Queues and Heaps

A priority queue is a structure into which we put values that have a size. When we remove an item from the priority queue, we always get the one with the largest size. You
can think of a priority queue as a waiting line in which each entering person has a priority
(his or her "size"). The person doesn't need to go to the end of the line but only to the position behind all others with the same or higher priority. The person (or thing) with the
highest priority is always first. When it comes time to remove a person from the line,
presumably to get served at some facility, the person at the head of the line gets service
next.

A heap is a structure that is useful in many ways, one of which is in implementing
priority queues. A heap is theoretically a binary tree structure that stores values with size.
As a binary tree, each node has zero, one, or two children. The largest item is always at
the root and each node contains a value that is larger than (or possibly equal to) the values
in any of its children. We shall see that it is usually possible to store this tree in an array
like structure. We shall see the details shortly, but the idea of implementing a priority
queue with a heap works because the largest item is easily available. We shall also see
that it is very efficient to insert an item into a heap (or remove an item) and keep the heap
property.

6.7.1   Heaps

We need to refine our definition of heap slightly. First we want a binary tree. This means
that each node has either zero, one, or two children. A node with no children is a leaf
node, and others are called interior nodes. The single node with no parent node is called
the root. The height of a node is the number of links between it and the root. In the tree
in Figure 6.3, the height of the node with a six in it is two. The height of a tree is the
maximum of the heights of the nodes. For the tree in Figure 6.3, the height is three. A
heap also has the property that only those nodes whose height is the height of the tree or
one less than the height have less than two children. Finally, we want all of the nodes at
height equal to the height of the tree to be as far to the left as possible. Therefore, the tree
in Figure 6.3 is a heap.

The reason for the restrictions on a heap are to make storage of the heap in an array as
efficient as possible. Suppose that we consider an array whose first subscript is one

(rather than the usual zero) and store the root of our heap there. Then for each node stored in a subscript k, the children of that node are stored in cells 2*k and 2*k+1.

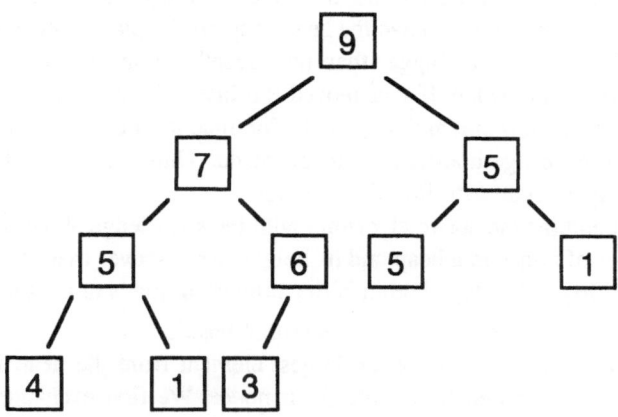

Figure 6.3. A heap shown as a tree.

Storing the heap of Figure 6.3 in this way leads us to an array such as shown in Figure 6.4. The restrictions on the heap guarantee that there are no gaps in the array between active node elements. Thus, the storage in an array is as dense as possible. This also means that, for a given height, there are about as many nodes in the tree as possible. Looked at in another way, in such a tree, each node is about as close to the root as possible. In fact, for a tree of height H, there are between 2*H and 2*(H+1)-1 nodes that can be stored. Thus in a tree of height ten, we can store over 1,000 nodes. But every node is no farther from the root than ten arcs.

| 9 | 7 | 5 | 5 | 6 | 5 | 1 | 4 | 1 | 3 |

Figure 6.4. The heap of Figure 6.3 shown as an array.

The reason that it is nice to store a heap in such an array is that moving both up and down the arcs of the tree is very easy. The children of a node can be found at fixed subscripts relative to the subscript of the given node. Also, the parent of the node in cell k is at subscript k/2. (For zero-based array storage, these formulas need to be adjusted slightly, however.)

Exercise. Give the formulas for parent and child access in a heap stored in a zero-based array, with the root at cell zero.

One can insert into a heap and maintain the heap property in the following way. Physically insert the value in the next available slot. For an array representation, this is the first empty cell in the array. For a tree, it is the left-most slot on the last row. Then compare that value with the value in the parent slot. If the value in the child is smaller or the same, then you already have the heap property in place. Otherwise, exchange the two values. If the value was bigger than the parent's value, it must also be bigger than the parent's other child value. If you moved the inserted value, repeat the process looking at the value in the new slot and its parent. Continue up the tree until you reach the root, or until some exchange doesn't need to be made. Thus *reheaping* the heap after an insert works along a single path from leaf to root.

If we combine the above algorithm with the knowledge about the relationship between the number of nodes in a heap and its height, we discover that the reheap operation takes only about $\log_2(n)$ time, where n is the number of nodes in the tree. In formulas like this we shall use lg as the name of the logarithm base 2.

Similarly, we can remove the largest element from the heap in the following way, which also takes about lg(n) time for n nodes. We first exchange the root node and the last node in the tree. The node in which the old root now lies will eventually be pruned away. First we *downheap* the structure, restoring the heap property. To do this we compare the root node with both of its children. If it is bigger than both we are done and we have a heap. Otherwise, we exchange the root and the larger of the children. We then move down to the original location of the value we promoted and continue as above from there, until we either reach a leaf or until we have a value that is bigger than all of the children. This process also follows a single path, but this time from root to leaf.

The STL does not provide a heap container class or class template. Instead it supplies six algorithms for maintaining heaps in any structure that has random access iterators. Since such a structure can be thought of as a generalized array, this is very general and useful. All of the heap operations occur in pairs. One element of each pair compares values using operator<. The other function uses a user-supplied comparison object. This is just an object from a class that implements an operator() to compare two values. There are requirements on such an operator. These were discussed in Section 4.3.3.

```
template <class RandomAccessIterator>
void make_heap
(   RandomAccessIterator first,
    RandomAccessIterator last
);

template
<class RandomAccessIterator, class Compare>
void make_heap
(   RandomAccessIterator first,
    RandomAccessIterator last,
    Compare comp
);
```

Algorithm make_heap constructs a heap from the elements given in the range of any random access iterator. It can work by successively reheaping starting with the first two elements and adding one each time. The time is proportional to n*lg(n), where n is the size of the range. There is actually a faster way. It takes only time proportional to n. If we first note that a leaf is automatically a heap, then we only need to start reheaping in the first node in the tree that actually has a child. In Figure 6.3, this is the node with the six. We just downheap from there. We then consider the other nodes farther to the left in the array, downheaping from each of them in turn as we go. Our starting node is actually the middle node in the array structure. With ten nodes, it is in slot five.

```
template <class RandomAccessIterator>
void push_heap
(   RandomAccessIterator first,
    RandomAccessIterator last
);


template
<class RandomAccessIterator, class Compare>
void push_heap
(   RandomAccessIterator first,
    RandomAccessIterator last,
    Compare comp
);
```

Algorithm push_heap assumes that the range [first, last-1) is a heap, and that we want to insert the item at location last. It restores the heap property so that the range [first, last) is a heap. It doesn't actually insert anything. It is typically used by applying it to a vector or array and first performing push_back followed by push_heap. This algorithm requires only logarithmic time in the number of elements in the heap.

```
template <class RandomAccessIterator>
void pop_heap
(   RandomAccessIterator first,
    RandomAccessIterator last
);

template
<class RandomAccessIterator, class Compare>
void pop_heap
(   RandomAccessIterator first,
    RandomAccessIterator last,
    Compare comp
);
```

Algorithm pop_heap starts with a heap in range [first, last). It rearranges the elements so that the old maximum value is in location last, and the range [first, last-1) is again a heap. It is the opposite of push_heap, though they are not necessarily strict inverses, since many rearrangements of the same values can constitute a valid heap. Again, this algorithm doesn't actually remove anything, though it is often followed by operation back which will then return the largest element and then pop_back, which will remove that value. This algorithm is logarithmic in its time behavior.

Finally, the STL has (two versions of) an algorithm that will rearrange a heap into a sorted range. Algorithm sort_heap assumes that it has a heap for a range and sorts that range in time proportional to n*lg(n). It does this by repeatedly performing pop_heap on a smaller and smaller range. The first call puts the largest value last and each successive call puts one more "next largest" value in the correct slot.

```
template <class RandomAccessIterator>
void sort_heap
(   RandomAccessIterator first,
    RandomAccessIterator last
);


template
<class RandomAccessIterator, class Compare>
void sort_heap
(   RandomAccessIterator first,
    RandomAccessIterator last,
    Compare comp
);
```

6.7.2 Priority Queues

The STL priority_queue container adaptor shows a nice relationship between containers, adaptors, and algorithms. It requires a container with a random access iterator and treats it as a heap. We also need to specify a comparison object to define the order of the values to be inserted. The protocol, however, is nearly the same as that of a queue. We push to enter into the priority queue and we pop to remove from it. As discussed in the last section, we push by first doing a push_back on the underlying container, and then calling push_heap. Popping performs the inverse operations. Here is a complete implementation.

```
template <class Container, class Compare>
// Compare = less<Container::value_type> >
class priority_queue
{
public:
    typedef Container::value_type value_type;
    typedef Container::size_type size_type;
```

```
protected:
    Container c;
    Compare comp;
public:
    priority_queue
    (   const Compare& x = Compare())
    : c(),
        comp(x)
    {
    }
    priority_queue
    (   const value_type* first,
        // Should be an iterator
        const value_type* last,
        // Should be an iterator
        const Compare& x = Compare()
    )
    :   c(first, last),
        comp(x)
    {   make_heap(c.begin(), c.end(), comp);
    }
    bool empty() const { return c.empty(); }
    size_type size() const { return c.size(); }
    value_type& top() { return c.front(); }
    const value_type& top() const
    {   return c.front();
    }
void push(const value_type& x)
    {   c.push_back(x);
        push_heap(c.begin(), c.end(), comp);
    }
    void pop()
    {   pop_heap(c.begin(), c.end(), comp);
        c.pop_back();
    }
};
```

Normally we don't use priority queues to store simple datatypes like ints or floats.
The most important usage is when we have a complex datatype and one of its fields is a
comparison field. We create a compare object that compares our objects based on this
field. The priority queue will then prioritize our objects based on values of this field. For
example, suppose we have person objects with a last name field (a string). We provide a
compare object that (using operator()) tells us which of two persons has a "smaller" last
name. Then if we insert these person objects into a priority queue, then when we dequeue
them, they will be ordered by last name: largest first, of course.

6.8   STL Generic Algorithms—Searching and Sorting

The deque and vector classes of the STL as well as arrays of C++ provide random access iterators. The generality of these iterators permits a large collection of algorithms to be written that will easily manipulate any of these structures. Sometimes we insert items into a container that can be compared with operator<. Other times we insert data that has no defined comparison. It is often necessary to find an item once it has been inserted into a container. This process is called *search*. If the items can be compared, then it is much faster to search a container if the container is sorted, with smaller items first and larger ones last, for example. Putting a container into such a sorted state is called *sorting*. The STL contains generalized algorithms for both searching and sorting of containers with random access iterators. Many of the algorithms don't require random access iterators.

6.8.1   Generalized Searching

First we will look at searching in situations in which the container may not be sorted. In this case any searching strategy that does not repeatedly look at the same components of the container is about as good as any other. The most common technique is called sequential search and it proceeds by searching from the first element to the last, comparing each element in turn with the target of the search. This is quite easily achieved with a for or while loop. For generality, however, it is advantageous that we not apply the operation to a container, but to a pair of iterators representing a range. Suppose we have iterators first and last, representing a range [first, last) in the usual way. Suppose we search for a value named target. Then either of the following two fragments will find the element if present.

```
while(first != last)
{   if( *first == target) return first;
    ++first;
}
return last;

for( ; first != last; ++first)
    if(*first == target) return first;
return last;
```

Of course, if we don't want to modify first then we need an auxiliary iterator to step across the range.

It is also possible that we don't want to compare the elements with operator==. In this case we would use a comparison predicate instead. This would be a function of two arguments that returns true if the first argument is considered to be the same as the second. The algorithm could use this in place of the operator== in the above.

Actually, the STL takes a somewhat different approach that increases the usefulness. Suppose that we drop the requirement that we are searching for a given value and think of searching for an item about which something of interest happens to be true. For example, if the elements have a feature called color, we might want to search for the first red item. In this case we could replace the comparison in the above fragments with a predicate that has a single argument and returns true if that element is red. For example,

```
while(first != last)
{  if( isRed(*first) ) return first;
   ++first;
}
return last;
```

The STL provides two algorithms that provide these services. They are called find and find_if. The first version uses operator==.

```
template<class InputIterator, class T>
InputIterator find
(  InputIterator first,
   InputIterator last,
   const T& value
);
```

This searches starting at first, looking for an element that is == to value. If it is not found, then last is returned. Otherwise an iterator to the location of the found item is returned. Note that we don't need random access iterators to do this. In particular, we may also use it to search lists and sets. We may even search for items as they come in from a stream, as they only need to look at one item at a time and only in the forward direction.

The second form of the find algorithm requires a unary predicate and will return an iterator to the first occurrence of a value for which that predicate returns true.

```
template
<class InputIterator, class unaryPredicate>
InputIterator find_if
(  InputIterator first,
   InputIterator last,
   unaryPredicate pred
);
```

When calling this function, you can pass a function for this unaryPredicate, or you can pass an object from a class that implements operator(). In other words, a function or a function object. The function or function object must have a single parameter and return a boolean value.

As you might expect, these algorithms are both linear in time behavior.

Suppose that you want to find several copies of an item in the container. In this case, you can call find several times, each time replacing *first* with the successor of the value returned on the previous call.

There is another possibility, however. Sometimes you want to find a location in a container at which there are adjacent items that are the same. Here we need to compare two items within the container rather than one item with something else. For this purpose, the STL provides two versions of adjacentFind. The first uses operator== and the second uses a binary predicate. They both return an iterator to the first element of a pair of "equal" values, or location last, if all adjacent pairs are distinct.

```
template <class ForwardIterator>
ForwardIterator adjacent_find
(  ForwardIterator first,
   ForwardIterator last
);


template
<class ForwardIterator, class BinaryPredicate>
ForwardIterator adjacent_find
(  ForwardIterator first,
   ForwardIterator last,
   BinaryPredicate pred
);
```

If you were to write these yourself, you would need to take a bit of care, remembering that the next to last location of the iterator represents the last actual location in the range and that this is never followed by an item to be compared with.

Another linear sequential search technique that is often needed is trying to determine if two ranges are the same, and if not, finding the first location at which they differ. The ranges need to be of the same length, of course, for this to be defined. Again, we could search for a the first location at which a pair of values, one from each range, are not == or for which a binary predicate returns false.

The STL provides two versions of algorithm mismatch for this purpose. We pass in two ranges by passing in three iterators. The first two iterators give the beginning and end (after the end, of course) locations of the first range, and the third iterator gives the beginning of the second range. The end of the second range will be implied by the length of the first range.

```
template <  class InputIterator1,
            class InputIterator2
         >
pair<InputIterator1, InputIterator2> mismatch
(  InputIterator1 first1,
   InputIterator1 last1,
   InputIterator2 first2
);
```

The algorithm returns a pair of iterators, one into each range. If all values are the same, then both iterators represent after the end locations in the two ranges. Otherwise they represent locations, one into each range, at which the values differ. Note that the ranges may overlap if needed. The second version is similar except that comparisons are done with a supplied binary predicate.

```
template <  class InputIterator1,
            class InputIterator2,
            class BinaryPredicate
       >
pair<InputIterator1, InputIterator2> mismatch
(  InputIterator1 first1,
   InputIterator1 last1,
   InputIterator2 first2,
   BinaryPredicate binary_pred
);
```

The last search algorithm that we shall consider here looks for one range within another. For example, you might want to search for the word "liberty" in a document represented as a string. While such a search proceeds linearly, it has quadratic time complexity. Note that there does exist a linear time algorithm (on the average) for this problem, though it is not implemented in at least some versions of the STL. This is because of its complexity and the fact that it is generally slow in typical use.

Algorithm search looks for one range duplicated within another. These ranges are represented by four iterators. The first range, given by the first two parameters, is the range to be searched. The last two iterators give the range to be looked for. If the target is found, search returns an iterator into the first range that represents the beginning of the target. If the target cannot be located, then last1 is returned.

```
template
<class ForwardIterator1, class ForwardIterator2>
ForwardIterator1 search
(  ForwardIterator1 first1,
   ForwardIterator1 last1,
   ForwardIterator2 first2,
   ForwardIterator2 last2
);
```

The algorithm is surprisingly simple since we may use mismatch.

```
while(first1 != last1)
{  pair
   <ForwardIterator2, ForwardIterator1> where =
      mismatch(first2, last2, first1);
   if (where.first == last2) return first1;
```

```
    ++first1
}
return last1;
```

There is a second version that uses a binary predicate for the comparison, as you would expect.

The algorithms we have been discussing here are all of a kind that the STL classifies as nonmutating sequence algorithms. In addition to the search algorithms, there are also function templates to determine directly if two ranges are equal, and to count ranges. The equal algorithm could be used in place of mismatch in implementing the search algorithm.

6.8.2   Sorting

We discussed two sorts in Chapter 2: selection sort and quicksort. Selection sort is too inefficient generally for inclusion in a general library such as the STL. Its main advantage is its simplicity. Another simple sort is called insertion sort, and it has the advantage that it behaves efficiently on small containers. The idea of insertion sort is to keep the range to be sorted in two sections, an initial sorted section and another unexamined section. This is shown in Figure 6.4.

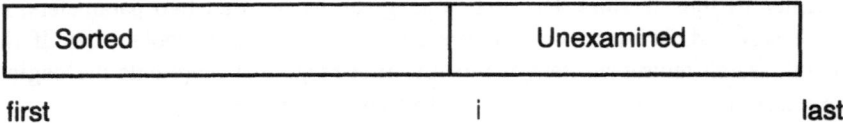

first   i   last

Figure 6.4. Loop invariant for the outer loop of insertion sort.

The idea is to keep this true while getting the iterator i up to the location of iterator last. We can do this by making a copy of the contents of cell i in a variable copy. This effectively leaves cell i "empty" since we know the value that was originally there. We can then slide elements to the right starting at cell i-1, leaving a new cell "empty" each time, until we come to the location j at which value copy actually belongs. Notice that each slide to the right requires only one statement be executed and on the average we will only have to slide about half of the elements in first...i-1 to the right. This inner loop is shown in Figure 6.5.

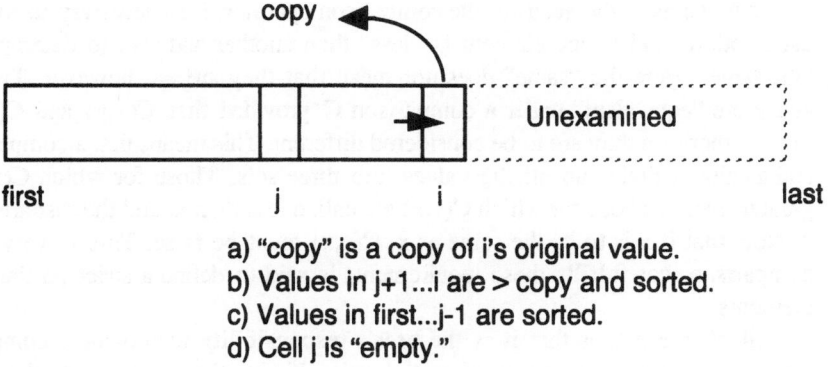

a) "copy" is a copy of i's original value.
b) Values in j+1...i are > copy and sorted.
c) Values in first...j-1 are sorted.
d) Cell j is "empty."

Figure 6.5. Inner loop invariant for insertion sort.

The sort algorithm of the STL uses a combination of insertion sort and quicksort. If the size of the range to be sorted is small, it uses insertion sort. Otherwise it uses quicksort. This gives the best average running time since for short ranges we don't need the recursive overhead of quicksort and for longer ranges we don't absorb the quadratic time behavior of insertion sort.

As indicated in Chapter 2, the use of quicksort implies that for some ranges (sorted ranges, for example) sort will take quadratic time. There is another sort algorithm, partial_sort, in the STL that can be guaranteed to be n * lg(n) in its running time, though slower on the average than sort. This algorithm will be discussed below in the section on the median.

The standard version of sort uses operator< to compare elements. There is another version that uses a binary comparison function instead. This comparison should return true if its first argument should come before the second in a sorted list. This comparison needs certain characteristics, however, if sorting is to be accomplished correctly. There are many other algorithms that also require the same behavior for the comparison.

```
template <class RandomAccessIterator>
void sort
(   RandomAccessIterator first,
    RandomAccessIterator last
);

template
<class RandomAccessIterator, class Compare>
void sort
(   RandomAccessIterator first,
    RandomAccessIterator last,
    Compare comp
);
```

To understand the needs of the comparison operator, it is necessary to know that it is used both to find if one element is "less" than another and also to determine if they are "the same." Here the "same" does not mean that they are ==, however. Two elements x and y are "equivalent" under a comparison C provided that C(x,y) and C(y,x) are both false. Otherwise they are to be considered different. This means that a comparison operator and a value x divide up all the values into three sets. Those for which C(x,y) are called greater than x. Those for which C(y,x) are called less than x, and the rest are *equivalent* to x. Note that if x is to be the same as x, C(x,x) must be false. This is very important. A comparison that fulfills these requirements is said to define a strict partial order on the elements.

All of this means that it is the user's responsibility to provide a comparison object that satisfies the requirements of partial order. If not, the sorting and other similar algorithms may not operate correctly. They may even loop infinitely. In particular, operator<= is not a valid candidate for a comparison operator. Again, we can pass a function for the comparison operator, or a function object.

Be aware that even with the first version of sort, which uses operator<, it is important that the version of operator< that is used also impose a strict partial order on the elements. The standard comparison on ints and floats does so, of course, but the programmer must be careful that other overloaded versions do as well.

Fairly often, sorting a container is not just a matter of picking some simple basis for the sort. We may have records of some kind with several fields. We might need to sort the data on one of these fields. If the contents of this field have repeated values, it may not be good enough to leave the order of elements with common values unspecified. For example, it might be necessary to sort employees in a large company by department. Within each department we might like the employees sorted alphabetically by name. To do this requires two sorts. The first is by name. The second is by department. There is a problem, however: in the second sort, there is no guarantee that the relative positions defined by the first sort won't be changed. Of course some rearrangement is necessary, but we mean that values with the same department field should not be rearranged relative to each other.

To achieve this requires that the second (and subsequent) sort be *stable*. A sort on a field is stable if values of that field that are equivalent are not rearranged relative to each other. Unfortunately, quicksort is not stable and so the STL sort algorithm is not stable either.

For this reason, the STL provides another algorithm (two versions) called stable_sort that is based on the merge sort process, which is stable.

```
template <class RandomAccessIterator>
void stable_sort
(   RandomAccessIterator first,
    RandomAccessIterator last
);

template
<class RandomAccessIterator, class Compare>
void stable_sort
```

```
(   RandomAccessIterator first,
    RandomAccessIterator last,
    Compare comp
);
```

The merge_sort algorithm will be discussed in the section on merge, which follows. Its two advantages over sort are that it is stable and is guaranteed to have n * lg(n) running time if there is enough extra memory available to make a copy of the range to be sorted.

6.8.3 Searching Sorted Containers

Once a container is sorted using some criteria, we can search it efficiently using compatible criteria. We examined binary search in Chapter 2. The STL includes a number of algorithms that implement binary search. The simplest, called binary_search, just returns a boolean value as to whether the target is present or not. The first version assumes that the data are sorted using operator<.

```
template <class ForwardIterator, class T>
bool binary_search
(   ForwardIterator first,
    ForwardIterator last,
    const T& value
);
```

This second version uses a binary predicate to compare elements. This should be the same predicate that was used to sort the data originally.

```
template
<class ForwardIterator, class T, class Compare>
bool binary_search
(   ForwardIterator first,
    ForwardIterator last,
    const T& value,
    Compare comp
);
```

These algorithms will require logarithmic time if the iterators are random access iterators. However, they also work on more general forward iterators, as the template parameters imply. In case the iterators are not random access, the time behavior will be linear. Therefore, it is possible to search lists and sets using binary_search. This is also true of the other algorithms discussed in this section.

Usually we want to know more than whether the target is present. We want to know where the element lies in the (sorted) container. Since duplicate values are possible, there can be many locations of a given target. There can also be none, as the target might be absent from the container. Algorithm lower_bound will return an iterator to the first occurrence of the target. Formally, it returns an iterator to the first location at which the target could be inserted while maintaining the sorted order. If the target is not present, this will be to the first value that is "larger" according to the sort criteria.

```
template <class ForwardIterator, class T>
ForwardIterator lower_bound
(   ForwardIterator first,
    ForwardIterator last,
    const T& value
);
```

There is another version that has an additional parameter giving a comparison operator to define the sort, and hence the search, criteria. There are also two versions of upper_bound, which gives the last location at which the target could be inserted.

Finally, equal_range returns a pair of iterators that would be returned individually by lower_bound and upper_bound.

```
template <class ForwardIterator, class T>
pair<ForwardIterator, ForwardIterator> equal_range
(   ForwardIterator first,
    ForwardIterator last,
    const T& value
);
```

All of the values from the first iterator returned up to, but not including the second, should refer to values that are equivalent to the target value. As usual, there is another version with the additional search predicate. Again, the behavior of these is logarithmic if the iterators are random access, and linear otherwise.

There are also a number of algorithms that operate on containers that are not necessarily sorted, but whose contents are sortable. For example, min_element will search a range, whether sorted or not, for the minimum value of the sort criteria.

```
template <class ForwardIterator>
ForwardIterator min_element
(   ForwardIterator first,
    ForwardIterator last
);
```

There are also corresponding max_element algorithms and versions of both that take the usual comparison operator. These return an iterator to the desired element or to last for an empty range.

Algorithm lexicographical_compare compares two ranges according to the following rule. We compare corresponding elements of the two ranges starting at their first elements. Let f be the element from the first range and s be that from the second. If f < s for a given comparison, stop the process and return true. If f > s, stop and return false. If they are the same, then proceed to the next pair of corresponding elements. If you come to the end of the first range, with all comparisons having come out "the same," then return true; otherwise, return false. Thus, lexicographical_compare tells us whether the first range represents a string of values that would come before that of the second in a dictionary-like ordering.

```
template
<class InputIterator1, class InputIterator2>
bool lexicographical_compare
(   InputIterator1 first1,
    InputIterator1 last1,
    InputIterator2 first2,
    InputIterator2 last2
);
```

In fact, if we apply this operation to ordinary C++ strings, it will give us the dictionary ordering. A second version takes an additional comparison operator.

Finally, we look at three algorithms that don't put a range in order, but rather destroy the order.

Algorithm random_shuffle puts a range into random order in linear time. It uses either a built-in random number generator, or one supplied as a parameter. It works by computing a random location to swap with each successive location.

```
template <  class RandomAccessIterator,
            class RandomNumberGenerator
        >
void random_shuffle
(   RandomAccessIterator first,
    RandomAccessIterator last,
    RandomNumberGenerator& rand
);
```

If supplied, this RandomNumberGenerator should be a function object of no parameters. It should return values in the interval [0, 1). The standard generator is built in and is approximately uniform. If this is what is desired, the third parameter need not be given. Also note that this algorithm does not require sortable elements. It works for any sort of contents, but does require random access iterators to define the range to be shuffled.

It is also possible to systematically generate all possible rearrangements, or permutations, of a range. Algorithm next_permutation will shuffle the elements in such a way that successive calls will generate all permutations. It also is guaranteed to generate them in lexicographical order. It requires linear time. It returns true unless there is no next_permutation, meaning that its input was the last permutation lexicographically. This will be true (and the algorithm will return false) if the range is sorted from largest to smallest. When it returns false it also rearranges the range, but in sorted (smallest to largest) order.

```
template <class BidirectionalIterator>
bool next_permutation
(  BidirectionalIterator first,
   BidirectionalIterator last
);
```

To generate all permutations, first sort the range and then repeatedly call next_permutation. It will require n! (n factorial) calls, where n is the length of the range. In this case, the first call will permute the last two elements. Starting with elements 1 2 3 4 5, the first 16 successive permutations are:

```
1 2 3 4 5
1 2 3 5 4
1 2 4 3 5
1 2 4 5 3
1 2 5 3 4
1 2 5 4 3
1 3 2 4 5
1 3 2 5 4
1 3 4 2 5
1 3 4 5 2
1 3 5 2 4
1 3 5 4 2
1 4 2 3 5
1 4 2 5 3
1 4 3 2 5
1 4 3 5 2
```

There is also a prev_permutation algorithm that also generates all permutations when called repeatedly, but in reverse lexicographical order. Both of these have versions with comparison operators as a final parameter as well.

6.9   Median and Other Order Statistics

The median of a set of values is the value that would appear in the middle location if the set were sorted. It is expensive to sort, however, so a more efficient means of finding the median and other similar *order statistics* is needed. The other common order statistics are quartiles, deciles, and percentiles. The three quartiles are the values in locations one-fourth, half and three-fourths of the way through the range of sorted data. The nine deciles are each one-tenth further along, so that in a collection of 200 items, they would be the values that would fall in slots 20, 40, etc. in the data if it were sorted. The 99 percentiles are each 1 percent of the data apart. The 37th percentile in a collection of 1,000 would be at the 370th location. Of course, if we ask for the 37th percentile in a list of 150, then we must choose between two slots. Rounding can be used to choose the slot, or we can (with some types of data) average the values in the two closest slots.

We can find the median in linear time by using a variation of the partition algorithm that we used to help implement quicksort in Chapter 2. If we separate that algorithm and rewrite it to use iterators, we get

```
template <class Iterator>
void partition_aux
(   Iterator b,
    Iterator& m,
    Iterator e
)
{   Iterator J = b; J++;
    m=b;
    while(J < e)
    {   if(*J != *b)
        {   m++;
            swap(*m, *J);
        }
        J++;
    }
    swap(*m, *b);
}
```

Exercise. What kinds of iterator do we require for partition_aux? Do we need a random access iterator or will a forward or bidirectional iterator suffice? Why?

Exercise. Rewrite partition_aux so that it performs the same function, but only requires a forward iterator.

The idea is to first partition the range, obtaining a location near the middle. If this location is to the left of the middle, we repartition only the right section. If, on the other hand, our returned iterator is actually to the right of the true middle, we recurse on the left part only. Notice, however, that we can't keep recomputing the mid on each recursion. We need the mid position of the original range, even though we recurse over portions of this range. We therefore write an auxiliary function.

```
template <class Iterator>
void median_aux
(   Iterator b,
    Iterator e,
    Iterator mid
)
```

```
{   if(b<e-1 && mid>=b && mid<e)
    {   Iterator t;
        partition_aux(b, t, e);
        if(t<mid)
            median_aux(t+1, e, mid);
        else if(t>mid)
            median_aux(b, t, mid);
    }
}
```

Exercise. What kinds of iterator do we require for median_aux? Do we need a random access iterator, or will a forward or bidirectional iterator suffice?

Median then, just calls median_aux. Note that calling median will rearrange your data, but not completely sort it. It does move the median into the middle location rather than return it. From that location it can be retrieved.

```
template <class RandomAccessIterator>
inline void median
(   RandomAccessIterator begin,
    RandomAccessIterator end
)
{   median_aux
    (begin, end, begin + (end-begin)/2);
}
```

Note the computation of the middle position. It can't be written as (end+begin)/2, since operator+ (with two iterators) is not an iterator operation. Operator-, however, returns an integer value, and integers can be added to random access iterators.

The median is not one of the algorithms in the STL. There are a number of similar algorithms that can be used to generate the median and other order statistics, however.

Algorithm nth_element places the nth element from the smallest into that location. It will partially rearrange the range, but not completely sort it.

```
template <class RandomAccessIterator>
void nth_element
(   RandomAccessIterator first,
    RandomAccessIterator nth,
    RandomAccessIterator last
);
```

For example, to find the median of an array you can use something like the following:

```
int A[300];
. . .
nth_element(A, A+150, A+300);
```

When this returns, the array will have been rearranged somewhat and the median will be in A[150]. These operations are linear on the average, but like the quicksort, they are quadratic in some cases. The version shown uses operator< to define the sorted order. The other version requires a comparison operator as the last parameter.

Related to the above are algorithms that will partially sort a range. The first of these (with two versions as usual) rearranges a range so that the first part consists of the elements in sorted order that would occur there if the entire range were sorted. The elements after the first part will not necessarily be in order, but the entire range is a permutation of the original.

```
template <class RandomAccessIterator>
void partial_sort
(   RandomAccessIterator first,
    RandomAccessIterator middle,
    RandomAccessIterator last
);
```

The subrange from the first to the second parameter is sorted. The other version of this takes a comparison operator.

There is also a version of partial sorting that makes a copy of the original range and then partially sorts this range, leaving the original unmodified.

```
template <  class InputIterator,
            class RandomAccessIterator
         >
RandomAccessIterator partial_sort_copy
(   InputIterator first,
    InputIterator last,
    RandomAccessIterator result_first,
    RandomAccessIterator result_last
);
```

If the second range, of size N, say, is smaller than the first, the algorithm leaves the N smallest elements of the first range in the second range in sorted order. If the second range is the same size or larger than the first, it places the entire first range into the second in sorted order starting at result_first. Other locations in the second range are not modified. In either case, partial_sort_copy returns a past-the-end value of the sorted range that it creates.

Partial_sort and partial_sort_copy are guaranteed to be n * lg(n) in running time. Partial_sort will sort an entire range by making middle equal to last. Likewise, partial_sort_copy will sort an entire range if the second range has length equal to that of the first.

Finally, we discuss two algorithms that don't exactly belong with the sort routines, but are similar in flavor. Algorithm partition also rearranges a range, but does so according to a predicate function rather than a comparison operator. Those elements for which the predicate returns true are placed before those for which it is false.

```
template
<class BidirectionalIterator, class Predicate>
BidirectionalIterator partition
(   BidirectionalIterator first,
    BidirectionalIterator last,
    Predicate pred
);
```

The other algorithm is like this but is stable in the sense that it won't permute two elements, both of which return true for the predicate, or both of which return false.

```
template
<class ForwardIterator, class Predicate>
ForwardIterator stable_partition
(   ForwardIterator first,
    ForwardIterator last,
    Predicate pred
);
```

These algorithms could be used to put small elements before large ones or red ones before nonred elements, etc. Algorithm partition is linear, as is stable_partition if there is memory available for a copy of the input range. Otherwise, stable_partition requires n*ln(n) time.

6.10 Merging

Merging is the process of creating a larger sorted list from two or more smaller sorted lists. In the simplest version we need three ranges: two for the inputs and a separate third one for the results.

```
OutputIterator merge
(   InputIterator1 first1,
    InputIterator1 last1,
    InputIterator2 first2,
    InputIterator2 last2,
    OutputIterator result
);
```

The algorithm proceeds by examining the first elements in each of the inputs. The smaller of these is copied to the output. The output iterator is advanced and also the iterator that was the source of the copy. The process proceeds from this point until one of the inputs is empty. The remainder of the other input range is then copied to the output. This process is linear in the sizes of the inputs. A second version takes a comparison operator as the last parameter, as we would expect.

Sometimes the two input ranges are two halves of a larger range. Note that each half still needs to be sorted. We desire to provide a sorted range as usual. If we want to store the results in the same range, we have two possibilities. The first and simplest uses some auxiliary storage and the algorithm above. It is somewhat more complex, though possible, to merge in place without additional space for a copy of our data. To explain this requires that we discuss another algorithm that rotates a range about a location within it.

```
template <class ForwardIterator>
void rotate
( ForwardIterator first,
  ForwardIterator middle,
  ForwardIterator last
);
```

Assuming that middle is within the range [first, last), this algorithm relocates the element at middle to the location first, rotating toward the left. Therefore, the old first element winds up just after the old last element. When we finish the element that was just before the original middle will be in last location. There is also a copying version rotate_copy, but we won't need that here for our inplace merge.

```
template <class BidirectionalIterator>
void inplace_merge
( BidirectionalIterator first,
  BidirectionalIterator middle,
  BidirectionalIterator last
);
```

This process merges the sorted range [first, middle) and the sorted range [middle, last) into a sorted range [first, last) without using additional space. It is similar to quicksort in some ways. It proceeds as follows. First, we compute the exact middle point of the left range, mid_left, and note what value, v, is stored there. This should be near the median value of the result. We then use lower_bound to find the first occurrence of this value (or a slightly larger one in case v is not present) in the right range. Call this location mid_right. Then we compute the smaller of middle-mid_left and mid_right-middle. We call this value s. We next rotate(mid_left, mid_left + s, mid_right). This leaves us with value v near the middle in its correct final position. It also leaves us with all values to the left of the mid_left + s smaller than v and all values to the right larger than or equivalent to v. Finally, the subranges [first, mid_left) and [mid_left, mid_left + s) are each individually sorted, as are the two corresponding subranges to the right of mid_left + s. We can then recursively apply the same process to the left side and the right side of the point mid_left + s. This leaves us with a sorted result. As described, the process requires n * lg(n) time for the same reason that the quick sort has this time complexity. However, the actual implementation will use merge and then copy back to the input range if space is available, making it linear in that case.

Finally we discuss a process called merge sort that forms the basis of the stable_sort described above. Merge_sort itself is not part of the STL.

We assume that we have a range of values that can be compared with operator< or with a comparison operator. Merge_sort proceeds by splitting the input range in the exact middle, assuming that there is more than one item. It then recursively sorts the two halves of this range and then merges the two halves together into a whole. You can use either merge or inplace_merge for this operation, depending on how much additional space is available. If space is available, the overall algorithm requires n * $\log_2(n)$ time. Other-

wise, it requires n * $(\log_2(n))^2$ time. This is still better than quadratic time.

Merge_sort is stable because neither the split nor the merge permute equivalent elements. It takes some careful thought to see that rotate, as used in the inplace_merge, swaps the left and right sides of the range to which it is applied, leaving relative locations within each half unaffected.

6.11   Summary

Make certain that you understand each of the following terms. You should also understand each of the algorithms discussed in this chapter.

binary search
container adaptor
decile
double-ended queue
heap
heap sort
insertion sort
nonmutating sequence algorithm
lexicographical order
median
merge sort
order statistic
partial order
percentile
permutation
priority queue
quartile
rotation
sequential search
stable sort

6.12 Exercises

1. Write a member function to read in a DiGraph that was written with archive.

2. Implement a heap container. Write reheap and downheap as described in the text.

3. Using a stopwatch object and the STL heap operations over a deque, verify that the make_heap operation is linear in its time requirements. Show that, over a wide range of deque sizes, doubling the size of the deque doubles the time necessary to make it into a heap. Use random data for your tests.

4. Implement an insertion sort generic algorithm, as described in the text.

5. Implement inplace_merge, as described in the text.

6. Use partition_aux to find other order statistics than just the median. Start with the first and third quartiles. The first quartile is larger than or equal to one fourth (quarter) of the data and less than or equal to three fourths of it. Now try the 20th percentile. This value is larger than or equal to 20 percent of the values. Test your functions on a large set of data. Write a general percentile function.

7. In the STL, container adaptors like stack and queue do not have iterators. Discuss why not. Can you find valid reasons? For the queue adaptor shown in the text, add an associated iterator. A queue iterator should produce the elements of the queue in the order from front to back. Should operator* of your iterator return copies of the elements? references to the elements? const references? Think about this before you start.

8. Give your own implementation of the first version of sort_heap. It should take a heap and produce a sorted container. Test it by transforming a random vector into a heap and then sorting it. Use a stopwatch object to determine experimentally what the running time can be expected to be as a function of the size of the heap.

9. Suppose you have a vector that contains items in no particular order and in which the current order need not be maintained. Then one possible search technique is random_search. Suppose we have N items in the vector and we have examined N-K of them already. Pick a random number i in the range [0,K). Look in cell i to see if that is the item of interest. If not, then swap cell i and cell N - K-1, reduce K, and repeat as necessary. Implement random_search. Compare its running time with that of sequential_search.

10. Draw a picture or series of pictures to illustrate random_search. Use Figure 6.4 and 6.5 as a rough guide.

11. Draw a picture or series of pictures to explain what happens in algorithm rotate. You may need to consider more than one case for a complete explanation. It might help to run the algorithm a few times so that you thoroughly understand it.

Chapter 7
Lists

7.1. Implementation Strategies of STL Lists

The STL provides a container class template list that is very useful in situations in which we need to frequently insert and remove items in the middle of a container. We looked at simple lists in Chapter 3 and examined the basic insert and removal algorithms there. STL lists provide bidirectional iterators. This means that the list should be built of doubly linked nodes so that we can easily traverse in both directions. We also want to provide after-the-end values for iterators. Therefore, a trailer node after the last actual data node will be useful.

The basic node type in a list implementation could look like Figure 7.1.

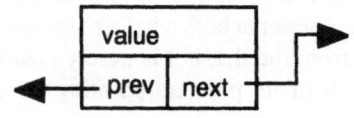

Figure 7.1. A node from a doubly-linked list.

If we chain a number of these nodes together we get something like Figure 7.2. Each node refers to the one that follows it and the one that precedes it. Somehow the process must stop. One way to do this is to set the pointer to the previous node of the first node and the pointer to the next node of the last node to be NULL, as is shown in Figure 7.2.

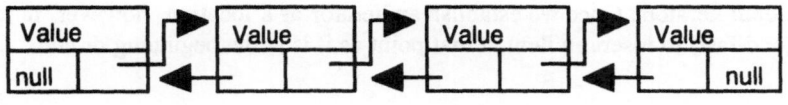

Figure 7.2. A sequence of nodes in a doubly-linked list.

If this is used, then a list as a whole could be represented by maintaining a pointer to each end of the list. This is shown in Figure 7.3.

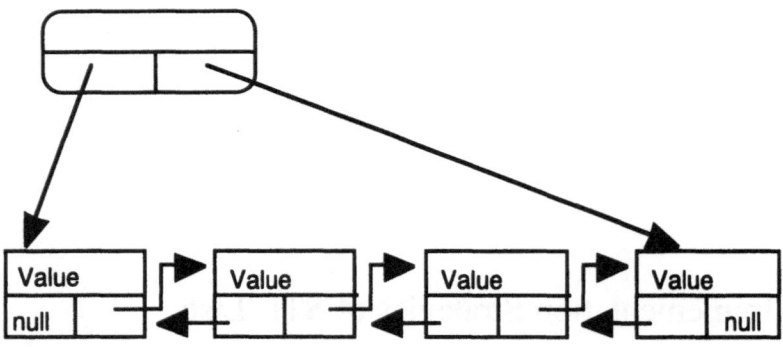

Figure 7.3. Representing a list with begin and end pointers.

Figure 7.3 does not show a trailer node. We could replace the null pointer in the rightmost node with a pointer to a trailer. There could be one trailer for all lists or there could be a separate trailer for each list.

The STL takes a slightly different approach, however. Each list has a node known as the header that is unique to each list. Both the previous pointer of the first node and the next pointer of the last point to this header. In turn, the header points to each of these. The list itself is implemented using a pointer to the header node. See Figure 7.4. Logically, the header node represents both a before-the-beginning and an after-the-end location. It does not hold data from the list, but is purely positional. An empty list consists of just a header node with both of its pointers pointing to itself. We call this structure circular linking.

An iterator into such a container can be represented as just a pointer to a node. The begin() iterator is a pointer to the node that follows the header. The end() iterator is a pointer to the header node. Iterators are a class here, since the distance between nodes is not fixed. We cannot do simple pointer arithmetic on a pointer to find the next node. Iterators maintain a pointer to a node and to execute operation++, we need to set the value of this pointer to the value of the next field in the node that the iterator currently references. Similarly, the prev field is used to execute operation--. There are actually separate classes for iterators and const iterators.

A list structure makes random access iterators extremely expensive, since the list must actually be traversed to do pointer arithmetic. For this reason, lists provide only bidirectional iterators. Once we establish an iterator at a location, however, it is just as simple (and fast) to insert an item at that point as it is at the beginning or end.

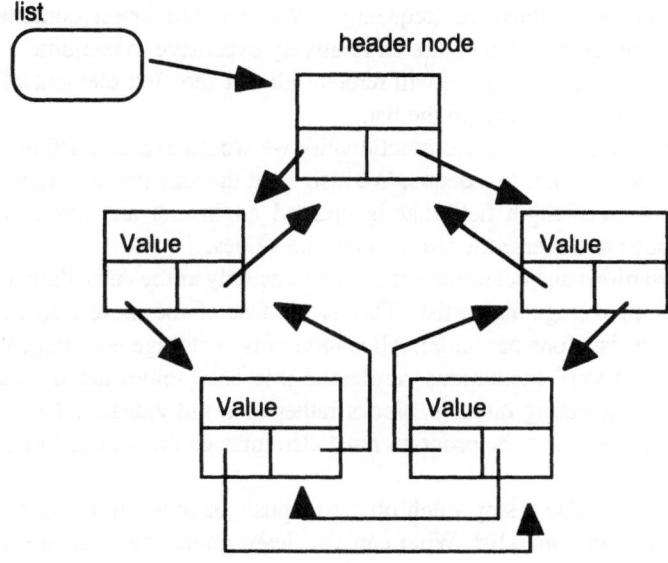

Figure 7.4. Lists in the STL.

7.2.   Properties of STL Lists

Lists have constructors to create empty lists, lists with any number of elements with the same value, a copy of another list, or a copy of the elements of any iterator range.

As noted above, lists have only bidirectional iterators. This means that some algorithms can't be used with lists. Sorting is the most important algorithm that we might like to have with lists. The sort routines of the STL require random access iterators, however. For this reason, list provides a member function sort. The sort member function is a stable sort and uses a variation on merge sort. Instead of trying to split the list in the middle, which would be somewhat expensive, it starts by merging the first two elements into a sorted minilist. It then repeats this with the next two, and then merges these two minilists into a list of four. It then repeats this process until it gets a list of eight, etc., until it has incorporated all the elements into the work list. It also does this merging without creating new nodes, since it just relinks the existing nodes into the work lists as it proceeds.

Another special member function splices all of the nodes of one list into another, making the first empty. We can also remove an item from one list and splice it into another without recreating a node. A third version splices an iterator range from one list into another. If movement of items from one list to another is frequent, splicing can be important to efficiency. This is exactly the case in the sort algorithm mentioned above. The ability to splice lists together in constant time makes lists useful in some algorithms in which containers must be frequently combined into larger containers. In contrast, the other containers in the STL are all relatively expensive to combine.

Member function unique will remove all but the first element of any consecutive sequence of equal elements in the list.

Lists also have the usual functionality we would expect, such as pushing and popping at both ends, similar to a deque. We also want the size function to work in constant time, so lists keep a length field that is updated on inserts and removals. Without this, we would need to traverse the list to count the values.

If insertions and deletions need to be done only at the ends, then a deque or vector will be faster on average than a list. This is because of the more frequent allocations that are needed for lists (one per node). Allocation of new storage is an expensive operation generally. Actual implementations can lessen this cost somewhat by maintaining blocks of nodes and allocating them in blocks rather than individually. This speeds the code, but complicates it, since the program must also manage these node blocks.

Experiment. Use a stopwatch object to push_back a few thousand items onto a vector and then again onto a list. What can you learn about the relative speed of a vector and a list on this operation?

If the primary need is to keep a collection sorted as insertions are done, rather than sorting it afterwards, then lists might be a good choice, but sets or multisets might be better. If processing is frequent and must be done according to the sort order, then lists might be better. Insertions would be faster for sets, though lists would have the edge during traversals.

Lists also have an advantage in that iterators are not invalidated by insertions, nor by deletions (with member erase) unless a deletion removes a value that the iterator references. In complex algorithms involving many iterators, it is not always easy to know how many iterators refer to a given location, so great care must be taken when deleting. Even if we resplice nodes from one list to another, any iterators referencing that item will stay valid, though this is not always an advantage.

One example of an application for which lists are ideal is in managing the objects to be drawn in a complex graphics system. Suppose each object is to be drawn in its own layer so that objects can partially overlap each other. Suppose that we also need to be able to rearrange the layers, moving some objects forward and others backward in the scene. One way to do this is to have a draw function that takes a list of objects to be drawn as an argument. This list is called a display list. The draw function draws them from last to first, representing the back of the scene to the front. In this way the objects properly overlap each other. A list is used since we want to be able to rearrange the layers. We do this just by changing the position of an object in its display list.

7.3 A Simple Implementation of Circular Lists

It is easy to build a circularly linked list with a header node that is less sophisticated than that of the STL. Our lists will only be singly linked which is a great simplification, but it leads to a few complications as well. We will build a class template CircleList, and two nested classes CircleList::Node, and CircleList::Iterator. We shall show these last two classes separately, though they are contained within the definition of CircleList. The nesting structure looks like the following:

```
template <class E>
class CircleList // singly linked circular list.
{ public:
    typedef Iterator iterator;
    typedef E value_type;
    typedef E& reference;
    typedef E* pointer;
...
  protected:
    class Node
    // Nested class. The nodes of the list.
    {  ...
    };
    class Iterator
    {  ...
    };
friend class Iterator;
    Node* head;
};
```

This permits us to use the template argument E within the Node and Iterator classes. The nested Node class is very simple.

```
class Node
// Nested class. The nodes of the list.
{  public:
   E value;
   bool header;
   Node *next;
   Node(E val, Node * n)
   :  value(val),
      next(n),
      header(false)
   {
   }
};
```

The class is entirely public. though it is nested within the protected part of its container class. It has a constructor that takes a value to be saved and another node that is to follow it in the list. The last node in a list will point to the head node of that same list. We need the boolean value *header* to distinguish header nodes from other nodes. This will help us implement after-the-end values of iterators. The other classes (CircleList and Iterator) will operate directly on the fields of Node.

The Iterator class is implemented using a Node pointer named *here* and a boolean value named *isEnd*. This latter variable is used to distinguish an iterator at the beginning of a CircleList from one after the end. Both of these Iterators will actually point to the head node of their list. The complication single linking introduces that we mentioned in the opening paragraph of this section is that when an iterator refers to a value within a node, it must actually point to the previous node. This is because it is expensive to back up in a singly linked list (we must run around the list to find the previous location), and many of our operations require modifying the node that points to the one under consideration. For example, to remove a value (and its node), we must change the pointer in the previous node, not the pointer in the node being removed which, after all, is about to be deleted.

We create a new Iterator by making it point to the head node of its list and setting isEnd to be true if the list is empty and false otherwise. An empty list's new Iterator is already at the end.

```
class Iterator
// This is only a forward iterator.
// An iterator points to the node before the
// one it logically references.
{   Iterator(const CircleList<E> *const L)
    :   here(L->head),
        isEnd(L->empty())
    {
    }
    . . .
private:
    CircleList<E>::Node *here;
    bool isEnd;

friend class CircleList;
};
```

An Iterator to the end of the list will also point to the head node, but its isEnd will always be true.

To de-reference an Iterator, we extract the value from the next node, not the current one.

```
reference operator*()const
{  return here->next->value;
}
```

We advance an Iterator with the usual node walk operation. However, we also advance to the header node if we move past the logical end of the list. Thus, if the here variable points to the last data node, then it logically references the following header node, so we move there and set isEnd to be true.

```
iterator& operator++()
{  here = here->next;
   if(here->next->header)
      here = here->next;
   if( here->header) isEnd = true;
   return *this;
}
```

Two Iterators are equal if they reference the same node and have equal isEnd values

```
bool operator==(const iterator& it)const
{  return here == it.here
         && isEnd == it.isEnd;
}
```

There is also a post increment operator++ and an assignment operator=, not shown here.

A CircleList itself is created by creating a new head node and linking it to itself in a self-circular way. We must reset the default values of the created node.

```
CircleList():head(new Node(E(), NULL))
{  head->next = head;
   head->header = true;
}
```

The copy constructor, destructor, and overloaded operator= are implemented in terms of two hidden helper functions free and copy, as is typically done. We will show copy and free later.

```
CircleList(const CircleList& L) // copy constructor
{  copy(L);
}

~CircleList(){ free(); }

CircleList& operator= (const CircleList& L)
```

```
{   if ( this == &L) return *this;
    free();
    copy(L);
    return *this;
}
```

A CircleList is empty whenever its head points to itself. Since we don't maintain a node count, we need to walk around the list to determine its size. It would be easy to fix this, of course. We push a new value onto the front of our list by creating a new node to hold it. Notice how the constructor of the Node class makes it easy to link the new node in using only a single statement here.

```
void push_front(const E& val)
{   head->next = newNode(val, head->next);
}
```

Most list operations use iterators. We provide the usual begin and end functions.

```
iterator begin()const
{   return iterator(this);
}

iterator end()const
{   iterator result(this);
    result.isEnd = true;
    return result;
}
```

For example, we can insert a new item into the middle of a list by moving an iterator to the point of insertion. The new value will be inserted before the logical position of the iterator (but after the physical position). The comments refer to the logical position.

```
void insert(iterator& i, const E& val)
// Insert before i.
{   i.here->next = newNode(val, i.here->next);
}
```

We can erase an element in the middle of a list by first moving an iterator to its location and then using CircleList::erase. This function removes the node after the one to which the iterator points, but it never removes the head node, which would destroy the list itself.

```
void erase(iterator& i)
        // Removes value at location of i and
        // moves to following location.
```

```
{   if(i.here->next == head)return;
    CircleList<E>::Node *temp
        = i.here->next->next;
    delete i.here->next;
    i.here->next = temp;
}
```

Note that, after erasing an element, the iterator refers to the following location auto-matically.

We can then erase all of the elements of a list with clear. We can also use erase to im-plement pop_front. We can then use clear to implement the hidden free function used in the destructor.

```
void clear()
    // Removes all elements from the list,
    // leaving it empty.
{   iterator i = begin();
    while(!empty()) erase(i);
}

void pop_front(){ erase(begin());}

void free()
{   clear();
    delete head;
}
```

7.3.1 Sorting a List

We can quicksort a list as easily as we do a vector or array. This is true even though we have only a forward iterator into a list. We provide two versions of sort, one defined in terms of iterators and the other that refers to only the list itself. Quicksort is not a stable sort and the STL requires its List class to have a stable sort. Therefore, this one isn't quite good enough. The STL sort uses a variation on merge sort.

```
void sort(iterator& start, iterator& done)
// PRE: done does not precede start.
{   if(start != done)
    {   iterator mid(done);
        partition_aux(start, mid, done);
        sort(start, mid);
        sort(++mid, done);
    }
}
```

The partition_aux is the same one we saw in an exercise in Section 6.9 when we studied order statistics. The second version can easily use the first.

```
void sort()
// NOT stable, Therefore does not meet STL
// requirements. Requires a forward_iterator
// version of partition_aux.
{   if(size() > 1) sort(begin(), end());
}
```

7.3.2   Recursive List Operations

The STL prefers to implement most algorithms independently of its containers since we can save effort and runtime code by doing so. However, as a general technique, there is a very interesting way to implement list operations within a list class using recursion. A list is a recursive data structure at the node level. The node consists of a value and another node. We can use this idea to write functions (at the node level) that parallel the node structure itself.

For example, we can copy a list by copying nodes recursively. To do so requires that the copy function (of the CircleList class) use a function that works at the node level. Recall that copy is used in the copy constructor and in operator=.

```
void copy(const CircleList& L)
{   head = new Node(E(),NULL);
    head->next = head;
    head->header = true;
    Node *here = L.head->next;
    head->next = copy_aux(here, head);
}
```

Member copy works by first creating a new head node for the list this. It then sets the next field of the head to be a pointer to a list that looks just like the list of elements of L, with the exception that this list must terminate with the head of this, rather than the head of L. We use the recursive function copy_aux to create this list of nodes. We pass in a pointer to the first actual data node of L and the head of this.

```
Node *copy_aux
(Node *here, Node *OriginalHead)
{   if(here->header) return OriginalHead;
    Node *n = new Node
            (   here->value,
                copy_aux
                (   here->next,
                    OriginalHead
```

```
                    )
                );
        return n;
    }
```

If we call copy_aux pointing to a header node, it returns the original head node it was sent. Otherwise, we create and return a new node that is constructed by taking the value from the list being copied, and the next from a recursive call of copy_aux, that automatically creates the rest of the list. Notice that this recursion creates the new list from the back forwards, since the recursion in the parameter position must return before the new operator completes. Some time spent understanding this function will be well spent.

For example, suppose we wish to copy a list containing 1, 2, and 3. Then the list's nodes can be represented as head -> [1] -> [2] -> [3] -> head, where the second head is the same as the first, closing the circle.

Copy_aux is passed the head of the new list being created and a pointer to [1]. It works by creating a new node with a 1 in it and with a next that it first gets from a recursive call that is passed the pointer to [2] and the same original head. This recursive call tries to create and return a node with a 2 in it and a next that it first gets from another recursive call: one with a pointer to [3] and the same original head.

This recursive call creates a node with 3 in it and a recursive call that passes a pointer to the head node of the list being copied. This last recursion, seeing that it is at a head node, returns the original head node of the list being created. It returns this node to the "3" recursion that pastes this node as the next node of the node it creates and passes this newly created node to the "2" recursion that uses it for the tail of the node it creates, etc., until we finally return back to the copy member that originally called copy_aux.

While this is difficult to explain and to understand at first, it is not especially difficult to program correctly, and it is a very powerful technique.

A similar technique could be used to replace the clear member function with a recursive equivalent. We again need an auxiliary function to get to the node level, where the recursion takes place.

```
    void clear_aux(Node * n)
    {   if( n == head) return;
        head->next = n->next;
        delete n;
        clear_aux(head->next);
    }

    void clear_rec()
    {   clear_aux(head->next);
    }
```

7.3.3   Some Difficulties with This Implementation

This implementation is simple, but it is not perfect, especially when we compare it to the STL specification. We noted above that the STL wants a stable sort defined for lists. The one presented here, while efficient, is not stable.

A more fundamental issue, however, is invalidation of iterators. If we have two iterators to two adjacent nodes and pass the first one to erase, then we have invalidated the second one, since it actually points to the node just erased. This is a very serious difficulty and limits the uses to which we can put iterators. If we have lots of iterators in a given algorithm, it is especially troublesome. If there is only one, it is not a difficulty.

Note also what happens if we have two iterators to the same location and we pass one of them to insert. Then the other iterator will still be valid, but it will reference the newly inserted value instead of the original. This might cause problems in some algorithms unless they were coded carefully.

Of course, the fact that we link singly and provide only forward iterators doesn't match the specification of the STL either, but this is easily remedied.

The most serious flaw in CircleList is discussed in the exercises.

7.4   An Alternate Implementation of Lists

In this section we shall look at an implementation of lists that has some very interesting properties, though it won't quite meet the specifications of the standard. The weakness will be in the STL requirement that insertions and deletions not invalidate iterators. We will also show a sort algorithm for lists that is interesting, but not stable. It therefore doesn't meet the standard either, though a different sort could be used instead.

The first interesting property of this implementation illustrates a classic computer science problem: that of the space-time tradeoff. It is often possible in algorithms and data structures to trade space for time, where more space can be exchanged for faster algorithms, or less space for slower ones. The programmer is encouraged not to be naive about space vs. time, however, especially when using a modern operating system. Sometimes a smaller program will also run faster since it has a better fit with respect to the page quota provided by a paged virtual memory management system such as UNIX. A smaller program loads faster and generates fewer page faults; therefore, it runs faster.

The classic implementation of doubly linked lists uses two pointers in each node as described above. This is true even when circular linking is used, as with the standard implementation of STL list. We then have iterators that use a single pointer to refer directly to some node. It is possible to turn this around, however, with one "pointer" in each node and two pointers to adjacent nodes in each iterator. This is a positive tradeoff in space, since we expect to have a lot of nodes, but few iterators. We put "pointer" in quotes above, since the value saved in a node won't actually be a pointer to another node. Instead it will be an access value that gives us the ability to generate a pointer to either the node to the left or the node to the right as needed. To fully explain this, we need to examine the properties of the exclusive or operator, called XOR, and represented in C++ by the standard operator^. For boolean values, XOR is true if and only if the two operands have different truth values. The usual mathematical symbol for XOR is $\otimes$.

Properties of XOR

(1) Commutative	$a \otimes b = b \otimes a$
(2) Associative	$a \otimes (b \otimes c) = (a \otimes b) \otimes c$
(3) Identity	$a \otimes 0 = a$
(4) Self Inverse	$a \otimes a = 0$
(5) Distinctness	$a \otimes b = 0$ if and only if $a = b$
(6) Cancellation	$(a \otimes x) \otimes x = a$
(7) Substitution	$a \otimes b = (a \otimes c) \otimes (c \otimes b)$

These properties can all be verified by looking at truth tables.

In this implementation (see [7]) of lists, we shall build a class template List<T>, where the nodes hold a value of type T and an *access* value. This access of a node is the XOR of pointers to the nodes to the immediate left and right of that node. This is depicted in Figure 7.5.

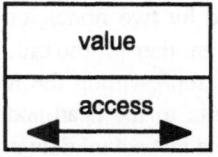

Figure 7.5. A node in an "access" list.

Iterators will be represented with normal pointers to two adjacent nodes. A few nodes of a list and one iterator are depicted in Figure 7.6. We have also informally named the nodes, a, b, c, and d. Then the iterator's left pointer refers to b.

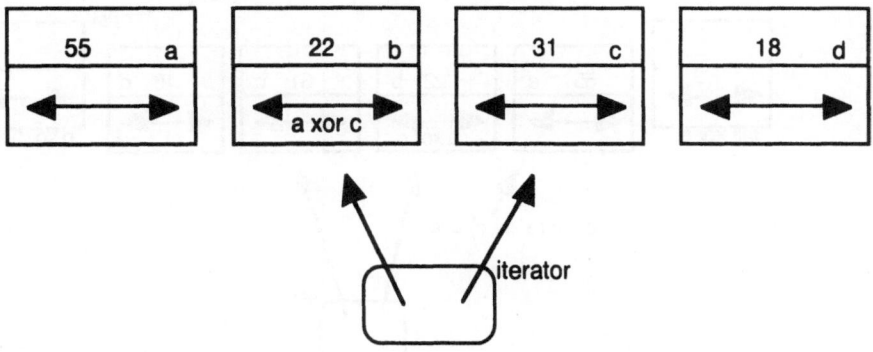

Figure 7.6. An iterator into an "access" list.

Then, if we have an iterator with pointers left and right and an access value, left->access = (a ⊗ c), we can form right ⊗ left->access = c ⊗ (a ⊗ c) = a by the commutative and cancellation properties. Likewise, we can get a pointer to node d, with left ⊗ right->access = b ⊗ (b ⊗ d) = d. Unfortunately, an iterator now refers to two nodes, and removing either of them will invalidate that iterator. It is also a consequence of this that we cannot navigate the list except with the use of iterators, since the access value alone is not enough information to navigate. We need the additional external pointers provided in the iterators.

Note. however, that the nodes are smaller, by one pointer, than in the classic implementation, though traversal takes longer since we must also compute xors as we go.

We can compute the xor of two pointers with the following function. It is a static member of the Node class. First we cast the two pointers to long values, then take the xor and finally cast the result back to a pointer to a node of the desired type.

```
static Node* ExclOr(Node* a, Node* b)
{   return (Node*)((long)a^(long)b);
}
```

So far we have seen List nodes and iterators, but we have not seen the lists themselves. A List is represented by two nodes, one for the head, which represents a before-the-beginning location, and another for the tail, representing an after-the-end location. An iterator can be thought of as representing the location of its right pointer. Therefore, the begin() iterator of a list points to the head node and the first actual data node. Likewise, the end() iterator points to the last actual data node and the tail node. An empty list can be thought of as an iterator that points to the head and tail nodes. This is shown in Figure 7.7 where we have four data nodes and the head and tail.

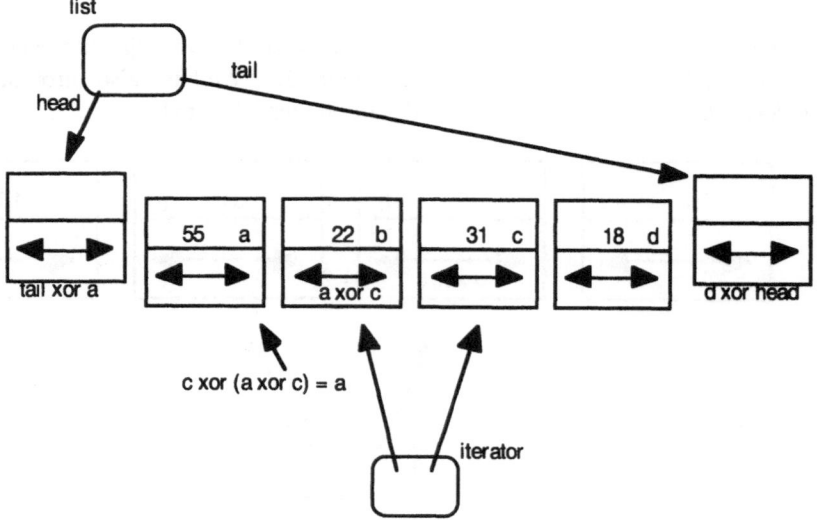

Figure 7.7 An "access" list with its nodes and an iterator.

This figure also illustrates the computation of a node pointer. If we xor the right pointer in an iterator (here a pointer to c) with the access value in the node to the left (here a xor c), we get a pointer to a node one step farther to the left (here a). This can be used as the basis of operator--. Reversing left and right in this description gives us operator++ from the Iterator class.

```
iterator& operator++()
{  List<data>::Node *temp = left;
   left = right;
   right = Node::ExclOr
          (temp, right->access);
   return *this;
}
```

Notice that the access values stored in the head and tail nodes imply that the logical representation is also circular, but with two extra nodes instead of one. It doesn't fit the philosophy of the STL, but this implementation mechanism can be used to create iterators and list operations that are completely left-right symmetric. We could use the same operations for moving left or right. This is because an iterator in this scheme faithfully represents the location between two nodes and does so in a symmetric way.

In this implementation an iterator really represents the position between two nodes. For this reason these iterators are sometimes called cursors because of the similarity of cursors in word processing programs that represent the position between two characters in a document. When we create an iterator, we locate it between the head and the first data node.

```
Iterator(const List<data> *const L)
:  left(L->head),
   right
   (  Node::ExclOr
      (  L->tail,
         L->head->access
      )
   )
{
}
```

As stated above, an iterator is said to reference its right location:

```
reference operator*()const
{  return right->value;
}
```

Unlike our simple CircleList, however, we can walk to the left as easily as to the right.

```
iterator& operator--()
{   List<data>::Node *temp = right;
    right = left;
    left = Node::ExclOr
            (temp, left->access);
    return *this;
}
```

Lists provide iterators to the beginning and the end of themselves, as usual.

```
iterator begin()const
{   return iterator(this);
}

iterator end()const
{   iterator result(this);
    result.right = tail;
    result.left = Node::ExclOr
                    (head, tail->access);
    return result;
}
```

Many of the remaining operations of this List class are the same as those of the CircleList class, since they just use iterators and do not depend on the implementation of the lists themselves.

Since we provide a bidirectional iterator in this class, we can also provide reverse iterators. A reverse iterator is one that iterates backwards from the usual way. To use them we first export a type from the List class.

```
typedef reverse_bidirectional_iterator
      <   iterator,
      data,
      data&,
      long
      >
reverse_iterator;
```

Reverse iterators are defined within the STL using a template with four parameters. The first is the iterator type it reverses. The next two are the value type and the reference type of the iterator it reverses, and the last is an integer type that can be used to represent differences between iterators. Here we assume long will work, though we could be more sophisticated about this.

Next we provide rbegin and rend:

```
reverse_iterator rbegin()
{   return reverse_iterator(end());
}
reverse_iterator rend()
{   return reverse_iterator(begin());
}
```

Finally, we need a constructor so that we can capture the position of a reverse iterator in an ordinary iterator. Reverse iterators work by maintaining an ordinary iterator called the base.

```
Iterator(List<data>::reverse_iterator& r)
:   left(r.base().left),
    right(r.base().right)
{
}
```

Having a reverse iterator type will allow us to apply many of the STL algorithms in the reverse of the usual order.

7.5   The Iterator Invalidation Problem and Its Solution

Suppose we wish to write a series of algorithms on lists that will require lots of iterators. Suppose also that the algorithms require frequent insertions and deletions from the lists. Then the invalidations that occur when we delete a node may be unacceptable. Note that iterators in the second implementation above also become invalid when we insert values. This is because such iterators refer to two adjacent nodes. If we put a new node between the two referenced by another iterator, we invalidate that iterator.

Lets examine a mechanism by which iterators may be updated automatically when the list that they reference becomes modified. To do this we will build a subclass of whatever list class we wish to extend. Before doing so, we should change all of the base class private data to protected so that we may get access to it in the subclass. The new class will be called SafeList. We will extend the "access" list of Section 7.4, for example.

In a safe list we require an additional member variable and also derived "safe" versions of the Iterator and Node classes. A SafeList will be built out of SafeNodes and will permit the use of SafeIterators, as well as ordinary iterators. A SafeIterator is one that is automatically updated when a node that it references becomes deleted, or when a node is inserted between the two that it references. The overall structure of our new template follows.

```
template <class data>
class SafeList:public List<data>
{
```

```
class SafeIterator:public List<data>::iterator
{  ...
   friend class SafeList<data>;
};

class SafeNode:public List<data>::Node
{  ...
   friend class SafeList<data>;
   friend class SafeIterator;
};
```

```
};
```

The extra variable of SafeList is actually a pointer to a List of SafeList iterator pointers.

```
List< SafeIterator *> *_Iterators;
```

The basic idea is that when we create a new safe iterator, we insert it into the _Iterators list of its SafeList. Then, when any change is about to be made to the nodes, the list notifies each of the iterators in its _Iterators list of the node to which the change is being made. If that node is of interest to an iterator, it has a chance to change its position, anticipating the change.

When we want a safe iterator, we ask a safe list for one using begin_safe.

```
iterator begin_safe()
{  SafeIterator result(*this);
   return result;
}
```

The constructor of the safe iterator inserts it into the safe list's iterator list.

```
SafeIterator(SafeList<data> & L)
:   Iterator(&L),
    _owner(L)
{
   if(!L._Iterators)
      L._Iterators
         = new List<SafeIterator *>();
   L._Iterators->push_front(this);
}
```

Then when a change is made, we can notify all of the iterators, though usually we don't notify the iterator that is responsible for the change, since it knows about the change already.

```
void insert
(List<data>::iterator& i, const data& val)
    // Creates a new location at this
    // position. Leaves the location with
    // the new value to the left. Notifies
    // all safe iterators of the change.
{   Node* oldLeft = i.left;
    Node* oldRight = i.right;
    List<data>::insert(i, val);
    Node* aNode = i.left;
    notifyOthers
        ( &i,oldLeft, oldRight, aNode);
}
```

We require a new member of SafeList to perform this notification:

```
void notifyOthers //Notify all except
                    // skip (may be NULL)
( List<data>::Iterator* skip,
  Node *N,
  Node *M = NULL,
  Node *ptr = NULL
)
{   if(_Iterators)
    { List< SafeIterator* >::
      Iterator nextIterator
          = _Iterators->begin();
      while
      (nextIterator != _Iterators->end())
      { if (*nextIterator != skip)
            (*nextIterator)->
      notify(N,M,ptr);
          ++nextIterator;
      }
    }
}
```

When an iterator gets the notify message, it must update itself.

```
void notify
( Node *N,
  Node *M,
  Node *ptr
)
{   if(!M) // Removing N
```

```
{   if(left == N)
        left = List<data>::Node::ExclOr
            (  right,
               ((SafeNode*)N)->getaccess()
            );
    else if (right == N)
        right = List<data>::Node::ExclOr
            (  left,
               ((SafeNode*)N)->getaccess()
            );
}
else // Inserting between N and M
    if(left == N && right == M)
    {  left = ptr;
        // NOT Symmetric, always Left.
    }
}
```

We need safe nodes as well, since SafeLists and SafeIterators won't be able to get access to the access value of the Node class. Therefore, we must provide members in SafeNode to get and set these access values.

Finally, when a SafeIterator is destroyed, it must get removed from the list's _Iterators list.

```
~SafeIterator()
{   ((SafeList<data> &) _owner)
        .deregister(this);
}
```

The deregister member of SafeList does the actual removal.

```
void deregister(SafeIterator *C)
{  if(_Iterators)_Iterators->remove(C);
}
```

This technique is not unique to lists. It can be applied as necessary to other container classes.

7.6   Techniques for STL Lists

Next we will return to the STL itself and show a few techniques for programming with lists. We will briefly illustrate some common problems and their solutions. Along the way we will also discuss some additional STL algorithms.

7.6.1 Finding an Item in a Sorted List

Suppose that we have a list that has been sorted with operator<. Suppose we need to search it for a value named target of type data. We may not be sure that target is present in the list at all. However, when we search sequentially from the beginning, we may stop searching when any of the following conditions is true.

(1) We reach the end of the list.
(2) We find the value we seek.
(3) We find a value bigger than the one we seek.

We can combine the last two conditions into one:

(2') We find a value not less than the one we seek.

Combining this with requirement (1), we get

```
List<data>:: iterator i = L.begin();
while( i != L.end() && *i < target) ++i;
```

Note that the order of the two conditions is important so that we don't move past the end of the list before checking to see if we have reached the end.

The find generic algorithm will search beyond the point at which the value would occur in a sorted list when it is not present and keep searching to the end of the list. However, algorithm find_if may be used in this case. This algorithm takes a predicate to determine when it should return a location.

```
bool notBigger(data v)
{   return ! (v < target);
}
...
List<data>::iterator i = find_if(L.begin(), L.end(),
notBigger);
```

Note that with both of these methods, we don't know at the end whether the value was found. We must do an additional check of iterator i. This is because both have a compound exit condition.

7.6.2 Inserting into a Sorted List

To insert a value into a sorted list without destroying the sort property, we first must move an iterator to the point of insertion and then use that iterator to insert. The methods of Section 7.6.1 leave us in an appropriate location for inserting the value target. This is because they leave us at the first location not less than the target, and insert inserts its parameter before the location of the iterator.

```
List<data>::iterator i = find_if(L.begin(), L.end(),
notBigger);
L.insert(i, target);
```

7.6.3   Applying an Arbitrary Function to Each Element of a List

Sometimes we need to apply some operation to each element of a list or other structure. If this is just a data-gathering operation (summing the elements, for example), then it can be applied to a list of const values using a const iterator. It might also be a data-modifying operation, however, in which case a normal iterator is used. If we are applying only data-gathering operations (const operations), then we may use algorithm for_each. This algorithm applies a function of one parameter to each of the elements of a range. If the function returns a value when called, these values are ignored. How does such a function do any work, then, if it is const and returns no usable value? The answer depends on nested scopes and global variables. For example, we can sum the elements of an array of float values with the following:

```
float total = 0.0;
void addNext(float v)
{   total += v;
}
...
for_each (L.begin(), L.end(), addNext);
```

In fact, for_each returns the function object that it was passed, though this value is often ignored, as here. This object can, of course, have member variables that were modified each time the object was called "as a function." These variables can collect information for us.

The for_each algorithm cannot be used to modify the contents of the list, but if the list contains values that are themselves mutable (as floats are not), then we could apply a function to each of them that would perhaps modify the state of the values stored. For example, if we had a list LS of Stacks and wanted to push the same value on each of the stacks in our list, we could use for_each with the following function:

```
void pushNext(Stack& S)
{   S.push(value);
}
```

Note that we only get to pass one parameter to the function for_each, so the value to be pushed on each stack must be a global value. Note that

```
for_each (LS.begin(), LS.end(), pushNext);
```

leaves us with a list of the same stacks, but each of those stacks has been modified. The reference parameter of pushNext is required so that we push onto the actual stacks in the list and not onto copies passed by value to pushNext.

For each does not depend on lists. It is defined in terms of input iterators, which makes it very general.

7.6.4 Splicing Lists

Splicing is an operation that is unique to lists and other linked structures. Instead of copying values from nodes or other similar cells, it is possible to relink the nodes themselves, first unpinning a node from its location in a list and then linking it into some other position in the same or another list. The list template has three member functions that accomplish this task. The first unlinks all of the nodes of one list as a unit and links them into the current list at the location of an iterator. Here, "at the location of an iterator" means just before the value that the iterator references. This can involve thousands of nodes, but takes constant time. Just the time to adjust a few pointers. It leaves the other list empty, however, and any iterators into that list will now refer to nodes of the current list.

```
void splice(iterator position, list<T>& x);
```

The second version unlinks a single value (node actually) from an iterator position i in a list x and relinks it into an iterator location named position in the current list.

```
void splice
(  iterator position,
   list<T>& x,
   iterator i
);
```

The last version unlinks a range from a given list back into a given position in the current list.

```
void splice
(  iterator position,
   list<T>& x,
   iterator first,
   iterator last
);
```

Splicing is especially useful when very large data values are stored in list nodes. We can move them around without the overhead of actually copying the values. Splicing also has the advantage that an iterator, which is logically a reference to a value, "moves" with the node automatically, leaving it a reference to the same value. When we move values between nodes, an iterator, being implemented as a pointer to a node, stays with the node and hence references a new value.

7.6.5 Merging Sorted Lists

The merge algorithm of the STL is defined in terms of input iterators, so is suitable for use with lists. It may be, however, that a splicing version is more appropriate in some situations. This would be the case if we didn't need the input ranges after the merge. We would also avoid allocator calls when splicing. As usual, splicing is especially useful when the values stored in the list are large and hence have a high copying cost. The STL provides this function as a member of the list template.

7.6.6 Reversing a List

The reverse algorithm can be used with lists, since it uses bidirectional iterators. The basic idea of reversing a range is to swap values at the extremes of a list (or other range) using two iterators, and then move both iterators toward the middle. The algorithm halts when they reach the middle. (Why?) A specialized version could be provided for lists that would avoid copying the elements. If the next and prev pointers in each node were switched, then the list would be reversed. This would also automatically reverse the direction of any iterators into the list.

For the "access" list implementation that we showed in Section 7.4, a list can be reversed simply by swapping the head and tail pointers in the list itself. This would have an unfortunate effect on iterators, however, as a bit of study will show.

7.6.7 Building a Spelling Dictionary

Suppose that we need to build a large sorted list of correctly spelled words for use as a spelling dictionary. The list needs to be sorted so that we can use binary search to find a given word in it quickly. Actually, there are other mechanisms as well that will provide quick lookups—hashing for example—but we focus on sorting here.

One way to build such a dictionary is to start with several large text files, such as on-line novels and technical reports and the like. We first read them into a sequential structure such as a list or a vector, with one word per location. Next we sort this list with an efficient algorithm. This might take a long time if there are a lot of words, as there should be. Next, we apply algorithm unique to the sorted structure, which removes all adjacent repeats of elements. This leaves us with exactly one copy of each word. If we do this separately with several files, we can merge them together with a specialized merge that doesn't create copies. (See algorithm set_union.)

Finally, we can write our sorted structure to a file for later use. When actually used as a spelling dictionary, it should not be stored in a list, however, as lookups would take too long. A sorted array or vector would be better, or a set, to be discussed in the next chapter. There are also specialized data structures that let us store such a word list efficiently. One such commonly used structure is called a trie (pronounced tree). Briefly, a trie is a tree in which each node has many children. The actual root of the tree is a dummy node, and its children hold the various possibilities for the first characters in the words of our word lists. For English, if we permit both capitalized and uncapitalized words, we need fifty-two children of the root. If any word begins "ab" (several do), then there is a b below the a node. If any word begins "abo" (several), then there is an o below the b node that is below the a node. Since "about" and "above" both occur in English, there is both a "v" and a "u" below our o node. When we traverse this tree, we get a correctly spelled word. When we reach a missing node, we complete a spelling. We will have more to say about trees in the next chapter.

7.6.8   A Merge Sort Suitable for Lists

The standard merge sort works by dividing a vector or array into two equal parts at the middle element. It then recursively sorts those two parts and then merges the sorted results into a sorted whole. When you think about what really happens in the recursion, however, you discover that since the division comes first in the original, it will come first in the recursions as well. This means that the algorithm works by first continually dividing and redividing, etc., until there is nothing left to divide (minilists of just one element, which are sorted of course), and then it starts to merge the little pieces together into sorted larger pieces. The important thing about the algorithm, however, is the merging, not where it gets the items to merge, or the order in which it does the many different merges that make up the whole.

Suppose that we start with an unsorted list. As an auxiliary storage structure we will use an array or a vector of lists. The lists in this array (say) are composed of nodes extracted from the list to be sorted by unsplicing them from the original and splicing them onto one of the lists of the array. When we unsplice a node from one list and splice it into another, we say we *transfer* the node. Initially this array is composed of empty lists, and in general each list in the array will be kept sorted.

We start the algorithm by transferring the first node of the original list into the first of the lists in the array. Next we take one node from the original list and merge it with the single element in the list in the array to get a two-element sorted work list. We install this work list as the second element of the array. We now repeat the above until we get a second two-element sorted list in the work list. We can now merge this with the other two-element list in the array to get a sorted four-element list that goes into the third slot in the array. Now we repeat all of the above until we obtain another four-element sorted list that we merge with the one we already have to get an eight-element list for the next slot of the array. This process continues until we empty the original array, though at the last stages we won't have work lists of the maximum length. This is no problem for merging, however. This entire process can be managed with a loop that on each pass creates a sorted list whose length is the next higher power of two by first creating one of the same length as the one on the previous pass and then merging with the one created on that pass.

Notice that we only need to move forward in each of the lists that we process, so this is easily done with only forward iterators or the equivalent. This technique can be used as the basis of the sort member of the list class.

7.7   Summary

Make certain that you understand each of the following terms:

circularly linked list
cursors
doubly linked list
iterator invalidation
nested classes
reverse iterators
splicing
xor

7.8   Exercises

1. Write a recursive member for CircleList that removes all elements between two iterators. The second iterator should be a past-the-end location for the range to be removed.

2. Notice that CircleList becomes more useful within the context of the STL if we rethink the idea of front and back. In particular, if we change the name of push_front to push_back, and front to back, we can use a CircleList with a Stack adaptor. Discuss this and implement it.

3. CircleList has a very serious flaw. What happens if we attempt the following?

```
CircleList<int> C;
C.push_front(5);
C.push_front(6);
C.insert(begin(), 7);
C.insert(end(), 8);
```

Analyze this problem and solve it.

4. Doubly link the CircleList class. Every node needs an additional pointer: previous, that points to the previous node. Change the Iterator class so that an iterator points to the node that contains the value it references. Note that this requires some changes to the Cir-

cleList members as well. Do we still need the isEnd field of Iterator? Be sure to do this exercise in a way that insertions and deletions don't invalidate other iterators, unless we delete a node that an iterator refers to.

5. Provide a bidirectional iterator for the doubly linked CircleList class of Exercise 4.

6. Build a safe version of your updated doubly linked circular list.

7. In Section 7.6.6, we mentioned a bad effect of reversing access lists by simply reversing their head and tail pointers. Carefully explain this problem.

8. Implement the merge sort algorithm discussed at the end of this chapter as a member function of the CircleList class discussed near the beginning.

9. Discuss the tradeoffs in space and time as well as the compromises in functionality of the different list implementations discussed in the text.

10. Should the STL have a singly linked list structure as well as list? Justify your answer.

11. What is the comparative cost of a free store allocation of a small block compared to a simple assignment statement? Devise an experiment to find out. Carry out the experiment and report on your results.

Chapter 8
Sets, Maps, Multisets, and MultiMaps

8.1. Sequential Versus Sorted Containers

In Chapter 2 and in 3 through 7, we studied container mechanisms in which there was a direct linear, or sequential, structure. Elements had a physical order. When we sort them we make their logical order conform in some way with the physical order. STL sorted containers are quite different. These containers are always kept logically sorted, so that if we write them out the values are reported in increasing order according to some rule. When we insert into a sorted container, it is placed somewhere internally consistent with that logical order. As we shall see, however, there is no necessary physical relationship between the logical position and its physical location. In fact, many different physical arrangements can be equivalent to the same logical one, since the physical structure is not sequential.

In some ways the term set for the STL template of that name is misleading, since STL sets require that the elements inserted obey a comparison relation. This relation is usually operator<, though we can substitute others. In mathematics we can have sets of things that can't be easily compared like this. Also, STL sets are always sorted, though order and sorting is not part of the mathematician's idea of set.

Otherwise the name is well chosen, since in a mathematical set, if we insert an item into it and it was already present, we don't change its state. This is true of STL sets also. In other words, a given value can only be present once in a set, if at all. Multisets, however, permit multiple inclusions of the same element. We can also perform set like operations on STL sets (and Maps, etc.). For example, set_union and set_intersection are STL algorithms, but they only work correctly if the containers that they operate on are sorted. Therefore, they work most naturally with structures such as sets and maps.

The four templates we discuss here are sets, multisets, maps, and multmaps. They are called sorted associative containers, though the word associative really only applies to maps and multimaps. Map and multimap containers are used to *associate* pairs of values together. Each pair consists of two parts, a key and a value. The keys must be comparable, and the containers are kept in key order. In a map, only one pair with a given key may be present at any time. With multimaps, a key may be present several times. Therefore a map is like a set of ordered pairs, with the first element (the key) being unique within the map. Mathematically this is called a *function*. Another name for a multimap is *relation*.

Sorted containers could be implemented many ways, of course, including with lists and vectors. We could even impose a set-like property on lists or vectors, but each of these structures has an important disadvantage. This is because to insert an item we need to know if it is present already. With a vector this can be easily determined using binary search. But then comes a difficulty, for which, lists would provide a better solution. Once we decide an item belongs (and we know where it belongs), we must make room for it somehow. In a vector we need to move other items, perhaps a lot of other items. With a list we can simply insert a new node at the desired location. So each of the existing structures has important advantages, but serious disadvantages for use as sorted containers. Therefore, we seek an alternate storage mechanism. It will take us around a bit of a diversion, but we shall get to this soon. Trees are what we need, but a certain kind of tree.

8.2   Binary Trees

Trees are linked structures like lists, but in a list a node is connected to at most two other nodes, while in a tree, a node can be connected to many other nodes. Mathematically a tree is a connected graph without cycles, meaning that there is exactly one path between any two vertices. Normally one vertex, or node, is singled out and called the root of the tree. Given a root, some nodes are connected to only a single other node. These are called leaves of the tree. All other nodes are called internal nodes. Of all the nodes connected to a given node (other than the root), one will be closer to the root than the others. The others are called the children of the given node. The one closer to the root is called the parent. The height of a node is the number of links from that node back to the root. The height of a tree is the maximum height of all of the nodes of the tree.

The simplest kind of tree is one in which each of the internal nodes are connected to three nodes, the parent and two children. These binary trees were discussed in Chapter 3. To implement binary trees, we need to implement the nodes and the links. The usual way is to implement the nodes with a class and the links with pointers. In Chapter 3 we provided only two pointers in each node: to the two (potential) children. This makes movement toward the root difficult and expensive, however, so we will provide a pointer to the parent node as well here. Therefore, a binary tree node is something like the following:

```
struct node
{   T _data;
    nodeptr _left;
    nodeptr _right;
    nodeptr _parent;
    node
    (   T data = T(),
        nodeptr parent = NULL,
        nodeptr left = NULL,
```

```
          nodeptr right = NULL
    )
    :   _left(left),
        _right(right),
        _parent(parent),
        _data(data)
    {
    }
};
```

Processes for manipulating these nodes are very similar to those for lists. It is just that there is about twice as much work. We also need to be careful that we don't try to make the same node the child of two others, because then we wouldn't have a tree anymore.

8.3   Binary Search Trees

A binary search tree is a binary tree, but it holds data that can be compared with something like operator<. The built-in types of C++ have such a comparison, though the comparison for strings (or any pointers) is quite meaningless. Therefore, the STL permits the user to define alternate comparison operations using function objects. A comparison object is either a binary function returning bool, or an object in a class that has such an operator() defined. For example, a comparison function to compare strings might be

```
class stringLess
{   bool operator(char* s1, char* s2)
    {   return strcmp(s1, s2) < 0);
    }
}
```

If we have two strings, a and b, and an object *compare* of type stringLess, then

```
compare(a, b)
```

returns true if string a comes before string b.

Given a type with a suitable comparison operation, a binary search tree keeps values of that type in a binary tree maintaining a certain "sort" property. In particular, for any given node storing a value v, all values that compare less than v will be in the left child subtree rooted at v's node and all values that compare greater than v will be to the right of that node. Those that are equivalent to v could be to the left or the right. We can quickly find a value if present in a binary search tree by starting at the root. If it is equal to the value we seek, we stop. If our value is smaller than the root, we search left, otherwise right. We can repeat the same process at each node, stopping when we find our target, or when we reach a missing node. It is here that we should insert the value if that is our goal.

An interesting feature of binary search trees is that if we list all of the elements by recursively listing all of the children to the left of a node before we list the value in that node, and all of the values in children to the right afterwards, then the values are listed in sorted order.

Another interesting feature of binary search trees is that they can provide very fast insertions and deletions of values. This is because a binary tree can hold a lot of nodes for a given height. If we only need to search a single path from root to leaf to insert or remove a value, then the time required can be logarithmically related to the number of nodes in the tree. This is because in a tree with all leaves at about the same height, up to about half of the nodes are in the leaves. So each time we increase the height by one, we double the potential number of nodes that the tree can hold. Given this potential high density of a binary tree, combined with the easy mechanism for finding a value or finding the place in which a new value could be put, we get very fast searches, inserts, and deletions.

8.4   Balanced Binary Search Trees

One potential problem with the above characterization of binary search trees is that "it ain't necessarily so." That is to say, binary search trees don't need to be *full*, or hold the maximum number of nodes for their height. In particular, we could think of a linked list as a binary search tree in which there are no left children and all "next nodes" represent right children. Here the height of the tree is the same as the length of the list, in which case searches take linear time, not logarithmic time. There is a huge difference between these for large values of n. For example, the log of one million (base 2) is about 20. This is quite a bit less than a million. Therefore, to achieve good running times for binary search trees, we must keep them balanced.

A balanced binary tree is one in which the leaf nearest to the root is not too much closer than the one farthest from the root. A good rule of thumb is that the farthest leaf should be no farther than twice the distance of the nearest leaf. This is reasonably easy to maintain by a variety of mechanisms while providing good performance. Keeping a tree full (where the farthest leaf is no more than one link farther than the nearest) is much harder to maintain as we insert and remove items, adding to the cost of doing so.

8.5   2-3-4 Trees

We digress for a moment and describe a slightly different kind of tree. See [6]. It is not a binary tree in that its nodes don't all have two children. In a *2-3-4 tree*, each node has either two or three or four children. It stores one less value than it has children, so a 4 node has 3 values stored in it. It is convenient to think of the values as being stored between the pointers that represent the children. The values in a node are stored in order. The values in a subtree stored below a node have values between the values that bracket that subtree's pointer. See, for example, the 3 node and its children shown in Figure 8.1.

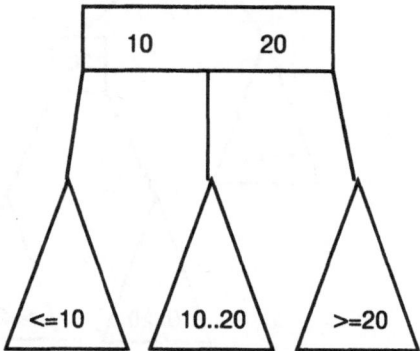

Figure 8.1. A 3 node with its subtrees.

It is possible to insert into a 2-3-4 tree keeping all of the leaves at exactly the same height. The tree only needs to be increased in height when all of its nodes are 4 nodes. For example, if the tree consists of a single 4 node it has height zero and stores three values. When we add the fourth value we can split the root node into a 2 node with one value and two children, a 2 node and a 3 node. This gives room for four values altogether. The height is one and all leaves are at height one.

The disadvantage of the 2-3-4 tree is the fact that the algorithms are all complicated by the several values stored in the nodes. It is much easier to maintain a binary tree with only one value in each node.

8.6   Red-Black Trees

A *red-black tree* can be thought of as a way to implement a 2-3-4 tree. A 2 node (binary node) in a 2-3-4 tree is, of course, the same as a binary tree node. A three node can be represented by two linked binary nodes as shown in Figure 8.2. Actually there are two different (symmetric) ways to represent this node.

To distinguish the "true root" of such a node (the node with the 10) from the node that implements the internal structure of the 2-3-4 node it represents, it is convenient to speak of the true root node as being black and the other as being red. Similarly, a 4 node in a 2-3-4 tree can be built from a black node and two red nodes. The resulting red-black tree is balanced in the sense defined above: no leaf is more than twice the height of any other. This can be seen from the observation that a red node always has black nodes both above and below it. And it comes from a completely balanced 2-3-4 tree.

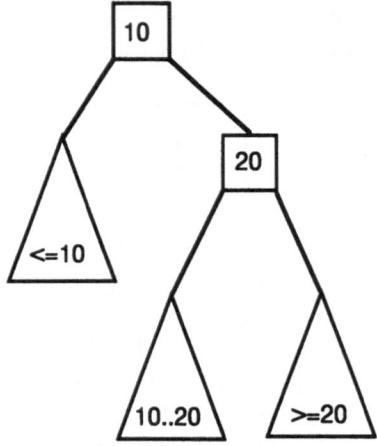

Figure 8.2. The 3 node of Figure 8.1 as two 2 nodes.

Figure 8.3 shows a red-black tree with twenty-two elements. The red nodes are marked with ovals. Figure 8.4 shows the equivalent 2-3-4 tree with the "colors" of the values preserved. This is not, of course, the only red-black tree that can hold these items. It depends on the order in which the items are inserted (55, 22, 33, 88, 11, 13, 42, 75, 8, 31, 17, 29, 34, 51, 93, 12, 9, 7, 63, 70, 15, 32). A different order would likely lead to a different tree.

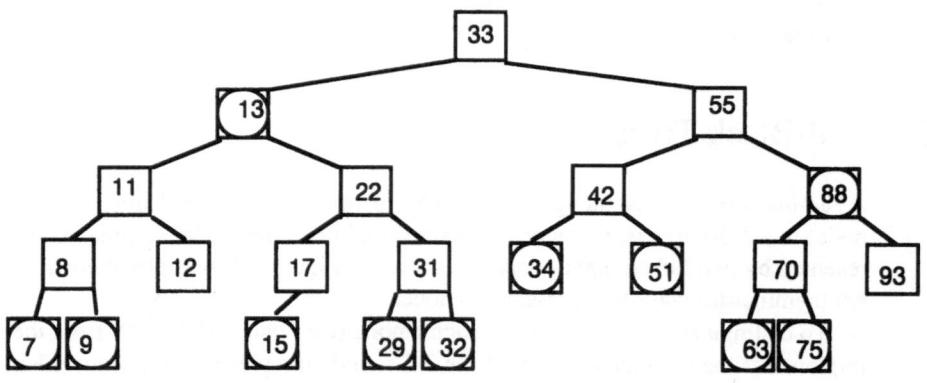

Figure 8.3. A red-black tree.

Note that the height of the red-black tree is four, while the leaf closest to the root has height three. In the 2-3-4 tree, however, all leaves are at height two.

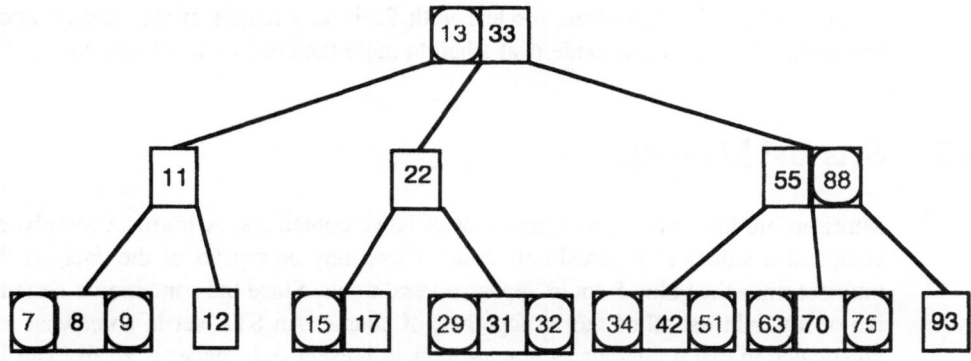

Figure 8.4. An equivalent 2-3-4 tree.

If we sort the input data before inserting it into the tree we get a dramatically different tree, as shown in Figure 8.5. As a red-black tree it has height six, though as a 2-3-4 tree the height is three. Note that the value 33 was the root of the first tree, but a leaf in this one.

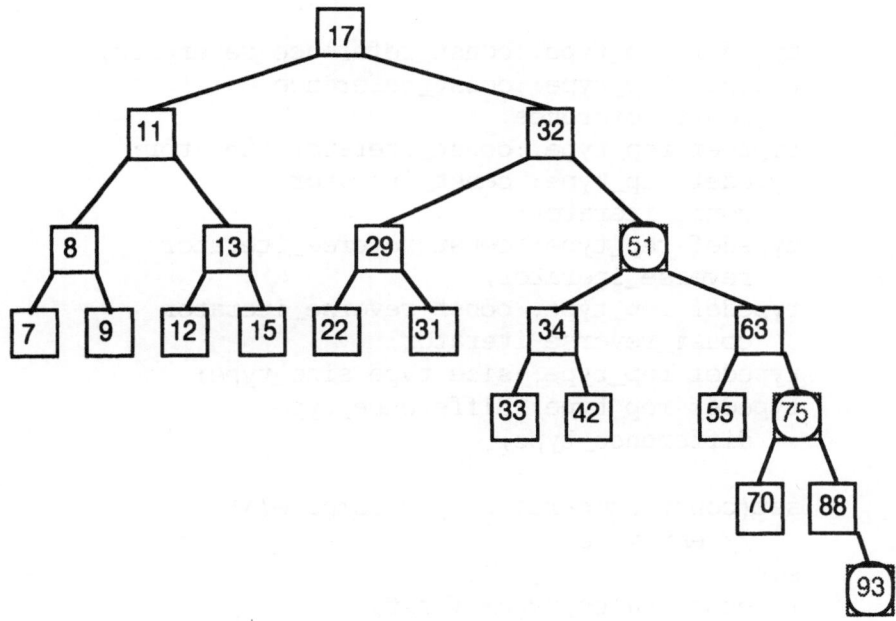

Figure 8.5. Another red-black tree with the same data.

Note that in this latter tree, the leaf with 93 is at a height of six, and no node has a height less than three. No node is at a height more than twice that of any other.

8.7   Sets and Multisets

Multisets are the simplest STL sorted associative containers. A multiset simply contains comparable values in a sorted collection. There may be repeats of the data, so that in a multiset<int> the value 5 could appear several times. Since the container is sorted, a listing of it would list all of the 5s together, of course. An STL set is somewhat more sophisticated in that it guarantees that an item is present only once, if at all. The interface of set and multiset is nearly identical, however. They support exactly the same operations. This interface is shown below.

```
template <class Key, class Compare>
class set
{ public:
    typedef Key key_type;
    typedef Key value_type;
    typedef Compare key_compare;
    typedef Compare value_compare;

    typedef rep_type::const_reference reference;
    typedef rep_type::const_reference
        const_reference;
    typedef rep_type::const_iterator iterator;
    typedef rep_type::const_iterator
        const_iterator;
    typedef rep_type::const_reverse_iterator
        reverse_iterator;
    typedef rep_type::const_reverse_iterator
        const_reverse_iterator;
    typedef rep_type::size_type size_type;
    typedef rep_type::difference_type
        difference_type;

    set(const Compare& comp = Compare());
        // empty set
    set
    (  const value_type* first,
       const value_type* last,
       const Compare& comp = Compare()
    ); // Create a set from an iterator range
    set(const set<Key, Compare>& x);
```

```
    set<Key, Compare>& operator=
    (   const set<Key,
        Compare>& x
    );

    key_compare key_comp() const;
        // returns the compare function
    value_compare value_comp() const;
        // returns the compare function
    iterator begin() const;
    iterator end() const;
    reverse_iterator rbegin() const;
    reverse_iterator rend() const;
    bool empty() const;
    size_type size() const;
    size_type max_size() const;
    void swap(set<Key, Compare>& x);
        // Swap contents of 2 sets.

    pair<iterator, bool> insert
    (   const value_type& x
    );
    iterator insert
    (   iterator position,
        const value_type& x
    );
    void insert
    (   const value_type* first,
        const value_type* last
    );
    void erase(iterator position);
    size_type erase(const key_type& x);
        // Returns number of elements erased.
    void erase(iterator first, iterator last);

    // set operations:
    iterator find(const key_type& x) const;
    size_type count(const key_type& x) const;
    iterator lower_bound(const key_type& x)
        const;
    iterator upper_bound(const key_type& x) const;

    pair<iterator, iterator> equal_range
    (   const key_type& x
    ) const;
};
```

Sets and multisets are one area in which the C++ standard is ahead of the state of C++ compilers (in early 1997). The actual standard for STL sets has a default value for the Compare template parameter (as well as for an allocator):

```
template < class Key,
           class Compare = less<Key>,
           class Allocator = allocator
       >
class set
{...
}
```

This means that the user does not need to specify the Compare function (or function object) if the standard less (which uses operator<) is the desired comparison. Most current compilers, however require the user to give the argument, so that to create a set you write something like

```
set< int, less<int> > tokens;
```

The Compare argument is only used as the default, however, and you can create a set using a different comparison by specifying it in the constructor. Note that the Allocator argument specified in the standard doesn't need to be given currently, as compiler writers assume a default allocator and don't give the user much opportunity to substitute another one currently. This will change as compilers are updated to accept default template parameters.

As usual, set exports several types. The most important one is value_type, which gives the type of values that may be inserted. It is the same as the Key type provided as the template parameter. The key_type and the value_type are the same for sets and multisets. We will see that they can be different when we examine maps and multimaps shortly.

Sets provide bidirectional iterators, so a number of the algorithms that require random access iterators can't be used. For this reason, some of those algorithms have specific analogs here. In particular, the set operations, find, lower_bound, upper_bound, and equal_range provide the functionality of the binary search algorithms provided elsewhere. Those generic algorithms require sorted ranges (which sets are) specified by random access iterators (which sets do not provide). As we have seen, the tree implementation of sets provides efficient search mechanisms, just as does binary search.

Note, however, that sets (and multisets) only provide const iterators. You can't use an iterator over a set to change a value in the set. This is because the only values are the keys themselves. To change the key requires repositioning the item. This is not a problem for maps and multimaps, since we store pairs in which the key is itself a const value. An iterator can be used there to modify the data part.

A few of the above function prototypes might not be obvious. One surprising member of the set interface is the insert function, since it returns a pair of an iterator and a bool. When we go to insert an item into a set, it might already be present. If it is not present, the insert function returns an iterator to the point of insertion and true for the bool. If it was already in the set, then we do not insert the new copy, but return an iterator to the original value and false for the bool. Since the equivalent multiset operation always inserts, it returns only the iterator to the newly inserted element.

One other insert member might be puzzling:

```
iterator insert
(   iterator position,
    const value_type& x
);
```

This function uses the position argument as a hint as to where to start looking for the proper location of the value. If the hint is accurate (namely an ancestor of the proper location), then the insert will be sped up.

The erase (value) member erases all copies of the value, which for a set is at most one. For a multiset, however, it might erase several elements. It returns the number deleted. We need to be careful in the interpretation of what is erased by this function. The algorithm does not use operator== to check for a match between the parameter and the item stored. Instead, it uses the comparison operator to look for equivalent values. Values are equivalent if the comparison operator applied in both directions returns false: i.e., !compare(a,b) && !compare(b,a).

Knowing that the implementation is a balanced binary tree, we can deduce the running time of most of the set/multiset operations. Insertion takes lg(N) time per item inserted, where N is the current size.

If we erase an item "by value," the time is logarithmic, but if we do so "by position," it is amortized constant. This is because we can avoid the search for the item initially. It is not actually constant, since the tree needs to be rebalanced after a deletion and that can take time, but as we are balancing a subtree, and the overall tree is growing smaller as we delete, the time averages out to a constant. The set operations are all logarithmic in running time.

One use of sets is in analyzing the variables in mathematical formulas or programming constructs. Consider the following fragment:

```
int x = 0;
while(x < 10)
    y = y + x;
```

Here we see a simple programming fragment that uses two variables. The usage of the two variables is somewhat different, however, since x is defined within the fragment itself, and y is not. We say that x has one definitional occurrence and two applied occurrences, while y has only two applied occurrences. We also say that the applied occurrences of x are *bound to the definitional occurrence*, since that definition determines what variable is used when the name x is used. We also say that the two occurrences of y are *free*, meaning not bound to any definition within this fragment.

Compilers and other language processors often need to know which variables are free and which are bound in a fragment of code such as a function body. One way to do this is using sets. When we see a definition of a variable we insert it into a set of *bindings*. When we see an applied occurrence, we check to see if that name is currently bound by examining the binding set. If so, we insert an item into the bound occurrence set, otherwise into the free occurrence set. If we come to the end of the scope of a definition (end of a function body, for example), we can remove the variables defined in that definition from the bindings set.

8.8   Maps and Multimaps

Maps and multimaps are similar to sets and multisets in that they keep a collection in sorted order using a binary tree structure as implementation. The interfaces are quite similar also. The big difference, however, is that maps and multimaps store pairs of values rather than just values. These pairs are special also. The first component of the pair is called its *key* and the second component is the *data*. The data can have any type whatever, but the keys need to define a compare operation. Maps and multimaps are ordered by key. A map or a multimap is just a simple database in which we want to store information distinguished by some characteristic called the key.

A phone book is such a database (like a multimap) in which the keys are the names of individuals or businesses and the phone numbers and other information are the data. A dictionary is another example of a sorted container of key-data pairs.

The pairs that are stored in maps and multimaps are sometimes called associations. It is from this that the terminology *sorted associative containers* for sets, multisets, maps, and multimaps arises. The reason that both key_type and value_type are exported from sets and multisets, when a single type would do, is to keep the interfaces between these classes as close as possible to each other. In maps and multimaps, the value_type is the pair type consisting of the key and data types.

When we create a map or multimap, we need to supply both key and data types as well as a compare operation on keys. For example,

```
map< int, char*, less<int> > errorDB;
```

defines a map with integer keys and string data using the standard operator< for its key comparison. One use of this structure might be to keep error numbers and the associated error messages together in a large program that wanted to do meaningful error reporting to its users. The program could generate error numbers and the map could be used to generate messages to the user.

Maps permit only a single occurrence of a given key to be present, so that they are set-like. In particular, two pairs with the same key but different data cannot be simultaneously present in a map, though they can be in a multimap. If you try to insert a pair into a map and another pair with an equivalent key is already present, the insertion will not be done. Instead you will get back an <iterator, bool> pair pointing to the already present pair and the bool false. You can use the iterator to erase the existing element and then re-insert the original pair if desired.

A map has two compare functions. The first, and the one given when the map is created, is the key_compare function. The other is called value_compare and compares pairs by comparing the keys in the pairs. The data values are ignored during the comparisons.

Maps also implement operator[] with a key_type argument so that subscript notation may be used to access data values. This is most natural when the key_type is an integer type, but is useful in any case. This operator is not present in the multimap interface. Otherwise, the map and multimap interfaces are like the set and multiset interfaces.

There is nothing inherent in the notion of a map or set that requires order. A proposal has been made to the C++ standards committee to provide an alternate notion of sets, multisets, maps, and multimaps to permit hashed implementations as well as sorted implementations. The runtime characteristics would also be somewhat different, but would add to the usefulness of the library. Hewlett-Packard provides a sample implementation appropriate to this proposal, which we will examine in the next chapter.

For that matter, we have been describing balanced binary trees as THE implementation of sets, etc. That is not precisely accurate, as the standard does not mandate an implementation. What the standard does require is a certain runtime behavior and certain rules concerning under which circumstances an iterator may be invalidated. For example, with these four classes, iterators are only invalidated when they refer to an item being removed from a structure. This is unlike the vector rules that permit iterators to be invalidated by insertions as well as deletions of unrelated items. It turns out that balanced binary trees, of which red-black trees are an example, have all of the required characteristics for sets, etc.

8.9   An Implementation of Red-Black Trees

In this section we will look at an implementation of red-black trees that is somewhat simpler than that typically used in the STL sorted associative containers. We make the following simplifications. We will provide after-the-end locations for iterators, but not before-the-beginning. This will make reverse iterators impossible, so we will implement only forward iterators. We won't provide as many exported types or all of the functions, though many others could be easily implemented. We will assume that operator< will be used to compare items. Finally, we will provide a structure suitable for multisets and multimaps only, as we won't restrict inserts.

Note that the elements stored in our tree (type T in the following code) could either be simple values, hence implementing a multiset, or key-data pairs, giving us an implementation of multimap.

What follows is the basic structure, showing nested node and iterator classes as well as the implementing variables. We omit only the function bodies.

```
template <class T>
class RedBlackTree
{  protected:
      struct node;
      typedef node* nodeptr;
      static nodeptr Z;
          // used to terminate all chains

      struct node
      {  enum color{red, black, none};
         T _data;
         color _color;
         nodeptr _left;
         nodeptr _right;
         nodeptr _parent;
         node(T data = T(), color c = none);
      };

      nodeptr _root;
          // This node is a dummy "header."
          // The actual tree is to its right.
      nodeptr _trailer;
          // This node is the root of an empty
          // tree and is the right child of the
          // rightmost logical entry in other
          // trees. It represents a past-the-end
          // location.
      long  _nodeCount;

   public:
      typedef T value_type;
      typedef T* pointer;
      typedef T& reference;

      RedBlackTree();

      bool empty()const;

      class iterator
          // Bidirectional Preorder iterator.
          // Inorder would be far superior.
      {  public:
             iterator(RedBlackTree<T> & t);
             bool operator==
             (  const RedBlackTree<T>::
```

```
              iterator& i
            ) const;
            T& operator*();
            iterator& operator++();
            iterator& operator--();
        protected:
            nodeptr _here;
            RedBlackTree<T>& _tree;
            friend class RedBlackTree<T>;
    };

    iterator begin()const;

    iterator end()const;

protected:

    enum rotation{left, right};

    nodeptr rotate
    ( bool rightRotation,
      nodeptr where
    );
    // where is the point of rotation.
    // If rightRotation is true we will rotate
    // right, otherwise the rotation will be
    // left. We must always rotate to the
    // right of the _root, however.

    nodeptr split
    ( const T& val,
      nodeptr grand,
      nodeptr parent,
      nodeptr here
    ); // Split a 4-node into 2 2-nodes.

public:
    iterator insert(const T& t);
    // Returns an iterator to the inserted
    // item.

    iterator find(const T& t);
    // Return an iterator to t's location if
    // present. Returns a past-the-end
    // location otherwise.
```

```
            iterator findNext(iterator from);
            // finds the next occurrence of *from or
            // returns end()

            void erase(iterator where);
            // Erase the item pointed to by where.
            // Works by finding a node near a leaf to
            // swap with the node at where. It then
            // removes this node and rebalances the
            // tree by working upwards from that leaf.

        friend class RedBlackTree<T>::iterator;
        friend class RedBlackTree<T>::node;
};
```

When we create a tree we give it two special nodes that do not contain tree data. The first is the _root node that serves as a physical root of the tree. The topmost (root) logical node in the tree will be the right child of _root. The second node is _trailer and represents a past-the-end value for this tree. It is always the leaf node farthest to the right in the tree and so is initially the right child of _root. There is another node Z that is used to terminate all node pointer chains. In other words, we don't use NULL to represent a missing value in the tree but a pointer to node Z. Z's left and right child pointers are Z itself. Note that there is only one node Z, even though we may have several trees. Using Z rather than NULL makes certain tests easier within the algorithms.

The nodes have _left, _right and _parent pointers as we saw at the beginning of this chapter. They also have a color field, with the color being defined in an enumeration that is also nested within the RedBlackTree::node class definition. We provide color none for the trailer nodes and the Z node. Note that the node class is protected, making it available within subclasses of RedBlackTree, but not to ordinary clients. The RedBlackTree::iterator class, by contrast, is public. We create a new node by setting its pointers all to Z.

```
            node(T data = T(), color c = none)
            :   _color(c),
                _left(Z),
                _right(Z),
                _parent(Z),
                _data(data)
            {
            }
```

The node Z presents special problems, since it must be created and initialized before the first tree is created. The declaration (nested) above is not sufficient, since it is declared static. We must also provide two additional fragments. The first is a definition of the node, which is done outside of the class definition.

```
template <class T>
RedBlackTree<T>::nodeptr RedBlackTree<T>::Z = NULL;
```

This defines storage for the node pointer and sets it to be null. We must also define the node itself and initialize it. This is handled by the RedBlackTree constructor, which tests to see if Z is NULL. The code here is a bit awkward. We initialize the fields of the new tree in the usual way, creating new nodes for the _root and _trailer. If Z is still NULL, however, the constructions of these two nodes will be incorrect since their creation refers to Z explicitly. Therefore, if we find Z NULL, we must redo part of that construction.

```
RedBlackTree()
:   _nodeCount(0),
    _root(new node()),
    _trailer(new node())
{   if(Z == NULL)
    {   Z = new node();
        Z->_left = Z;
        Z->_right = Z;
        Z->_parent = Z;
        _root->_left = Z;
        _root->_parent = Z;
        _trailer->_left = Z;
        _trailer->_right = Z;
    }
    _root->_right = _trailer;
    _trailer->_parent = _root;
}
```

Therefore, an empty RedBlackTree looks like the structure in Figure 8.6. Note that the Z node, while it has a _parent pointer, does not point back to the parent since there is actually only one Z node in the whole system.

Recall that an invariant of a red-black tree is that a red node has black nodes both above and below it. This is essential in understanding the correctness of the following. A black node with both of its children red is a 4 node in the equivalent 2-3-4 tree and a black node with exactly one red child represents a 3 node. The work involved in keeping the tree balanced when we insert and delete is carried by two auxiliary routines, rotate and split. The latter splits a 4 node into two equivalent 2 nodes without changing the balance. Operation rotate transforms a left or right 3 node into the opposite, shortening one path and lengthening the other.

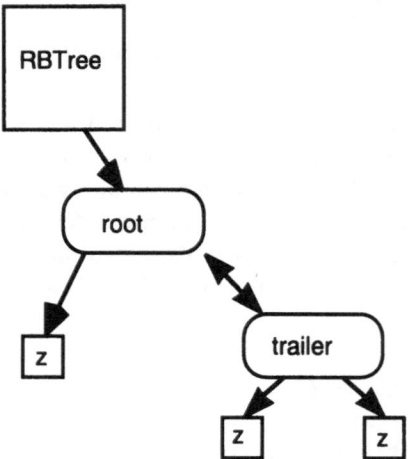

Figure 8.6. An empty RedBlackTree.

Rotation can be done either to the left or the right. In Figure 8.7 we show a left rotation. A right rotation would transform in the other direction. Notice that the C node gets *promoted* while the A node gets *demoted*. Likewise, E moves up and B moves down as do any nodes below B. D stays at the same level, but changes its parent from C to A. This, then, has the effect of lengthening some paths and shortening others. We haven't shown color here, since rotate is used in various contexts and the colors are adjusted elsewhere. A rotation one direction about a node, followed by a rotation in the opposite direction about its parent, is called a double rotation. A double rotation is shown in Figure 8.8 and Figure 8.9. Note that node D stays at the same height, nodes F and G rise one level and Node C moves down one level. The nodes below these move accordingly.

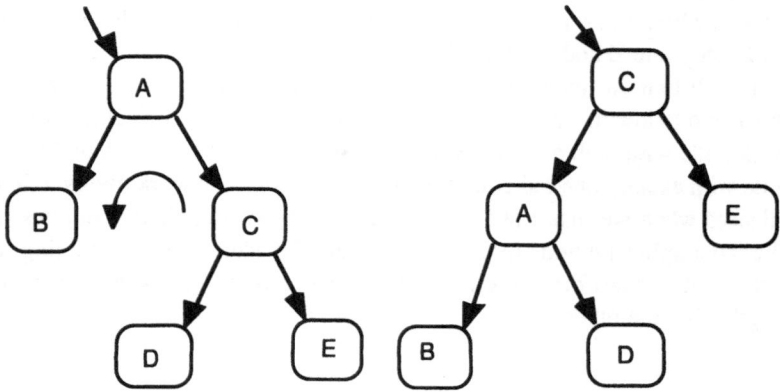

Figure 8.7. The effect of a left rotation.

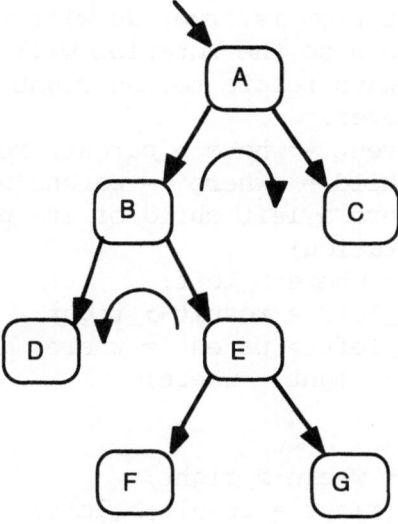

Figure 8.8. Before a double rotation (left about B, then right about A).

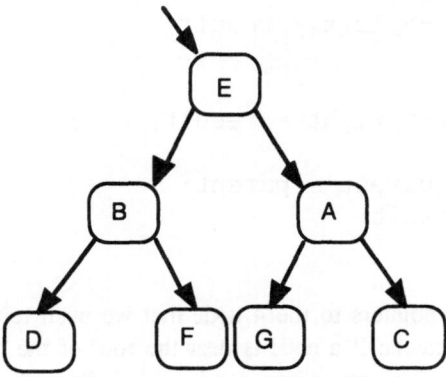

Figure 8.9. After a double rotation.

The rotate function returns the new root of the tree fragment. It also pins this new fragment properly into the tree.

```
nodeptr rotate
( bool rightRotation,
   nodeptr where
)
```

```
// where is the point of rotation.
// If rightRotation is true, we will rotate
// right, otherwise the rotation will be left.
// We must always rotate to the right of the
// _root, however.
{   nodeptr parent = where->_parent, result;
    bool leftChild = (where == parent->_left);
        // Is here a left child of its parent?
    if(rightRotation)
    {   result = where->_left;
        where->_left = result->_right;
        where->_left->_parent = where;
        result->_right = where;
    }
    else
    {   result = where->_right;
        where->_right = result->_left;
        where->_right->_parent = where;
        result->_left = where;
    }
    where->_parent = result;
    if(leftChild)
    {   parent->_left = result;
    }
    else
    {   parent->_right = result;
    }
    result->_parent = parent;
    return result;
}
```

Split requires pointers to the 4 node that we wish to split as well as pointers to its parent and grandparent. If a node is near the root of the tree the parent and grandparent could be the same. This procedure is only called after we verify that the node is indeed a 4 node. Note that it may do a double rotation (about parent then about grand) or only a single rotation. The first parameter passed in (val) is a data value that is used to determine if the double rotation needs to be done. Split is used only in insert and the val passed is the value being inserted. We need a double rotation if the values in the parent and grandparent nodes are on opposite sides of val with one larger and the other smaller than val.

While we could technically turn a 4 node into two 2 nodes simply by recoloring the two red nodes, this would lengthen paths on the equivalent 2-3-4 tree, unbalancing it. We need to avoid this unbalancing. The node at which we split is necessarily originally black. We want to make the split node red so as not to lengthen a path in the equivalent 2-3-4 tree. There are actually a number of cases that can all be handled by proper use of Boolean values. The hardest case is when the parent of the split node is red. We must then make further adjustments. If the parent were black then just coloring is enough, but not if it is already red. If so, we do a single or double rotation to readjust the local height of the tree and fix the colors.

```
nodeptr split
(   const T& val,
    nodeptr grand,
    nodeptr parent,
    nodeptr here
)
// Split a 4-node into 2 2-nodes.
{   here->_color = node::red; // it was black
    here->_left->_color = node::black;
    here->_right->_color = node::black;
    if(parent->_color == node::red)
        // then the grandparent must be black
    {   grand->_color = node::red;
        if (   (val < grand->_data)
               != (val < parent->_data)
            ) // double
            parent = rotate
                    ( val < parent->_data, parent);
        here = rotate(val < grand->_data, grand);
        here->_color = node::black;
    }
    _root->_right->_color = node::black;
    return here;
}
```

Note that the logical root of the tree is _root->_right and it never needs to be red. The last statement of split before the return guarantees that we don't leave it red with the other changes. Split is used in insert as we search down the tree for the location in which to insert the new element. We split any 4 node that we encounter along the way. It also shortens the path along which we search because we are about to lengthen that path by inserting the new element at a leaf along that path.

Insert works by starting at the root of the tree, and moving left or right at each node depending on the value there and the value to be inserted until we reach a leaf. As we search, we split any 4 nodes that we find, biasing the rotations so as not to lengthen the path on which the new item will lie. The reason we want to break up four nodes is that we can't insert into them. That is to say, if we were working in 2-3-4 tree and wanted to insert into a 2 node or a 3 node, all we would need to do is promote it to a larger node and insert into the result with no change in tree heights or balance. We can't do that with 4 nodes so we try to eliminate them.

We will also return an iterator to the location of the insert. In the STL version, though not in this one, the returned iterator can be used as the hint for further inserts. If the tree is empty, it is, of course, easier to do the insertion.

```
iterator insert(const T& t)
// Returns an iterator to the inserted item.
{   _nodeCount++;
    iterator result(*this);
    if(empty())
    {   nodeptr newRoot = new node
                        (t, node::black);
        newRoot->_right = _trailer;
        _trailer->_parent = newRoot;
        _root->_right = newRoot;
        newRoot->_parent = _root;
        result._here = newRoot;
    }
    else
    {   nodeptr grand = _root;
        parent = _root;
        here = _root;
        do
        {   grand = parent; parent = here;
            if( here != _root && t < here->_data)
                here = here->_left;
            else here = here->_right;
            // Split any 4-nodes you encounter
            if (   here->_left->_color == node::red
                    &&
                    here->_right->_color == node::red
                )
                here = split
                        (t, grand, parent, here);
        } while(here != _trailer && here != Z);
        nodeptr temp = here;
        here = new node(t,node::black);
        here->_right = temp;
            // Preserve the trailer.
        if(temp == _trailer)
            _trailer->_parent = here;
        here->_parent = parent;
        if(t < parent->_data)
            parent->_left = here;
        else
            parent->_right = here;
```

```
      result._here = here;
      here = split(t, grand, parent, here);
   }
   return result;
}
```

As we search for the insert point we keep track of the grandparent and parent nodes of the current search point. This aids in the splits that we will do. The final split treats the newly inserted value as if it were the middle value in a 4 node and splits that node also.

The erase operation is much harder than insert. We will only outline it here. The only version of erase that we consider is one that is passed an iterator to the point at which we want to remove a value. If we don't have such an iterator we can use find to obtain one. The difficulties arise because the erase location need not be a leaf. We search the tree from the erase point for a suitable value to replace the one we are removing. This can be the largest value to the left of the value being removed, or the smallest value to the right. A moment's reflection shows that either of these could occupy the location of the item being removed without destroying the binary search tree property. Once we find this node we will unpin it from its current (leaf) location and repin it at the erase point. This leaves any iterators to it intact. We can then delete the leaf node, but we must also rebalance the tree. This is the hard part.

Rebalancing works by starting at the leaf location that was deleted and moving upwards, attempting to lengthen the path on which we search without shortening other paths. This can be done in some cases by rotations. When we can do this we quit. If we work all the way back to the root without doing so, then we must shorten all paths in the tree to account for the one shortened path on which the deleted item was originally found. The details are very tedious.

The find operation looks for a value and returns one equal to it. In the STL version we would not use operator== to determine when we had found a match, but rather the induced equivalence relation defined by the comparison operation. In either case we search from the root, moving left or right as determined by the values that we find. If we do not find the item desired, then we return a past-the-end iterator, namely an iterator to the trailer. Note that we may safely ignore the color of the nodes when searching, so that the added structure of a red-black tree does not slow lookups. This is an important advantage of the technique.

```
iterator find(const T& t)const
// Return an iterator to t's location if
// present.
// Returns a past-the-end location otherwise.
{  iterator result(*this);
   nodeptr here = _root->_right;
   while(here != Z && here->_data != t)
      if(here->_data < t)
         here = here->_right;
      else
```

```
            here = here->_left;
    if(here == Z) here = _trailer;
    result._here = here;
    return result;
}
```

Operation findNext searches from an iterator for the next item that has the same value as that at the iterator location. Note that this search may proceed upwards or downwards in the tree. The iterator does all of the work in its operator++, as we shall see.

```
iterator findNext(iterator from)
// finds the next occurrence of *from or
// returns end()
{   iterator result = from;
    iterator top = find(*from);
    // top is the topmost occurrence of the
    // desired value. If we reach it we have
    // returned all of the values.
    do
    {   ++result;
    } while (   result._here != _trailer
             && result != top
             && *result != *from
           );
    if(result == top) result._here = _trailer;
    return result;
}
```

The nested iterator class has interface, as shown above and repeated here, along with the simpler operations. It uses the preorder protocol to move over the elements using operator++. This is far from ideal, since an inorder protocol would actually list the elements in their natural order. An exercise will correct this situation.

```
        class iterator
        // Bidirectional Preorder iterator.
        // Inorder would be far superior.
        {   public:
                iterator(RedBlackTree<T> & t)
                :  _here(t._root->_right),
                   _tree(t)
                {  }
                bool operator==
                (   const RedBlackTree<T>::
                        iterator& i
                ) const
```

```
            { return _here == i._here; }
            T& operator*(){return _here->_data;}
            iterator& operator++();
            iterator& operator--();
        protected:
            nodeptr _here;
            RedBlackTree<T>& _tree;
            friend class RedBlackTree<T>;
    };
```

An iterator is implemented using a node pointer to mark the current location and also a reference to the tree over which it iterates. The reference to the tree helps us to know the root and trailer of that tree when we arrive at them.

Operator++ needs to move to the next preorder node from its current position. If we are currently at the trailer there is nowhere to move to. Otherwise if there is a left node (not Z), then we need to move there. If there is no left node but there is a right one, then that is our final position. Finally, if we are at a leaf, then we must search upwards until we have a node to the right that we haven't visited yet. This means that the first time that we move upward from a left child to its parent and that parent has a right child, that the right child is the next node. The implementation of operator-- is similar.

```
iterator& operator++()
{   if( _here == _tree._trailer){return *this;}
    if( _here->_left != Z)
        _here = _here->_left;
    else if(_here->_right != Z)
        _here = _here->_right;
    else
    {   nodeptr old;
        do
        {   old = _here;
            _here = _here->_parent;
        } while (  _here->_right == Z
                    || _here->_right == old
                );
        _here = _here->_right;
    }
    return *this;
}
```

8.10 Summary

Make certain that you understand each of the following terms:

balanced binary tree
binary search tree
binary tree
logarithmic running time
red-black tree
2-3-4 tree

8.11 Exercises

1. Build an inorder iterator for the RedBlackTree class discussed in the text.

2. Modify RedBlackTree to make it more suitable for implementing sets. When you create a RedBlackTree, pass a parameter that indicates whether inserts should always be done, or only when the item to be inserted is not already present.

3. Predict what will happen if we add value 100 to the tree in Figure 8.5.

4. Modify the RedBlackTree class so that it uses a comparison operator in place of operator<. The comparison operator should be a template parameter.

5. Investigate AVL trees in the literature. Other data structures and algorithms text books may be helpful. What is available on the World Wide Web?

6. Investigate the structure called the B-Tree. These are used extensively in databases to store large files. How are these related to 2-3-4 trees?

7. Build a node class suitable for implementing 2-3-4 trees.

8. Write a program to produce figures like Figure 8.5.

9. Give RedBlackTree a const reference type and a const iterator type.

10. Give RedBlackTree a way to return the size of the tree. The size is the number of elements stored.

11. Give RedBlackTree a member that will erase all copies of a given element and return the number of items erased.

12. Using the RedBlackTree as the implementation, build the template Multiset with the following interface:

```
template <class Key, class Compare>
class Multiset
{ private
    typedef RedBlackTree<Key, Compare> rep_type;
 public:
// typedefs:
    typedef Key key_type;
    typedef Key value_type;
    typedef Compare key_compare;
    typedef Compare value_compare;
    typedef rep_type::const_reference reference;
    typedef rep_type::const_iterator iterator;

// allocation/deallocation
    Multiset () {}
    Multiset
    (  const value_type* first,
       const value_type* last
    ) {}
    Multiset (const Multiset <Key, Compare>& x){}
    Multiset <Key, Compare>& operator=
    (  const Multiset <Key, Compare>& x
    ) {}

// accessors:
    key_compare key_comp() const {}
    value_compare value_comp() const {}
    iterator begin() const {}
    iterator end() const {}
    bool empty() const {}
    long size() const {}

// insert/erase
    iterator insert(const value_type& x) {}
    iterator insert
    (  iterator position,
       const value_type& x
    ) {}
    void insert
    (  const value_type* first,
       const value_type* last
    ) {}
```

```
        void erase(iterator position) {}
        long erase(const key_type& x) {}
        void erase(iterator first, iterator last) {}

// multiset operations:
        iterator find(const key_type& x) const {}
        size_type count(const key_type& x) const {}
        iterator lower_bound(const key_type& x) const{}
        iterator upper_bound(const key_type& x) const{}
};
```

13. In Chapter 5 we saw a DiGraph class built from STL vectors. It is also possible to build a digraph using a **map** from graph nodes to lists of graph nodes. Discuss and implement this idea.

14. In Chapter 5 we saw a DiGraph class built from STL vectors. It is also possible to build a digraph using a **multimap** from graph nodes to graph nodes. Discuss and implement this idea.

Chapter 9
Hash Tables

9.1. Hashed Associative Containers and the STL

The Standard Template Library does not currently have hashed data structures, though it might have in the future, as a proposal has been made to the standards committee to adopt them. This chapter is based on two separate implementations that have been suggested as the basis of further action by the committee. One of these is by Robert Fraley of Hewlett-Packard and the other is by Javier Barreirro and David Musser of Rensselaer Polytechnic Institute.

Hashing is an alternative means of providing for sets, multisets, maps, and multi-maps, though not sorted structures. Hashing attempts to provide an alternate mechanism by which items may be stored and quickly retrieved when there is no natural ordering possible on the elements. Elements to be placed in hashed containers have other requirements placed on them, however. The advantage of hashed structures over binary tree implementations is that some of the operations such as insert and find can be made to be constant time rather than logarithmic. Giving up the sorted order may be either an advantage or a disadvantage, depending on the anticipated use.

A hashed structure is one in which the physical placement of an item is somehow determined by the value to be inserted and in which that location can be determined by performing simple computations on the inserted value. An item is later found either by exhaustively searching for it, or by repeating the computation. This is most useful in the case of maps, where the computation is done on the key of the pair being inserted. The retrieval "by key" is then simply done by repeating the computation on the key whose data is desired. The elements of hashed storage were introduced in Chapter 3.

While hashed structures are not currently part of the standard, they are a mature extension of it that meshes well with the other elements. The four containers hash_set, hash_multiset, hash_map, and hash_multimap are similar to their tree-based counterparts except for the sort requirements and except for more stringent requirements on the efficiency of some operations. The hashed containers provide iterators, as we would suspect. The formal proposal only requires forward iterators, but it is not difficult to provide for bidirectional iterators, as was done in one of the two implementations here discussed. The cost is relatively small in both time and space. It is actually easier to provide bidirectional iterators because parts of the implementation can be built with vectors and lists, each of which provide (at least) bidirectional iterators.

An interface for an implementation of hash_set might have the following outline. (This would look slightly different if template member functions were implemented in the C++ compiler.)

```
template <class Key, class Hasher, class Equal>
class hash_set
{ public:
    typedef Key key_type;
    typedef Key value_type;
    typedef Hasher hasher;
    typedef KeyEqual key_equal;
    typedef ... size_type;
    typedef hash_set<Key, Hasher, Equal>
        self_type;

    typedef pointer;
    typedef reference;
    typedef const_reference;
    typedef difference_type;

// constructors/destructor
    hash_set
    (   size_type size=1009,
        const Hasher& hash = Hasher(),
        const Equal& comp = Equal(),
        auto_rehash_modes rm
            = auto_rehash_intermittent,
        size_type ts = 4,
        size_type grow_power = 3
    );
    hash_set
    (   const value_type* first,
        const value_type* last,
        size_type size,
        const Hasher& hash,
        const Equal& comp = Equal()
    );
  hash_set(const self_type & x);

  ~hash_set();

// Extraction
    const Key & extract_key
```

```
    (   const value_type & x
    ) const; // Simply returns its input.

// Assignment
    self_type & operator=(const self_type & x);
    void swap(self_type & xx);

// Insertion and deletion
    pair<iterator,bool> insert
    (   const value_type& x
    );
    void insert
    (   const value_type* first,
        const value_type* last
    );
    void erase(iterator position);
    size_type erase(const Key& x);
    void erase(iterator first, iterator last);

// Accessors
    key_equal          key_eq() const;
        // Get the equivalence op.
    hasher             hash_funct() const;
        // Get the hash function.
    iterator           begin();
        // Actually a const_iterator
    const_iterator     begin() const;
    iterator           end();
    const_iterator     end() const;
    reverse_iterator   rbegin();
    const_reverse_iterator   rbegin() const;
    reverse_iterator   rend();
    const_reverse_iterator   rend() const;
    bool               empty() const;
    size_type          size() const;
    size_type          max_size() const;

// Find operations:
    iterator find(const Key& x);
    const_iterator find(const Key& x) const;
    pair<iterator, iterator> equal_range
    (   const Key& x
    );
    pair<const_iterator, const_iterator>   equal_range
    (   const Key& x
    ) const;
```

```
// Hash specific operations
 Vector::size_type bucket_count() const;
 void resize (size_type new_size);

// Iterators -- bidirectional here, only Forward
// are required.
   class iterator;
      // bidirectional const_iterator
   typedef iterator const_iterator;
   class reverse_iterator;
   typedef reverse_iterator
      const_reverse_iterator;
};
```

The first template parameter is the kind of values to be inserted into the set. For hash_map and hash_multimap, we would need another parameter for the data type. The second parameter is a function object that defines a hash function on the Key type. A hash function must take as input a value of the key type and produce an unsigned long int as output. Moreover, the hash function should ideally *uniformly* *cover* the unsigned longs, which means that a given Key is as about as likely to be in any given range of unsigned longs as it is in any other range of the same length. The hash function must also be able to reproduce the value for a given Key when it is called again on that same key.

The third template parameter is a comparison object that determines when two values of the Key type can be considered equivalent. This is most important for sets and maps, where we insist that only one value of a given key be present. It is this function object Equal rather than operator== that determines equivalence. Note that the comparison operator behaves like an equality operator, not like the "less than" test that is used with sets and maps.

Given this comparison operator, we can also define the equal_range function to return a range of values that contains all stored keys equal to the parameter. This requires, however, that the hasher and the comparison operator have a very precise relationship to each other. It is necessary that the hash function return the same value for any values that the comparison operator determines are equal. Otherwise such equal values would be stored in different buckets, making equal_range impossible (or at least extremely expensive). For some sets of data this can be a very difficult requirement. If so, a binary tree-based class might be preferable.

Most of the member functions are familiar. Member extract_value is provided for consistency. In maps and multi_maps it returns a key for a given value, but here the key and value types are the same, so it just returns its input. The parameters of the constructors set various characteristics of the implementation as will be discussed below.

The iterators provided are all const_iterators. In particular, this means that operator* applied to an iterator returns a const reference to the value stored rather than a reference to it. In hash_sets and hash_multisets, changing the value (which is the key itself) would be disastrous, as the key determines the placement of the value within the structure. If it could be freely changed but remained in its old location, then the new value could not be found. In hash_map and hash_multimap, there are distinct iterators and const_iterators, since the iterator only gives access to the data part of the pair in those cases and the data in the pair can be freely modified. In fact, one of the main purposes of maps and multi-maps in general is to store such updatable values.

One final note about these structures. Suppose we have a hash_multiset that stores several values that are equivalent according to the Equal comparison type. Then an iterator will report these values consecutively. Likewise, equal_range will return a pair of iterators that bracket all of the values. This feature is not common in hash structures generally, which normally place no such requirements on retrieval order at all. In fact, the values with "equal" keys will be stored together. (Caveat. If your equal comparison isn't compatible with your hasher, it is possible that two values are "equal" but hash to different buckets. The above only applies to those values stored in the same hash bucket.)

9.2   Simple Hashing—Separate Chaining

In this and the next few sections we will examine some hash storage mechanisms in some detail. The first, separate chaining, is very common. The components consist of a hash function, the hasher that will produce integers in a given fixed range; an index structure such as an array or a vector; and a collection of buckets, each of which is a list or a vector. The most common implementation uses an array for the index and lists for the buckets. The data values are stored in the buckets. When we insert an item whose key is A, we first pass A through the hasher, resulting in an integer in the same range as the subscript range of the index. The item A then belongs in the bucket with that index. We then index into the index array to obtain a reference to the list onto which to insert the item A. Retrieval of A follows the same path. We pass A through the hasher, and use the result to index a list. We now know which list the item is on if present at all. We must then search that list for an item with key A. When found we may return an iterator to this location. See Figure 9.1. The name separate chaining arises from the notion of a linked list as a chain. The name is used even though the buckets might be implemented as vectors rather than lists.

An iterator into such a structure could be implemented as an index integer and a pointer to a list node. It would be advanced by moving down the current list to the end and then moving to the beginning of the next nonempty list. If we use vectors for the buckets then bidirectional iterators are easy to provide, but not random access iterators, since the sizes of the vectors are all different. Random access would therefore be too inefficient. Using STL lists for the buckets also permits bidirectional iterators. If we use singly linked lists, however, we can only provide forward iterators. There would be some space and time advantage in doing so, since the back pointers in the lists don't need to be saved or updated.

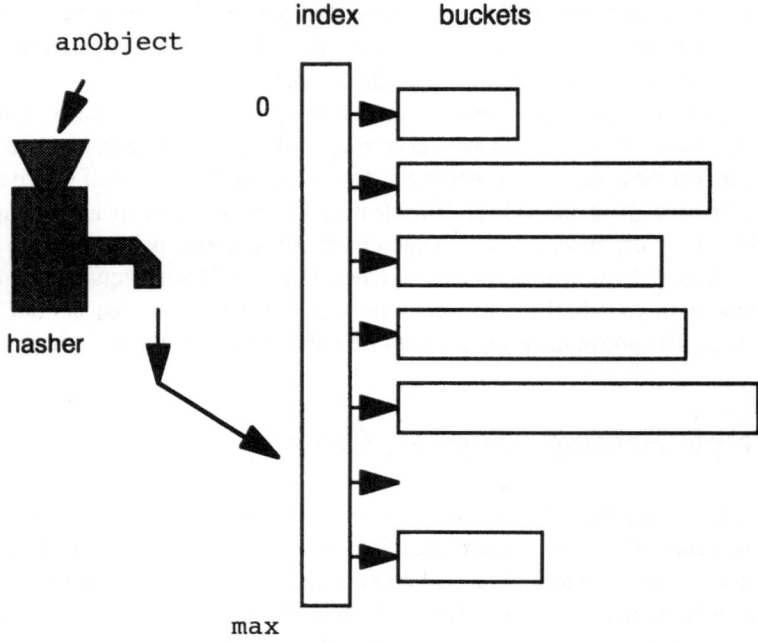

Figure 9.1. Separate chaining hashing.

The special requirements of the STL (proposal), namely making equivalent values, appear as if they are stored together, seems to imply that lists (or singly linked lists) should be used rather than vectors. This is because the easiest way to implement the requirement is to actually store such items together. This implies that an item when inserted won't always be inserted at the beginning (or end) of its bucket, but might need to be inserted in the middle. Lists would be better for this, of course. The after-the-end position of the last list is the after-the-end position of the entire hash structure.

9.3   Simple Hashing—Circular Hashing

Sometimes we want to store items in a hash structure and we know exactly what values will be stored, including, of course, the exact number of values to be stored. For example, in a compiler, we might need to store information about the keywords (reserved words) of the language being translated. Since these words form a fixed finite set of values, we can use them as keys into another kind of hash structure, one that uses circular hashing. In this method we avoid the buckets altogether. We have a hasher, of course, and a storage structure that can be an array or vector of values. The result of passing the key through the hasher is used as the index into the storage at which the associated item belongs. Recall that collisions may occur when we compute with the hash function. Collisions are caused when two distinct keys produce the same index value. If we can arrange a hasher that does not produce any collisions on the set of keys being stored (a perfect hash function), then no more needs to be done. Retrieval again uses the hasher to compute the index at which the item may be found. See Figure 9.2.

Iteration over such a structure can simply walk through the storage array or vector, taking account of the fact that some cells may be empty.

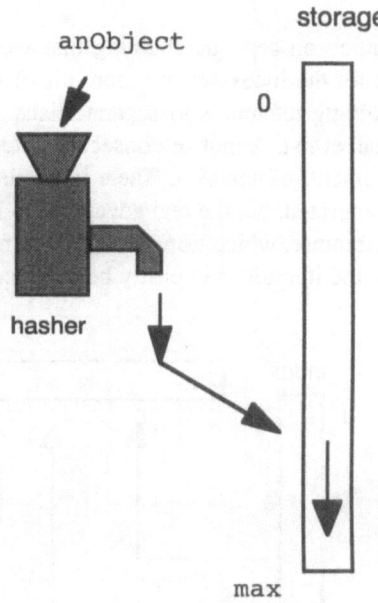

Figure 9.2. Circular Hashing

If collisions can occur, then we need to be a bit more sophisticated. If we hash a key to an index when inserting and find that the cell is already occupied, then we can simply begin a search from there for the next empty cell. If we come to the end of the structure, then we wrap around to the beginning and continue the search. Retrieval must then also follow the same path, starting at the value given by the hasher, searching circularly for the key. The search may terminate when we come to an empty cell or return to the item we started with.

The outline above fails, however, if items may also be deleted from the hash table. If an item between the hash index of a key and the cell it is actually stored in is removed, then the search will stop at the empty cell and report failure of the search even when the desired key is still present. This can be fixed by keeping two bits in each storage cell. The first tells whether the cell is currently filled or empty. The second tells whether the cell has ever been used. This second bit is originally off (false) for all cells, but is turned on when the cell is first filled. It is not turned off if the cell is later emptied. The search can then use this bit while searching, terminating when it comes to a cell that has never been used.

9.4   Variations on Simple Hashing

There is a simple variation on separate chaining that works well with the STL. In this method we use a vector for the index set but store all of the values in a single list. The index set, instead of holding references to separate lists, one per bucket, holds iterators into a single list: the bucket list. A pair of consecutive iterators in the index array form a range that defines the contents of a bucket. There is some space advantage in that only a single list needs to be generated, but the real advantage is in simplifying the operation of iterators into the hash structure, which now need only to move down a single list. Again, if it is an STL list, then the iterators can easily be bidirectional. See Figure 9.3.

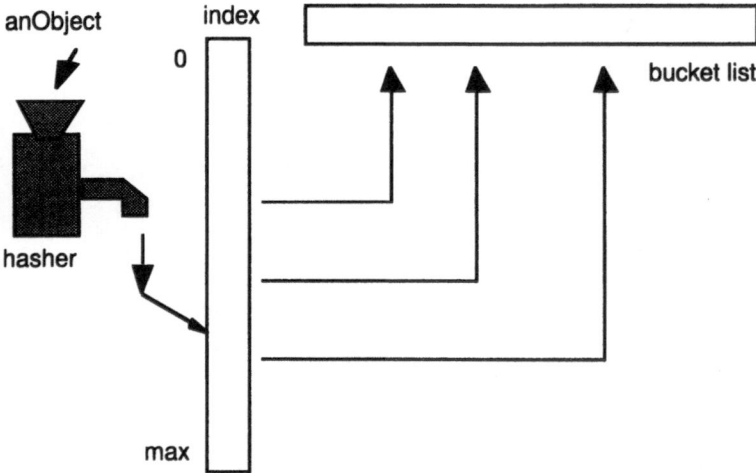

Figure 9.3. A variation on separate chaining.

A list is used rather than a vector, since we need to be able to keep equivalent items in a bucket together. Notice that during a retrieval the hasher yields us an iterator at which to begin the search. We only need to search a single bucket, however. We can either store a bucket number with the value to aid us with this, or we can just use the following iterator as a termination point. We could even use STL generic algorithms that search a range.

Achieving good performance in any of these structures depends fundamentally on keeping the buckets small. This is because we must linearly search a bucket (but only one) for an item. If our hash function is poor, we might have a lot of buckets, but all values concentrated in only a few. The storage would be much slower than expected. The worst case, of course, is when only one bucket is not empty. We must also tailor the number of buckets to the number of data items to be stored. Sometimes the number of values to be stored can be well determined in advance, in which case it is easy to choose a good number of buckets. The best situation is when each bucket contains exactly one item. This can only be achieved through marvelous good luck in general. However, if you know the keys in advance and there is a relatively small number of them, then it is possible to find a *minimal perfect* hash function. This is one that produces no collisions but also produces a minimal range of outputs so that if there are exactly n keys, then the hash function will produce exactly n values in the range 0...n-1. Finding such a function is computationally expensive, however. It would be worth doing so if the set of keys is stable and the program is to be used often.

9.5   Hash Functions

Obtaining good overall behavior from a hash table depends in important ways on the quality of the hash function that is used. A poor function guarantees poor performance. Most hash tables depend on the user supplying a hash function that produces integers or long integers. The system itself will then reduce the integer produced by the hasher to a suitable range for the index structure. Since this is usually done by remaindering, the hasher must provide good behavior relative to the remainder function.

When you spread butter on bread, you like to get uniform coverage, with no lumps or gaps. The same is true of a desirable hasher. You would like to take the values that will be inserted (the keys, actually) and spread them uniformly over the integers with no gaps. They don't need to satisfy any locality constraints with "similar" keys producing similar integers—quite the contrary—but they do need to cover the integers with no gaps and no "lumps." A lump would occur if more than an average number of keys mapped to the same integer. It is a bit more involved than that, even. Suppose more keys bunched up at multiples of 367, say, than at other integers. Suppose that we happened to have 367 cells in the index. Then remaindering by 367 would put more than an average number of keys in the same bucket, which would degrade performance.

Suppose that our keys are an integer type. Then we might be able to use the key itself as the value of the hasher, though this would depend on the actual integers used as keys in the values stored. If we store only keys with small integer values, then we will not get good coverage. For this reason, an integer key is often multiplied by a fairly large prime integer to get a hash value. A prime number is one with no integer factors other than itself and 1. If the integer chosen is large enough that multiplication often overflows the 16 or 32 bits used to store an int or long, all the better.

If the keys are floats, then there is a nice way to generate an integer, assuming that there is an integer type that requires the same number of bits as the floating type (float, or double) that we are using for keys. Consider the struct type

```
struct confuse
{   double real;
    unsigned long integer;
}
```

Then a hasher like

```
unsigned long hasher(double d)
{   confuse c;
    c.real = d;
    return c.integer;
}
```

will produce random seeming long values from doubles. This assumes that double and long require the same 32 bits, however.

Strings are more problematical. This is because strings usually hold words in human languages like English, which do not have uniform distributions of characters. For this reason the following is a poor hasher on strings.

```
unsigned long hasher(char * c)
{   unsigned long result = 0;
    for(int i = 0; i < strlen(c); ++i)
        result += *c++;
    return result;
}
```

This function has difficulties, since a string is more likely to be short than long, giving values more likely to be small than large, though this could be compensated for with a suitable multiplier, and because there are likely more vowels than consonants in the string c. A better one dips into the character encodings.

```
unsigned long hasher(char * c)
{   unsigned long result = 0;
    for(int i = 0; i < strlen(c); ++i)
    {   result += *c++;
        result <<= 1;
    }
    return result * bigPrime;
}
```

This function shifts the result left one bit for each character added. This is equivalent to multiplying by two each time, but has the effect that the order in which the characters appear also affects the result.

If the type of the key is a struct or class, then some suitable field (or fields) of it might be used to construct the hasher, provided that when that field changes we consider that we have a different key. Remember that the hasher must be functional so that if we give it the "same" key twice, we get the same integer back.

If the key is a pointer, then you must choose a field or fields of the value pointed to to construct a hasher. In some systems, the value (an address) of the pointer works for a hash value, but it is not often wise to depend on it. Some systems relocate objects in the free store, so that a value might have one address for a while and then be moved, giving it a different address and therefore any pointer to it a different value. This will almost assuredly be the case if your system uses a garbage collector to manage memory on the free store.

9.6   Reorganization of a Hash Table

The STL proposal for hash tables requires that certain operations such as find be done in constant time. With the implementations suggested above, this will not be the case if the hash table grows without bound. This is because the buckets will also grow in size, making the searches increasingly costly. In that case a search will take time proportional to a fraction of the size of the table, but that is still linear, not constant time.

To achieve constant search times in a growing table, the bucket sizes must be kept limited. This requires two things: a good hash function and an increasing number of buckets. In fact, the number of buckets must be allowed to grow (and probably shrink) as the number of elements changes. This leads us to the idea of self-reorganizing hash tables. There are two basic methods: periodic and continuous reorganization. The easiest to describe is the periodic variation. Suppose that as we perform table operations, we keep some statistic about the table such as the number of elements stored or the number of elements we need to examine when executing find. When our statistic surpasses some trigger point, we execute a special reorganizing operation.

One method of reorganizing is very common. Suppose that the number of buckets is always a power of 2, such as 32, 64, etc. Then when it is time to reorganize, we double the number of buckets and then examine each element in the table at that time and redistribute it to a new bucket. If the last step in the hash function is taking the remainder modulo the number of buckets, then the nature of division allows us to conclude that any item is either already in the bucket that it belongs in, or it belongs in the bucket half the length of the new index farther on. In other words, if it is in bucket n before reorganization, then it belongs either in n or n+k, where k was the old number of buckets. (See Figure 9.4.) This is because m mod 64, for example, is either m mod 32 or 32 + m mod 32.

We also need to modify the last step of the hash function to divide now by the new number of buckets. Each bucket will thus be about half of its length before reorganization. The buckets at index n and n+ k are called *buddy* buckets.

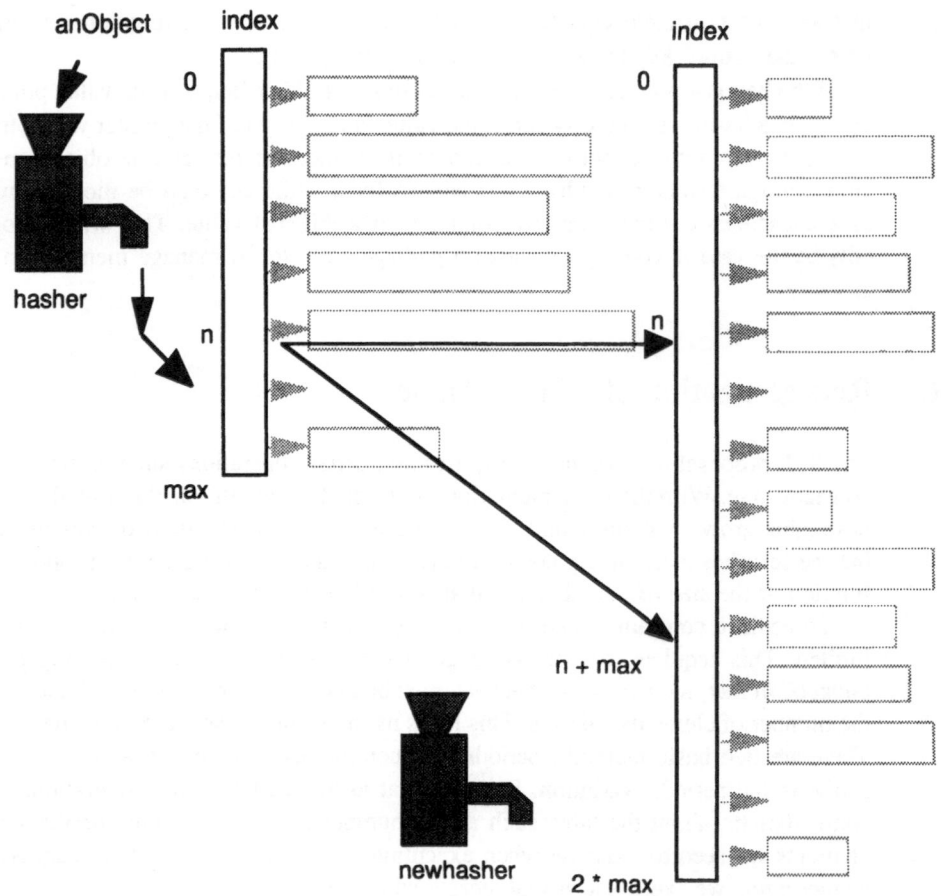

Figure 9.4. Before and after reorganizing a hash table.

You can likewise shrink the number of buckets in half as the table shrinks in overall size by folding buckets into one and readjusting the hasher accordingly. Note that changing the number of buckets also requires changing the length of the index, making vector the structure of choice for this. Likewise, lists are useful for the buckets when reorganizing, since we can simply unpin the elements from one list and pin them into another as necessary. This avoids calling the allocator, which can be a large time savings.

While periodic expansion works and does achieve constant search times (when the hasher is a good one), it has one unfortunate feature. The constant search time is only amortized constant time, and the insert or search that triggers a reorganization will be very costly. Some applications cannot afford such a situation. In some circumstances an application can anticipate when it won't be very busy and can trigger a reorganization anticipating future growth, but that is not always possible.

Expansion of a hash table can also be done continuously—with every insert. This works as follows. Suppose that we start with a small number of buckets, even just one. Then, every time we do an insert we expand the number of buckets by one. We then adjust the hasher appropriately and rehash all elements into the new buckets. This is simpler than you might expect, however, since if all is chosen well we only need to rehash the elements in one other bucket (the buddy), and those elements will belong either where they are originally or in the new bucket. The implementation of this idea is closely related to that of the periodic expansion discussed above.

To achieve this, suppose that we keep two values: maxBuckets and currentBuckets. maxBuckets is always a power of 2, and just after a major reorganization, currentBuckets is half of maxBuckets. The hasher uses remainders modulo maxBuckets at the end, except that if the result is greater than currentBuckets, the hasher reduces it by maxBuckets/2.

When we insert a new item, we increase currentBuckets by one. If that leaves the value less than maxBuckets, we just create a new bucket by increasing the size of the index, and then insert the new item into the new structure. We must also rehash the buddy bucket which is maxBuckets/2 slots below the new bucket. When currentBuckets eventually reaches maxBuckets, we must also double maxBuckets and adjust the hasher accordingly. This is the major reorganization step. The table can also be decreased in size symmetrically, by folding a bucket that we are removing into its buddy.

Note that if we store the buckets in a single list, then increasing the number of buckets is very easy. We just increase the size of the index and store an after-the-end iterator to the end of the bucket list into the new index cell.

Continuous reorganization makes each insert more expensive, but avoids the problem of a periodic expansion being so time-consuming that it might halt the application for an appreciable time. We are still subject to some of this effect, however, if we use STL vectors for the index. This is because the vector itself is self-organizing and requires periodic reallocation of storage. Notice that the index grows at the same rate as the hash table in this case, but vectors use reserve space so the reallocations would be less frequent than with the above periodic scheme. Using a deque for the index would even avoid some of this, since its major reorganizations are very infrequent. On the other hand, deque operations are a bit slower than vector operations.

Note that the average size of each bucket is only one with the continuous scheme just described. This doesn't mean that all buckets will have only one item, of course. This depends on the hasher. If it is a good one, they should all be small.

9.7   Using Hashed Structures

One of the major components of a compiler that translates languages such as C++ into machine code is a symbol table. When the programmer defines a new name, such as a function name or a variable name, the compiler makes an entry in the symbol table for the new name and stores information about the name along with it. Then, when the name is seen again, the compiler looks in the symbol table to see if the name has been defined, and if so, what kind of thing it represents to verify that the current usage is legal. Since names are frequently used in programs and since we want compiling to be fast, the lookup step in the symbol table must be fast. Hashed structures are often used to build symbol tables. Balanced binary trees are another good choice also. Thus a hash_map or hash_multimap might be a good choice as the basis of a symbol table. The keys would be the names defined by the programmer, and the data values would be objects holding the other information.

Some database programs use hashed structures for at least part of the data in the database. In fact, any program that requires fast retrieval by key should consider a hash structure as an implementation. However, doing so requires paying attention to the characteristics of the hash function that is to be used and verifying its adequacy somehow: either analytically, or through testing. The programmer should be prepared to try several hash functions on the anticipated set of values and the designed structure of the table to see if behavior will be good or poor.

One situation occurs in which hash tables should not be considered. Suppose you have a situation in which the keys are repeated very frequently, perhaps because there are only a very small number of keys, but they are associated in a nonunique way with a large set of data. Then you are guaranteed that all data will fall into a small number of buckets no matter what else you do. In a case like this, a balanced tree would be a much better choice, so use a multimap rather than a hash_multimap.

All of the algorithms that are defined in terms of forward iterators work with hash tables. In addition, so do those that work with bidirectional iterators if the specific implementation provides these. Sorting and binary searching won't work with hash tables, of course, nor is there a specialized sort algorithm provided within these classes as there is with the list class, because the idea of sorting is inconsistent with a hashed structure. If the data stored in a hashed structure permit comparisons and need to be sorted, then an iterator could be used to transfer them to a vector or tree-based structure first.

9.8   Elements of an Implementation

Let us examine a simple class that is similar in flavor to the hash table implementations suitable for the STL, but simpler in many ways. This class will show how to grow the number of buckets in the table incrementally as we insert data. We will not enforce the STL requirement that hash keys with equal values be kept together, however. Nor will we shrink the number of buckets as we erase data from the hash table.

9.8.1   The Hash Table

Our implementation uses a vector to hold the index and a single list to hold all of the buckets, as was discussed in Section 9.4. To do this the index entries will be list iterators. Two successive entries in the index vector give a range of entries in the bucket list that defines a single bucket. This implementation will be aided by the ability to decrement an iterator, since we can then insert before the position of the beginning of a bucket and then decrement the begin iterator for that bucket.

The advantage of this implementation is not its simplicity, because it complicates insertion as we shall see. It does make hash table iterators easy to build, since all a hash table iterator needs to do is iterate over a single list. Therefore, we just use a list iterator rather than build a new one.

While we want the hash buckets to be small, so that searching for a value within a bucket will be fast, there is no advantage to having empty buckets. Therefore, we will start with no buckets at all in an empty hash table. We will then add one additional bucket for each entry that we insert into the table. This keeps the average length of the buckets to be one. We also continually split buckets, so that no bucket has a chance to grow by much unless the hash function is extremely bad.

As usual we define a number of types for export. These include the type of the data to be stored and two iterator types. These are bidirectional iterators. We also export the type of the hash function object and the comparison object.

Actually, we do more than that. When the user constructs a hash table, an object defining a hash function object and one defining a comparison object are passed as template parameters. These are used internally in the hash_table constructor to create a hasher function object and a compare function object that are maintained as member variables. This lets us return these objects as the results of member functions. Thus a client can have access to the actual hashing object and the comparison object. An example will be shown in Section 9.8.3.

```
template <class T, class HASHER, class EQUAL>
class hash_table
{ public:
    typedef T key_type;
    typedef list<key_type >::iterator iterator;
    typedef list<key_type >::const_iterator
        const_iterator;

    typedef HASHER hash_type;
    typedef EQUAL equal_type;

    hash_table()
    :   maxbuckets(1),
        halfbuckets(0),
        currentbuckets(0),
        index(),
        buckets(),
        compare(EQUAL()),
        hasher(HASHER())
    {   index.push_back(buckets.end());
        // Creates the after-the-end iterator.
    }

    hash_type hash_function(){return hasher;}
```

```cpp
   equal_type comparer(){return compare;}

   long size()const{ return buckets.size();}
   bool empty()const{return buckets.empty();}
   iterator begin(){return buckets.begin();}
   iterator end(){return buckets.end();}
   const_iterator begin()const
   {  return buckets.begin();
   }
   const_iterator end() const
   {  return buckets.end();
   }
   . . .
private:
   unsigned long maxbuckets;
   unsigned long halfbuckets;
      //(always half of maxbuckets)
   unsigned long currentbuckets;

   vector<iterator > index;
   list<T> buckets;

   hash_type hasher;
   equal_type compare;
}
```

Note that a number of the member functions of hash_table just return information about the buckets list.

Variable maxbuckets is always a power of 2 and is the maximum number of buckets that we can have before a major reorganization. This value is used in the hash function that reduces the value returned by the hasher to one in the legal range for the index vector. Member variable halfbuckets is maintained as a convenience and is always half of max-buckets. Currentbuckets is the current number of buckets that grows by one for each in-sert. When currentbuckets reaches maxbuckets, we do a major reorganization.

The hash function that we actually use is not the one provided by the hasher, but the value returned by hasher reduced to the legal range for the index. We first call the hasher to get an unsigned long. Then we reduce this value modulo the maxbuckets value. Then if that value is less than currentbuckets, we are done. However, when the value is greater than or equal to the currentbuckets variable, we have an illegal bucket number. Therefore, we return the number of the buddy bucket instead. The buddy of any bucket is the one at a distance halfbuckets away. In this case the buddy is always before the one that we just computed, so we reduce the value by halfbuckets.

```cpp
unsigned long hash(const key_type& t) const
{  unsigned long result = hasher(t);
```

```
    result %= maxbuckets;
    if (result >= currentbuckets)
       result -= halfbuckets;
    return result;
}
```

Suppose that we have been inserting a few entries into our hash table. For each insert we are going to expand the number of buckets by one. We will then have to rehash all of the entries of the buddy of the new bucket, which distributes those values between their original buckets and the one newly added. This gives us average bucket size one, but we can hardly assume each bucket has only one element. Therefore, there will certainly be empty buckets. If we think about what the index looks like, we will see a potential problem. Each entry in the index vector is an iterator to the beginning of a bucket. This means that index[i] is the begin() iterator for bucket i, but also that index[i+1] is the after-the-end iterator for that same bucket. If we have empty buckets, however, then the begin and end iterators point to the same place, which is the after-the-end location. This will either be the end of the entire bucket list or to some list element. In the latter case, there are several iterators to the same list location: the begin() iterator of the corresponding bucket, and the begin iterators of all of the empty buckets immediately to the left of that bucket. If we insert into one of these buckets, we will have to adjust all of the iterators of empty buckets to the left. This gives us the insert algorithm.

The insert is done at the end of the bucket rather than at the beginning, since if the bucket isn't empty, then we don't need to adjust other iterators in this case. But if the bucket into which we insert an item is empty, then its iterator entry in the index list must be made to point to the new entry. Also, the index iterators of any empty buckets to the left must be made to point to the new item also. Figure 9.5 shows the situation in which buckets 1 and 2 are empty. Their begin and end iterators are the same. They are also equal to the begin iterator of bucket 3.

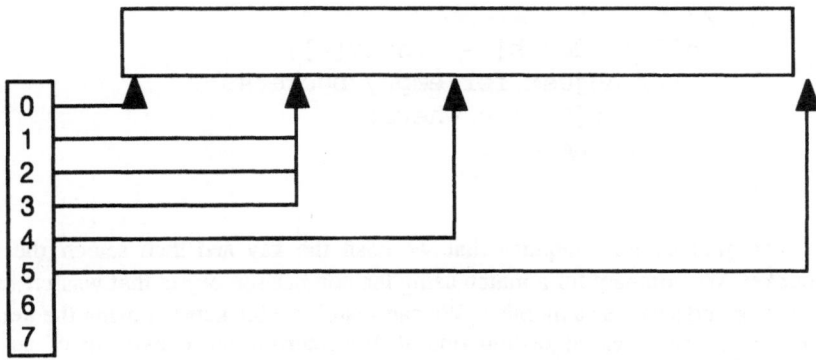

Figure 9.5. Two empty buckets.

If we now insert into bucket 2, we will be left with a situation like Figure 9.6.

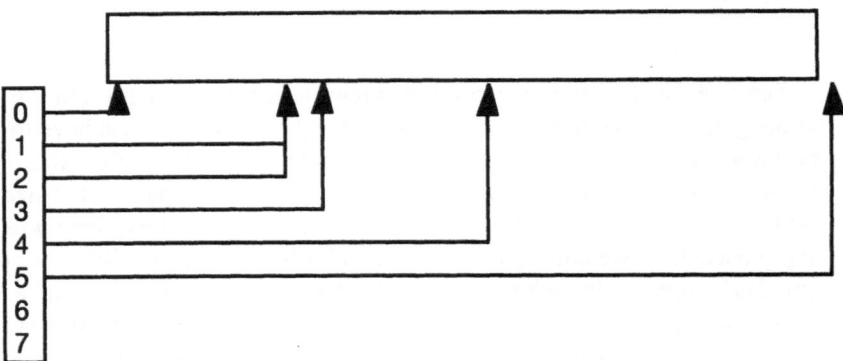

Figure 9.6. After inserting into bucket 2.

The insert member is shown next. Note the adjustments to iterators to empty buckets to the left of the insert point. If the hash function is adequate, there will be few empty buckets. However, in the worst case this is linear in the number of buckets.

```
iterator insert(key_type t)
{   expand();
    unsigned long b = hash(t);
    unsigned long w = b+1;
    iterator where
        = buckets.insert(index[w], t);
    // Inserts "before" the beginning of the
    // next bucket-- i.e. at the end of bucket
    // b.
    while(index[b] == index[w])
        // Adjust for empty buckets.
        index[b--] = where;
    return where;
}
```

To find an item requires that we hash the key and then search the corresponding bucket. We compare for a match using the comparison object that was created in the constructor and saved as a member. We can search the buckets list using the iterators saved in the index vector and algorithm find_if. We return a pair consisting of an iterator and a boolean. The boolean tells whether or not we found the item. If so, the iterator points to it.

```
pair<iterator, bool> find(const key_type& t)
{   if(buckets.size() > 0)
    {   unsigned long bucket = hash(t);
        iterator where = ::find_if
            (   index[bucket],
                index[bucket+1],
                bind1st(compare,t)
            );
        if(where != index[bucket+1])
            return
                pair<iterator, bool>(where, true);
    }
    return
        pair<iterator, bool>
        (   index[currentbuckets], false
        );
}
```

There are two versions of this algorithm. The other is identical except that it returns a const iterator within the pair, as is a const function as well. This is good practice in general, but vital for our use here, since set_hash has only const iterators, but map_hash has nonconst iterators and we intend to build both using this class.

Since we aren't reorganizing when we remove items, the erase algorithm is as follows. Note again that we must adjust all iterators to the item that is being removed. There may be several if this item is at the beginning of its bucket and there are empty buckets to the left. We return the number of items erased. We repeatedly use find to locate the item to be removed. When we find an item, we must increment the iterator to its bucket if that iterator points to the item being removed. We also depend on the fact that the comparison object is consistent with the hash function, though the dependence is subtle here. Note that we only hash once here to find a bucket number and we check for empty buckets only to the left of that bucket.

```
int erase(key_type t)
{   int result = 0;
    unsigned long where = hash(t);
    pair<iterator, bool> loc = find(t);
    while(loc.second)
    {   int i = where;
        while(index[i] == loc.first)
            ++index[i--];
        buckets.erase(loc.first);
        result++;
        loc = find(t);
    }
```

```
        return result;
}
```

Critical to efficiency overall is the expand member that adds a new bucket for each insertion. We maintain two values: currentbuckets, the current number of buckets; and maxbuckets, the maximum number of buckets before a major reorganization. When currentbuckets reaches maxbuckets, we double maxbuckets. Actually a major reorganization is very little extra work. Its main purpose is to define the basic divisor for the hash function. We also maintain variable halfbuckets as a convenience. It is always half of maxbuckets and is the distance between any bucket and its buddy bucket. When a bucket is created, its buddy bucket is split. The code is a bit longer than the other members and contains a loop. Since buckets are small on the average, the loop won't be iterated too often. We also need to be careful about the empty bucket problem when removing items from one bucket and inserting them into another. If we remove the first item from a bucket with empty buckets to the left, we adjust. If we insert into an empty bucket with empty buckets to its left, we also adjust. We use the splice algorithm to avoid calling the allocator.

The algorithm also uses shifts rather than multiplies. The shift operator<< effectively and quickly multiplies an integer by two. Some compilers will actually use this operator instead of multiplication when you multiply by any power of 2.

```
void expand()
{   currentbuckets++;
    index.push_back(buckets.end());
    if(currentbuckets > maxbuckets)
    {   halfbuckets
            = maxbuckets; maxbuckets <<= 1;
    }
    unsigned long buddy
        = currentbuckets -1 - halfbuckets;
    // split the buddy bucket.
    for
    (   iterator start = index[buddy];
        start != index[buddy+1];
        // nothing
        )
    {   iterator next = start;
        ++next; // Remember the "next" item.
        if(hash(*start) != buddy)
            // must move this item
        {   if(next == index[currentbuckets-1])
            // can just adjust pointers
            {   --index[currentbuckets-1];
                unsigned long adjust
                    = currentbuckets-2;
```

```
            while(index[adjust] == next)
                --index[adjust--];
            return;
        }
        else // must actually move it
        {   unsigned long k = buddy;
            while(start == index[k])
                ++index[k--];
            buckets.splice
            (   index[currentbuckets-1],
                buckets, start
            );
            iterator temp
                = index[currentbuckets-1];
            k = currentbuckets - 1;
            while(index[k] == temp)
                --index[k--];
        }
        start = next;
    }
    else ++start;
    }
}
```

9.8.2 Sets and Maps

A minimal implementation of sets based on the hash table above is shown next. Note that most of the members just pass on instructions to the hash_table representation. Note, however, that the iterator is a const_iterator. This is required by the notion of the hash implementation. If we change the value of an element in a set, it should be hashed to a different location. We could, of course, do this internally, but the easiest way is to disallow changes to the values. You can erase a value and then insert a modified value rather than change a value saved in the set.

We maintain the set property (unique inserts) by checking to see if an element is already present before inserting it. We can use the find member of the hash_table representation for this.

```
template <class KEY, class HASHER, class EQUAL>
class set_hash
{public:
    typedef hash_table<KEY, HASHER, EQUAL>
        ::const_iterator iterator;
        // bidirectional const iterator
    typedef KEY key_type;
```

```
typedef KEY value_type;
typedef HASHER hash_type;
typedef EQUAL equal_type;

set_hash(): rep(){}

hash_type hash_function()
{   return rep.hash_function();
}
equal_type comparer(){return rep.comparer();}

iterator insert (key_type t)
{   pair<rep_type::iterator, bool> where
        = rep.find(t);
    if(!where.second)
        return rep.insert(t);
    return where.first;
}

int erase(key_type t){ return rep.erase(t); }

iterator find(const key_type& k) const
{   pair<iterator, bool> where = rep.find(k);
    if(where.second) return where.first;
    return end();
}

iterator begin()const{ return rep.begin();}
iterator end()const{return rep.end();}
bool empty() const { return rep.empty();}
int size()const{return rep.size();}

protected:
    typedef hash_table<key_type, HASHER, EQUAL>
        rep_type;
    rep_type rep;
};
```

Note that since find is const and returns a const iterator, it uses the second version of hash_table::find; the one that is itself const returning a const iterator.

The code for map is nearly identical. The exception is that we save pairs instead of keys, and we don't require const iterators, though we permit them. We protect against changing the keys in a pair by storing const KEY values rather than KEY values in the pairs. Therefore, we can return (nonconst) iterators to these pairs, knowing that only the data value in the pair can be changed.

```
template
<  class KEY,
   class DATA,
   class HASHER,
   class EQUAL
>
class map_hash
{public:
    typedef pair<const KEY, DATA> value_type;
    typedef KEY key_type;
    typedef hash_table<value_type, HASHER, EQUAL>
        ::iterator iterator;
        // bidirectional iterator
    typedef KEY key_type;
    typedef DATA& reference;
    typedef HASHER hash_type;
    typedef EQUAL equal_type;

    map_hash(): rep(){}

    iterator insert (KEY t, DATA v)
    {   value_type p(t,v);
        pair<rep_type::iterator, bool> where
            = rep.find(p);
        if(!where.second)
            return rep.insert(p);
        return where.first;
    }

    hash_type hash_function()
    {   return rep.hash_function();
    }
    equal_type comparer(){return rep.comparer();}

    int erase(KEY t)
    {   value_type p(t,DATA());
        return rep.erase(p);
    }

    iterator find(const key_type& k)
    {   pair<iterator, bool> where
            = rep.find(value_type(k,DATA()));
        if(where.second) return where.first;
        return end();
    }
```

```
iterator begin(){ return rep.begin();}
iterator end(){return rep.end();}
bool empty() const { return rep.empty();}
int size()const{return rep.size();}

reference operator[](const key_type& k)
{   return (*(insert(k, DATA()))).second;
}   // NOTE that this inserts the DATA default
    // value into the map for your key if the
    // key is not originally present.

protected:
    typedef hash_table<value_type, HASHER, EQUAL>
        rep_type;
    rep_type rep;
};
```

We depend here on the fact that the hash depends on only the key. We can find a value knowing only the key by putting a dummy value into the data slot of the pair we seek.

We also provide an operator[] to permit index-like searching of the map. We supply a key between the brackets and get a reference to the associated value if present, and to the default value of the data type otherwise.

9.8.3   Using the Sets and Maps

Before we can create a set or a map, we must create the hash and comparison objects that it will use. This is easiest in the case of a set, since we have only the keys to worry about. For example, if we want to create a set of int values, we can use the following hash function and comparison object. We multiply the key value by a large prime number to guard against the insertion of a lot of small integers that would tend to overload some buckets. Note that the inthasher and the compare template provide consistent values: If two integers are the same according to compare<int>(), then the hash values are the same also.

```
class inthasher
{public:
    unsigned long operator()(const int& m) const
    {   return m * 1073741827;
    }
};

template <class T>
class compare : public binary_function<T, T, bool>
{public:
```

```
    bool operator()
    (   const T& first,
        const T& second
    ) const
    { return first == second;
    }
};
```

The compare function object should derive from the binary function class to be consistent with the rest of the STL. We can now create a set of ints with the following:

```
set_hash <int, inthasher, compare<int> > intSet;
```

To use maps requires a bit more work. First we need a hasher that works on pairs, but considers only the key to create the value. Suppose we want to build a map with ints for both keys and data values.

```
class pair_hasher
{public:
    unsigned long operator()
    (   const pair<const int,
        int>& m
    ) const
    {   return m.first * 1073741827;
    }
};
```

We also need a comparison object that is consistent with this and compares only the keys of a pair. Again, this should be derived from binary_function.

```
template <class T, class S>
class compare_pair : public
binary_function<pair<T,S>, pair<T,S>, bool>
{ public:
    bool operator()
    (   const pair<T,S>& first,
        const pair<T,S>& second
    ) const
    { return first.first == second.first;
    }
};
```

Now a map from ints to ints may be created with

```
map_hash
<   int,
    int,
    pair_hasher,
    compare_pair<const int, int>
> hashMap;
```

We could then read pairs from a file and insert them into our map with the following fragment of code.

```
ifstream aFile("somedata.in");
int k, v;
while(aFile>>k)
{   aFile>> v;
    hashMap.insert(k,v);
}
```

9.9   Design Issues

A number of important pieces have been left out of this implementation and some other features could be improved with better design. First, efficiency demands that we shrink the number of buckets at least occasionally. Otherwise, we get too many empty buckets and the adjustments necessary for empty buckets start to play a dominant role.

Another place at which we could improve the efficiency is in our separation of functionality between hash_table and the classes built from it. In particular, we could avoid extra searching by giving the hash_table class itself knowledge of whether it was being used in a set-like or multiset-like way. When we insert an item into a set, we search to see if it is present. If it is not we insert it, but that requires an extra search also. We could do it all with one search if the implementation had an insert_only_if_not_present member or something equivalent.

Another interesting idea is to provide additional constructors, so that we don't need to use the default value of the compare class as the comparison object. We could provide a constructor that passes in a comparison object to be used. This would permit us to parameterize the comparison class, adding to flexibility. We could do all of this for the hasher class as well, of course.

9.10   Extending the Standard Template Library

We see in the hashed structures provided in this proposal what it takes to extend the STL with an additional container. We need to define the container type, of course, and give it the usual exported types. We also need to give it an interface that includes all of the required container interface elements, such as insert and erase. We also need to define and perhaps construct an associated iterator type—especially if ordinary pointers won't work for the new container. Careful analysis needs to be done to assure that the new container will work with the appropriate generic algorithms, and on those occasions that this is impossible, provide special analogs of them as appropriate. Efficiencies of all of the member functions need to be given careful analysis.

More importantly, before attempting to add the new structures to the STL, the programmer should analyze the container and its iterator to be sure that it is designed with sufficient generality to be useful in a wide range of problems. This analysis of usefulness is closely related to the efficiency considerations mentioned above.

For example, it would be difficult to design a graph container to integrate with the STL, not because graphs aren't useful. Indeed many graph problems are very important. However, graphs can already be built with the existing elements as was shown earlier. Also, it would be difficult to design a graph interface with sufficient generality to satisfy critics. This is because there are very many ways to build graphs, each with different efficiency constraints, and each suitable for a certain set of problems, but unsuitable for many others.

9.11   Summary

Make certain that you understand each of the following terms:

> bucket
> circular hashing
> continuous reorganization
> hash table reorganization
> periodic reorganization
> separate chaining

9.12   Exercises

1. Build a hash table class template with a vector index and using STL lists for buckets. Use one list per bucket. Your template arguments should include at least the value type to be inserted and a hash function for values of that type.

2. Build a periodic reorganizer for your hash table. Use the total size of the table as the trigger. When the number of elements doubles, double the number of buckets. Does this give us amortized constant search times assuming a perfectly uniform hash function?

3. Build an iterator class for your hash table. Note that insertions should not invalidate iterators (even in the presence of reorganizations), and deletions do so only when they delete the item that an iterator references. The advantage of this implementation is that the

"empty bucket" problem of the hash_table shown in the text does not occur in this implementation.

4. Modify the hash table implementation described in the text so that it continuously shrinks the hash table structure when we remove items. Shrink one bucket per erasure.

5. Build a multiset_hash class similar to our set_hash. Base it on either the hash table implementation given in the text, or the one developed in the earlier exercises.

6. Build a multimap_hash class similar to our map_hash. Base it on either the hash table implementation given in the text, or the one developed in the earlier exercises.

7. Improve the hash_table class as suggested in Section 9.9. Reimplement the set_hash and map_hash classes to take advantage of the changes in hash_table.

8. Construct a set of data that can be inserted into either a red-black tree or a hash table. Provide relative timings of the two structures on a series of inserts and also on a series of deletes. Use the implementations discussed in this chapter and the previous one. Are the experimental timings consistent with the theory?

9. See Exercise 8. If you have access to the reference hash implementation (See [8]), then do the same for the STL set and hash_set structures.

10. From your experience in computer science, what additional structures could/should be added to the STL? Write an essay detailing your choice and the reasons. If you think that it is complete, write an essay justifying your decision.

Appendix
STL Summary

A.1 Algorithms Prototypes

A.1.1 Maximum and Minimum

```
template <class T>
inline const T& min(const T& a, const T& b);

template <class T, class Compare>
inline const T& min(const T& a, const T& b, Compare comp);

template <class T>
inline const T& max(const T& a, const T& b);

template <class T, class Compare>
inline const T& max(const T& a, const T& b, Compare comp);

template <class ForwardIterator>
ForwardIterator max_element
(  ForwardIterator first,
   ForwardIterator last
);

template <class ForwardIterator, class Compare>
ForwardIterator max_element
(  ForwardIterator first,
   ForwardIterator last,
   Compare comp
);

template <class ForwardIterator>
ForwardIterator min_element
(  ForwardIterator first,
```

```
      ForwardIterator last
);

template <class ForwardIterator, class Compare>
ForwardIterator min_element
(   ForwardIterator first,
    ForwardIterator last,
    Compare comp
);
```

A.1.2 Generalized Numeric Operations

```
template <class InputIterator, class T>
T accumulate
(   InputIterator first,
    InputIterator last,
    T init
);

template <  class InputIterator,
            class T,
            class BinaryOperation
         >
T accumulate
(   InputIterator first,
    InputIterator last,
    T init,
    BinaryOperation binary_op
);

template <  class InputIterator1,
            class InputIterator2,
            class T
         >
T inner_product
(   InputIterator1 first1,
    InputIterator1 last1,
    InputIterator2 first2,
    T init
);

template <  class InputIterator1,
            class InputIterator2,
            class T,
```

```
            class BinaryOperation1,
            class BinaryOperation2
      >
T inner_product
(  InputIterator1 first1,
   InputIterator1 last1,
   InputIterator2 first2,
   T init,
   BinaryOperation1 binary_op1,
   BinaryOperation2 binary_op2
);

template <class InputIterator, class OutputIterator>
OutputIterator partial_sum
(  InputIterator first,
   InputIterator last,
   OutputIterator result
);

template <  class InputIterator,
            class OutputIterator,
            class BinaryOperation
      >
OutputIterator partial_sum
(  InputIterator first,
   InputIterator last,
   OutputIterator result,
   BinaryOperation binary_op
);

template <class InputIterator, class OutputIterator>
OutputIterator adjacent_difference
(  InputIterator first,
   InputIterator last,
   OutputIterator result
);

template <  class InputIterator,
            class OutputIterator,
            class BinaryOperation
      >
OutputIterator adjacent_difference
(  InputIterator first,
   InputIterator last,
   OutputIterator result,
```

```
    BinaryOperation binary_op
);
```

A.1.3 Nonmutating Sequence Operations

```
template <  class InputIterator1,
            class InputIterator2
         >
pair<InputIterator1, InputIterator2> mismatch
(   InputIterator1 first1,
    InputIterator1 last1,
    InputIterator2 first2
);

template <  class InputIterator1,
            class InputIterator2,
            class BinaryPredicate
         >
pair<InputIterator1, InputIterator2> mismatch
(   InputIterator1 first1,
    InputIterator1 last1,
    InputIterator2 first2,
    BinaryPredicate binary_pred
);

template <class InputIterator1, class InputIterator2>
inline bool equal
(   InputIterator1 first1,
    InputIterator1 last1,
    InputIterator2 first2
);

template <  class InputIterator1,
            class InputIterator2,
            class BinaryPredicate
         >
inline bool equal
(   InputIterator1 first1,
    InputIterator1 last1,
    InputIterator2 first2,
    BinaryPredicate binary_pred
);
```

```
template <class InputIterator, class Function>
Function for_each
(   InputIterator first,
    InputIterator last,
    Function f
);

template <class InputIterator, class T>
InputIterator find
(   InputIterator first,
    InputIterator last,
    const T& value
);

template <class InputIterator, class Predicate>
InputIterator find_if
(   InputIterator first,
    InputIterator last,
    Predicate pred
);

template <class ForwardIterator>
ForwardIterator adjacent_find
(   ForwardIterator first,
    ForwardIterator last
);

template <class ForwardIterator, class BinaryPredicate>
ForwardIterator adjacent_find
(   ForwardIterator first,
    ForwardIterator last,
    BinaryPredicate binary_pred
);

template <class InputIterator, class T, class Size>
void count
(   InputIterator first,
    InputIterator last,
    const T& value,
    Size& n
);

template <class InputIterator, class Predicate, class Size>
void count_if
(   InputIterator first,
```

```
    InputIterator last,
    Predicate pred,
    Size& n
);

template <class ForwardIterator1, class ForwardIterator2>
inline ForwardIterator1 search
(   ForwardIterator1 first1,
    ForwardIterator1 last1,
    ForwardIterator2 first2,
    ForwardIterator2 last2
);

template <  class ForwardIterator1,
            class ForwardIterator2,
            class BinaryPredicate
        >
inline ForwardIterator1 search
(   ForwardIterator1 first1,
    ForwardIterator1 last1,
    ForwardIterator2 first2,
    ForwardIterator2 last2,
    BinaryPredicate binary_pred
);
```

A.1.4 Mutating Sequence Operations

```
    template <class InputIterator, class OutputIterator>
    OutputIterator copy
    (   InputIterator first,
        InputIterator last,
        OutputIterator result
    );

    template <  class BidirectionalIterator1,
                class BidirectionalIterator2
            >
    BidirectionalIterator2 copy_backward
    (   BidirectionalIterator1 first,
        BidirectionalIterator1 last,
        BidirectionalIterator2 result
    );
```

```
template <class OutputIterator, class Size, class T>
OutputIterator fill_n
(  OutputIterator first,
   Size n,
   const T& value
);

template <class T>
void swap(T& x, T& y);

template <class ForwardIterator1, class ForwardIterator2>
ForwardIterator2 swap_ranges
(  ForwardIterator1 first1,
   ForwardIterator1 last1,
   ForwardIterator2 first2
);

template <  class InputIterator,
            class OutputIterator,
            class UnaryOperation
         >
OutputIterator transform
(  InputIterator first,
   InputIterator last,
   OutputIterator result,
   UnaryOperation op
);

template <  class InputIterator1,
            class InputIterator2,
            class OutputIterator,
            class BinaryOperation
         >
OutputIterator transform
(  InputIterator1 first1,
   InputIterator1 last1,
   InputIterator2 first2,
   OutputIterator result,
   BinaryOperation binary_op
 );

template <class ForwardIterator, class T>
void replace
(  ForwardIterator first,
   ForwardIterator last,
```

```
        const T& old_value,
        const T& new_value
    );

    template <class ForwardIterator, class Predicate, class T>
    void replace_if
    (   ForwardIterator first,
        ForwardIterator last,
        Predicate pred,
        const T& new_value
    );

    template <  class InputIterator,
                class OutputIterator,
                class T
            >
    OutputIterator replace_copy
    (   InputIterator first,
        InputIterator last,
        OutputIterator result,
        const T& old_value,
        const T& new_value
    );

    template <  class Iterator,
                class OutputIterator,
                class Predicate,
                class T
            >
    OutputIterator replace_copy_if
    (   Iterator first,
        Iterator last,
        OutputIterator result,
        Predicate pred,
        const T& new_value
    );

    template <class ForwardIterator, class Generator>
    void generate
    (   ForwardIterator first,
        ForwardIterator last,
        Generator gen
    );
```

```
template <class OutputIterator, class Size, class Generator>
OutputIterator generate_n
(   OutputIterator first,
    Size n,
    Generator gen
);

template <   class InputIterator,
             class OutputIterator, c
             lass T
         >
OutputIterator remove_copy
(   InputIterator first,
    InputIterator last,
    OutputIterator result,
    const T& value
);

template <   class InputIterator,
             class OutputIterator,
             class Predicate
         >
OutputIterator remove_copy_if
(   InputIterator first,
    InputIterator last,
    OutputIterator result,
    Predicate pred
);

template <class ForwardIterator, class T>
ForwardIterator remove
(   ForwardIterator first,
    ForwardIterator last,
    const T& value
);

template <class ForwardIterator, class Predicate>
ForwardIterator remove_if
(   ForwardIterator first,
    ForwardIterator last,
    Predicate pred
);
```

```
template <class InputIterator, class OutputIterator>
inline OutputIterator unique_copy
(  InputIterator first,
   InputIterator last,
   OutputIterator result
);

template <  class InputIterator,
            class OutputIterator,
            class BinaryPredicate
        >
inline OutputIterator unique_copy
(  InputIterator first,
   InputIterator last,
   OutputIterator result,
   BinaryPredicate binary_pred
);

template <class ForwardIterator>
ForwardIterator unique
(  ForwardIterator first,
   ForwardIterator last
);

template <class ForwardIterator, class BinaryPredicate>
ForwardIterator unique
(  ForwardIterator first,
    ForwardIterator last,
   BinaryPredicate binary_pred
);

template <class BidirectionalIterator>
inline void reverse
(  BidirectionalIterator first,
   BidirectionalIterator last
);

template <class BidirectionalIterator, class OutputIterator>
OutputIterator reverse_copy
(  BidirectionalIterator first,
   BidirectionalIterator last,
   OutputIterator result
);
```

```
template <class ForwardIterator>
inline void rotate
(  ForwardIterator first,
   ForwardIterator middle,
   ForwardIterator last
);

template <class ForwardIterator, class OutputIterator>
OutputIterator rotate_copy
(  ForwardIterator first,
   ForwardIterator middle,
   ForwardIterator last,
   OutputIterator result
);

template <class RandomAccessIterator>
inline void random_shuffle
(  RandomAccessIterator first,
   RandomAccessIterator last
);

template <class RandomAccessIterator, class
RandomNumberGenerator>
void random_shuffle
(  RandomAccessIterator first,
   RandomAccessIterator last,
   RandomNumberGenerator& rand
);

template <class BidirectionalIterator, class Predicate>
BidirectionalIterator partition
(  BidirectionalIterator first,
   BidirectionalIterator last,
   Predicate pred
);

template <class ForwardIterator, class Predicate>
inline ForwardIterator stable_partition
(  ForwardIterator first,
   ForwardIterator last,
   Predicate pred
);
```

A.1.5 Sorting Related Operations

```
template <class RandomAccessIterator>
void sort(RandomAccessIterator first, RandomAccessIterator
last)

template <class RandomAccessIterator, class Compare>
void sort
(   RandomAccessIterator first,
    RandomAccessIterator last,
    Compare comp
);

template <class RandomAccessIterator>
inline void stable_sort
(   RandomAccessIterator first,
    RandomAccessIterator last
);

template <class RandomAccessIterator, class Compare>
inline void stable_sort
(   RandomAccessIterator first,
    RandomAccessIterator last,
    Compare comp
);

template <class RandomAccessIterator>
inline void partial_sort
(   RandomAccessIterator first,
    RandomAccessIterator middle,
    RandomAccessIterator last
);

template <class RandomAccessIterator, class Compare>
inline void partial_sort
(   RandomAccessIterator first,
    RandomAccessIterator middle,
    RandomAccessIterator last,
    Compare comp
);

template <class InputIterator, class RandomAccessIterator>
inline RandomAccessIterator partial_sort_copy
(   InputIterator first,
    InputIterator last,
```

```
        RandomAccessIterator result_first,
        RandomAccessIterator result_last
);


template <  class InputIterator,
            class RandomAccessIterator,
            class Compare
        >
inline RandomAccessIterator partial_sort_copy
(   InputIterator first,
    InputIterator last,
    RandomAccessIterator result_first,
    RandomAccessIterator result_last,
    Compare comp
);

template <class RandomAccessIterator>
inline void nth_element
(   RandomAccessIterator first,
    RandomAccessIterator nth,
    RandomAccessIterator last
);

template <class RandomAccessIterator, class Compare>
inline void nth_element
(   RandomAccessIterator first,
    RandomAccessIterator nth,
    RandomAccessIterator last,
    Compare comp
);

template <class ForwardIterator, class T>
inline ForwardIterator lower_bound
(   ForwardIterator first,
    ForwardIterator last,
    const T& value
);

template <class ForwardIterator, class T, class Compare>
inline ForwardIterator lower_bound
(   ForwardIterator first,
    ForwardIterator last,
    const T& value,
```

```
      Compare comp
);

template <class ForwardIterator, class T>
inline ForwardIterator upper_bound
(   ForwardIterator first,
    ForwardIterator last,
    const T& value
);

template <class ForwardIterator, class T, class Compare>
inline ForwardIterator upper_bound
(   ForwardIterator first,
    ForwardIterator last,
    const T& value,
    Compare comp
);

template <class ForwardIterator, class T>
inline pair<ForwardIterator, ForwardIterator> equal_range
(   ForwardIterator first,
    ForwardIterator last,
    const T& value
);

template <class ForwardIterator, class T, class Compare>
inline pair<ForwardIterator, ForwardIterator> equal_range
(   ForwardIterator first,
    ForwardIterator last,
    const T& value,
    Compare comp
);

template <class ForwardIterator, class T>
bool binary_search
(   ForwardIterator first,
    ForwardIterator last,
    const T& value
);

template <class ForwardIterator, class T, class Compare>
bool binary_search
(   ForwardIterator first,
    ForwardIterator last,
    const T& value,
```

```
    Compare comp
);

template <  class InputIterator1,
            class InputIterator2,
            class OutputIterator
        >
OutputIterator merge
(   InputIterator1 first1,
    InputIterator1 last1,
    InputIterator2 first2,
    InputIterator2 last2,
    OutputIterator result
);

template <  class InputIterator1,
            class InputIterator2,
            class OutputIterator,
            class Compare
        >
OutputIterator merge
(   InputIterator1 first1,
    InputIterator1 last1,
    InputIterator2 first2,
    InputIterator2 last2,
    OutputIterator result,
    Compare comp
);

template <class BidirectionalIterator>
inline void inplace_merge
(   BidirectionalIterator first,
    BidirectionalIterator middle,
    BidirectionalIterator last
);

template <class BidirectionalIterator, class Compare>
inline void inplace_merge
(   BidirectionalIterator first,
    BidirectionalIterator middle,
    BidirectionalIterator last,
    Compare comp
);
```

A.1.6 Set Operations on Sorted Structures

```
template <class InputIterator1, class InputIterator2>
bool includes
(   InputIterator1 first1,
    InputIterator1 last1,
    InputIterator2 first2,
    InputIterator2 last2
);

template <  class InputIterator1,
            class InputIterator2,
            class Compare
       >
bool includes
(   InputIterator1 first1,
    InputIterator1 last1,
    InputIterator2 first2,
    InputIterator2 last2,
    Compare comp
);

template <  class InputIterator1,
            class InputIterator2,
            class OutputIterator
       >
OutputIterator set_union
(   InputIterator1 first1,
    InputIterator1 last1,
    InputIterator2 first2,
    InputIterator2 last2,
    OutputIterator result
);

template <  class InputIterator1,
            class InputIterator2,
            class OutputIterator,
            class Compare
       >
OutputIterator set_union
(   InputIterator1 first1,
    InputIterator1 last1,
    InputIterator2 first2,
    InputIterator2 last2,
    OutputIterator result,
```

```
      Compare comp
);

template <   class InputIterator1,
             class InputIterator2,
             class OutputIterator
        >
OutputIterator set_intersection
(   InputIterator1 first1,
    InputIterator1 last1,
    InputIterator2 first2,
    InputIterator2 last2,
    OutputIterator result
);

template <   class InputIterator1,
             class InputIterator2,
             class OutputIterator,
             class Compare
        >
OutputIterator set_intersection
(   InputIterator1 first1,
    InputIterator1 last1,
    InputIterator2 first2,
    InputIterator2 last2,
    OutputIterator result,
    Compare comp
);

template <   class InputIterator1,
             class InputIterator2,
             class OutputIterator
        >
OutputIterator set_difference
(   InputIterator1 first1,
    InputIterator1 last1,
    InputIterator2 first2,
    InputIterator2 last2,
    OutputIterator result
);

template <   class InputIterator1,
             class InputIterator2,
             class OutputIterator,
```

```
                class Compare
        >
OutputIterator set_difference
(   InputIterator1 first1,
    InputIterator1 last1,
    InputIterator2 first2,
    InputIterator2 last2,
    OutputIterator result,
    Compare comp
);


template <  class InputIterator1,
            class InputIterator2,
            class OutputIterator
        >
OutputIterator set_symmetric_difference
(   InputIterator1 first1,
    InputIterator1 last1,
    InputIterator2 first2,
    InputIterator2 last2,
    OutputIterator result
);


template <  class InputIterator1,
            class InputIterator2,
            class OutputIterator,
            class Compare
        >
OutputIterator set_symmetric_difference
(   InputIterator1 first1,
    InputIterator1 last1,
    InputIterator2 first2,
    InputIterator2 last2,
    OutputIterator result,
    Compare comp
);
```

A.1.7 Heap Operations

```
template <class RandomAccessIterator>
inline void push_heap
(   RandomAccessIterator first,
    RandomAccessIterator last
);
```

```
template <class RandomAccessIterator, class Compare>
inline void push_heap
(   RandomAccessIterator first,
    RandomAccessIterator last,
    Compare comp
);

template <class RandomAccessIterator>
inline void pop_heap
(   RandomAccessIterator first,
    RandomAccessIterator last
);

template <class RandomAccessIterator, class Compare>
inline void pop_heap
(   RandomAccessIterator first,
    RandomAccessIterator last,
    Compare comp
);

template <class RandomAccessIterator>
inline void make_heap
(   RandomAccessIterator first,
    RandomAccessIterator last
);

template <class RandomAccessIterator, class Compare>
inline void make_heap
(   RandomAccessIterator first,
    RandomAccessIterator last,
    Compare comp
);

template <class RandomAccessIterator>
void sort_heap
(   RandomAccessIterator first,
    RandomAccessIterator last
);

template <class RandomAccessIterator, class Compare>
void sort_heap
(   RandomAccessIterator first,
    RandomAccessIterator last,
    Compare comp
);
```

A.1.8 Lexicographical Compare Operations

```
template <class InputIterator1, class InputIterator2>
bool lexicographical_compare
(   InputIterator1 first1,
    InputIterator1 last1,
    InputIterator2 first2,
    InputIterator2 last2
);

template <   class InputIterator1,
             class InputIterator2,
             class Compare
         >
bool lexicographical_compare
(   InputIterator1 first1,
    InputIterator1 last1,
    InputIterator2 first2,
    InputIterator2 last2,
    Compare comp
);
```

A.1.9 Permutation Generator Operations

```
template <class BidirectionalIterator>
bool next_permutation
(   BidirectionalIterator first,
    BidirectionalIterator last
);

template <class BidirectionalIterator, class Compare>
bool next_permutation
(   BidirectionalIterator first,
    BidirectionalIterator last,
    Compare comp
);

template <class BidirectionalIterator>
bool prev_permutation
(   BidirectionalIterator first,
    BidirectionalIterator last
);
```

```
template <class BidirectionalIterator, class Compare>
bool prev_permutation
(   BidirectionalIterator first,
    BidirectionalIterator last,
    Compare comp
);
```

A.1.10 Miscellaneous Operations

```
template <class InputIterator, class Distance>
inline void distance
(   InputIterator first,
    InputIterator last,
    Distance& n
);
// constant time for random access iterator else linear

template <class InputIterator, class Distance>
inline void advance(InputIterator& i, Distance n);
// constant time for random access iterator else linear
```

A.2   Containers

Note that only the public members are shown here.

A.2.1   Sequential Containers

```
template <class T>
class deque
{ public:
    typedef T value_type;
    typedef Allocator<T> data_allocator_type;
    typedef Allocator<T>::pointer pointer;
    typedef Allocator<T>::reference reference;
    typedef Allocator<T>::const_reference const_reference;
    typedef Allocator<T>::size_type size_type;
    typedef Allocator<T>::difference_type difference_type;
    typedef Allocator<pointer> map_allocator_type;

    class iterator
    : public random_access_iterator<T, difference_type>
    { public:
```

```
      iterator();
      reference operator*() const;
      difference_type operator-(const iterator& x) const;
      iterator& operator++();
      iterator operator++(int);
      iterator& operator--();
      iterator operator--(int);
      iterator& operator+=(difference_type n);
      iterator& operator-=(difference_type n);
      iterator operator+(difference_type n) const;
      iterator operator-(difference_type n) const;
      reference operator[](difference_type n);
      bool operator==(const iterator& x) const;
      bool operator<(const iterator& x) const;
   };

   class const_iterator
   : public random_access_iterator<T, difference_type>
   { public:
      const_iterator();
      const_iterator(const iterator& x);
      const_reference operator*() const;
      difference_type operator-
          ( const const_iterator& x) const;
      const_iterator& operator++();
      const_iterator operator++(int);
      const_iterator& operator--();
      const_iterator operator--(int);
      const_iterator& operator+=(difference_type n);
      const_iterator& operator-=(difference_type n);
      const_iterator operator+(difference_type n) const;
      const_iterator operator-(difference_type n) const;
      const_reference operator[](difference_type n);
      bool operator==(const const_iterator& x) const;
      bool operator<(const const_iterator& x) const;
   };

   typedef reverse_iterator
   <  const_iterator,
      value_type,
      const_reference,
      difference_type
   >
   const_reverse_iterator;
```

```
    typedef reverse_iterator
    <iterator, value_type, reference, difference_type>
    reverse_iterator;

    deque();
    deque(size_type n, const T& value = T());
/*  If template members are available:
    template<class Iterator>
        deque(Iterator first, Iterator last);
*/
    deque(const T* first, const T* last);
    deque(const deque<T>& x);
    deque<T>& operator=(const deque<T>& x);
    ~deque();
    iterator begin();
    const_iterator begin() const;
    iterator end();
    const_iterator end() const;
    reverse_iterator rbegin();
    const_reverse_iterator rbegin() const;
    reverse_iterator rend();
    const_reverse_iterator rend() const;
    bool empty() const;
    size_type size() const;
    size_type max_size() const;
    reference operator[](size_type n);
    const_reference operator[](size_type n) const;
    reference front();
    const_reference front() const;
    reference back();
    const_reference back() const;
    void push_front(const T& x);
    void push_back(const T& x);
    void pop_front();
    void pop_back();
    void swap(deque<T>& x);
    iterator insert(iterator position, const T& x);
    void insert(iterator position, size_type n, const T& x);
/*  If template members are available:
    template <class Iterator> void insert
    (   iterator position,
        Iterator first,
        Iterator last
    );
*/
```

```
      void insert
      (   iterator position,
          const T* first,
          const T* last
      );
      void erase(iterator position);
      void erase(iterator first, iterator last);
};

template <class T>
class list
{ public:
      typedef T value_type;
      typedef Allocator<T> value_allocator_type;
      typedef Allocator<T>::pointer pointer;
      typedef Allocator<T>::reference reference;
      typedef Allocator<T>::const_reference const_reference;
      typedef Allocator<list_node> list_node_allocator_type;
      typedef Allocator<list_node>::pointer link_type;
      typedef Allocator<list_node>::size_type size_type;
      typedef Allocator<list_node>
         ::difference_type difference_type;

      typedef reverse_bidirectional_iterator
      <   const_iterator,
          value_type,
          const_reference,
          difference_type
      >
      const_reverse_iterator;

      typedef reverse_bidirectional_iterator
         <iterator, value_type, reference, difference_type>
         reverse_iterator;

      list();
      list(size_type n, const T& value = T());
      list(const T* first, const T* last);
      list(const list<T>& x) ;
      ~list() ;
      list<T>& operator=(const list<T>& x);
      iterator begin();
      const_iterator begin() const;
      iterator end() { return node; }
      const_iterator end() const;
```

```
reverse_iterator rbegin();
const_reverse_iterator rbegin() const;
reverse_iterator rend();
const_reverse_iterator rend() const ;
bool empty() const;
size_type size() const;
size_type max_size() const;
reference front();
const_reference front() const;
reference back();
const_reference back() const;
void swap(list<T>& x);
iterator insert(iterator position, const T& x);
void insert
(   iterator position,
    const T* first,
    const T* last
);
void insert
(   iterator position,
    const_iterator first,
    const_iterator last
);
void insert(iterator position, size_type n, const T& x);
void push_front(const T& x);
void push_back(const T& x);
void pop_front();
void pop_back();
void erase(iterator position);
void erase(iterator first, iterator last);
void splice(iterator position, list<T>& x);
void splice(iterator position, list<T>& x, iterator i);
void splice
(   iterator position,
    list<T>& x,
    iterator first,
    iterator last
);
void remove(const T& value);
void unique();
void merge(list<T>& x);
void reverse();
void sort();

// Nested iterator classes
```

```
class iterator : public bidirectional_iterator
<T, difference_type>
{ public:
      iterator();
      bool operator==(const iterator& x) const;
      reference operator*() const;
      iterator& operator++();
      iterator operator++(int);
      iterator& operator--();
      iterator operator--(int);
};

class const_iterator
: public bidirectional_iterator <T, difference_type>
{ public:
      const_iterator();
      const_iterator(const iterator& x);
      bool operator==(const const_iterator& x) const;
      const_reference operator*() const;
      const_iterator& operator++();
      const_iterator operator++(int);
      const_iterator& operator--() ;
      const_iterator operator--(int);
};

};

template <class T>
class vector
{ public:
   typedef Allocator<T> vector_allocator;
   typedef T value_type;
   typedef vector_allocator::pointer pointer;
   typedef vector_allocator::pointer iterator;
   typedef vector_allocator::const_pointer const_iterator;
   typedef vector_allocator::reference reference;
   typedef vector_allocator::const_reference
      const_reference;
   typedef vector_allocator::size_type size_type;
   typedef vector_allocator::difference_type
      difference_type;
   typedef reverse_iterator
         < const_iterator,
           value_type,
           const_reference,
```

```
        difference_type
      > const_reverse_iterator;
    typedef reverse_iterator
        <iterator, value_type, reference, difference_type>
    reverse_iterator;

    iterator begin();
    const_iterator begin() const;
    iterator end();
    const_iterator end() const;
    reverse_iterator rbegin();
    const_reverse_iterator rbegin() const;
    reverse_iterator rend();
    const_reverse_iterator rend() const;
    size_type size() const;
    size_type max_size() const;
    size_type capacity() const;
    bool empty() const;
    reference operator[](size_type n);
    const_reference operator[](size_type n) const;
    vector() : start(0), finish(0), end_of_storage(0);
    vector(size_type n, const T& value = T());
    vector(const vector<T>& x);
    vector(const_iterator first, const_iterator last);
    ~vector();
    vector<T>& operator=(const vector<T>& x);
    void reserve(size_type n;
    reference front();
    const_reference front() const;
    reference back();
    const_reference back() const;
    void push_back(const T& x);
    void swap(vector<T>& x);
    iterator insert(iterator position, const T& x);
    void insert
    (   iterator position,
        const_iterator first,
        const_iterator last
    );
    void insert (iterator position, size_type n, const T& x);
    void pop_back();
    void erase(iterator position);
    void erase(iterator first, iterator last);
};
```

A.2.2 Sorted Associative Containers

```
template <class Key, class T, class Compare>
class map
{ public:
   typedef Key key_type;
   typedef pair<const Key, T> value_type;
   typedef Compare key_compare;

   class value_compare
   :  public binary_function <value_type, value_type, bool>
   { public:
        bool operator()
        (  const value_type& x,
           const value_type& y
        ) const;
   };

   typedef rep_type::pointer pointer;
   typedef rep_type::reference reference;
   typedef rep_type::const_reference const_reference;
   typedef rep_type::iterator iterator;
   typedef rep_type::const_iterator const_iterator;
   typedef rep_type::reverse_iterator reverse_iterator;
   typedef rep_type::const_reverse_iterator
      const_reverse_iterator;
   typedef rep_type::size_type size_type;
   typedef rep_type::difference_type difference_type;
   map(const Compare& comp = Compare());
   map(const value_type* first, const value_type* last,
   const Compare& comp = Compare());
   map(const map<Key, T, Compare>& x);
   map<Key, T, Compare>& operator=
   (  const map<Key, T, Compare>& x
   );
   key_compare key_comp() const;
   value_compare value_comp() const;
   iterator begin();
   const_iterator begin() const;
   iterator end();
   const_iterator end() const;
   reverse_iterator rbegin();
   const_reverse_iterator rbegin() const;
   reverse_iterator rend();
   const_reverse_iterator rend() const;
```

```cpp
    bool empty() const;
    size_type size() const;
    size_type max_size() const;
    Allocator<T>::reference operator[](const key_type& k);
    void swap(map<Key, T, Compare>& x);
    pair<iterator, bool> insert(const value_type& x);
    iterator insert(iterator position, const value_type& x);
    void insert
    (   const value_type* first,
        const value_type* last
    );
    void erase(iterator position);
    size_type erase(const key_type& x);
    void erase(iterator first, iterator last);
    iterator find(const key_type& x);
    const_iterator find(const key_type& x) const;
    size_type count(const key_type& x) const;
    iterator lower_bound(const key_type& x);
    const_iterator lower_bound(const key_type& x) const;
    iterator upper_bound(const key_type& x);
    const_iterator upper_bound(const key_type& x) const;
    pair<iterator, iterator> equal_range(const key_type& x);
    pair <const_iterator, const_iterator> equal_range
        (const key_type& x) const;
};

template <class Key, class T, class Compare>
class multimap
{ public:
    typedef Key key_type;
    typedef pair<const Key, T> value_type;
    typedef Compare key_compare;

    class value_compare
    :   public binary_function<value_type, value_type, bool>
    { public:
        bool operator()
        (   const value_type& x,
            const value_type& y
        ) const;
    };

    typedef rep_type::reference reference;
    typedef rep_type::const_reference const_reference;
    typedef rep_type::iterator iterator;
```

```
typedef rep_type::const_iterator const_iterator;
typedef rep_type::reverse_iterator reverse_iterator;
typedef rep_type::const_reverse_iterator
   const_reverse_iterator;
typedef rep_type::size_type size_type;
typedef rep_type::difference_type difference_type;
multimap(const Compare& comp = Compare());
multimap
( const value_type* first,
  const value_type* last,
  const Compare& comp = Compare()
);
multimap(const multimap<Key, T, Compare>& x);
multimap<Key, T, Compare>& operator=
   (const multimap<Key, T, Compare>& x);
key_compare key_comp() const;
value_compare value_comp() const;
iterator begin();
const_iterator begin() const;
iterator end();
const_iterator end() const;
reverse_iterator rbegin();
const_reverse_iterator rbegin() const;
reverse_iterator rend();
const_reverse_iterator rend() const;
bool empty() const;
size_type size() const;
size_type max_size() const;
void swap(multimap<Key, T, Compare>& x);
iterator insert(const value_type& x);
iterator insert(iterator position, const value_type& x);
void insert
( const value_type* first,
  const value_type* last
);
void erase(iterator position);
size_type erase(const key_type& x);
void erase(iterator first, iterator last);
iterator find(const key_type& x);
const_iterator find(const key_type& x) const;
size_type count(const key_type& x) const;
iterator lower_bound(const key_type& x);
const_iterator lower_bound(const key_type& x) const;
iterator upper_bound(const key_type& x);
const_iterator upper_bound(const key_type& x) const;
```

```
      pair<iterator, iterator> equal_range(const key_type& x);
      pair<const_iterator, const_iterator> equal_range
          (const key_type& x) const;
};

template <class Key, class Compare>
class set
{ public:
    typedef Key key_type;
    typedef Key value_type;
    typedef Compare key_compare;
    typedef Compare value_compare;
    typedef rep_type::const_reference reference;
    typedef rep_type::const_reference const_reference;
    typedef rep_type::const_iterator iterator;
    typedef rep_type::const_iterator const_iterator;
    typedef rep_type::const_reverse_iterator
        reverse_iterator;
    typedef rep_type::const_reverse_iterator
        const_reverse_iterator;
    typedef rep_type::size_type size_type;
    typedef rep_type::difference_type difference_type;
    set(const Compare& comp = Compare());
    set
    (   const value_type* first,
        const value_type* last,
        const Compare& comp = Compare()
    );
    set(const set<Key, Compare>& x);
    set<Key, Compare>& operator=(const set<Key, Compare>& x);
    key_compare key_comp() const;
    value_compare value_comp() const;
    iterator begin() const;
    iterator end() const;
    reverse_iterator rbegin() const;
    reverse_iterator rend() const;
    bool empty() const;
    size_type size() const;
    size_type max_size() const;
    void swap(set<Key, Compare>& x);
    pair<iterator, bool> insert(const value_type& x);
    iterator insert(iterator position, const value_type& x);
    void insert
```

```
    (   const value_type* first,
        const value_type* last
    );
    void erase(iterator position);
    size_type erase(const key_type& x);
    void erase(iterator first, iterator last);
    iterator find(const key_type& x) const;
    size_type count(const key_type& x) const;
    iterator lower_bound(const key_type& x) const;
    iterator upper_bound(const key_type& x) const;
    pair<iterator, iterator> equal_range
        (const key_type& x) const;
};

template <class Key, class Compare>
class multiset
{ public:
    typedef Key key_type;
    typedef Key value_type;
    typedef Compare key_compare;
    typedef Compare value_compare;
    typedef rep_type::const_reference reference;
    typedef rep_type::const_reference const_reference;
    typedef rep_type::const_iterator iterator;
    typedef rep_type::const_iterator const_iterator;
    typedef rep_type::const_reverse_iterator
        reverse_iterator;
    typedef rep_type::const_reverse_iterator
        const_reverse_iterator;
    typedef rep_type::size_type size_type;
    typedef rep_type::difference_type difference_type;
    multiset(const Compare& comp = Compare());
    multiset
    (   const value_type* first,
        const value_type* last,
        const Compare& comp = Compare()
    );
    multiset(const multiset<Key, Compare>& x);
    multiset<Key, Compare>& operator=
        (const multiset<Key, Compare>& x);
    key_compare key_comp() const;
    value_compare value_comp() const;
    iterator begin() const;
    iterator end() const;
    reverse_iterator rbegin() const;
```

```
    reverse_iterator rend() const;
    bool empty() const;
    size_type size() const;
    size_type max_size() const;
    void swap(multiset<Key, Compare>& x);
    iterator insert(const value_type& x);
    iterator insert(iterator position, const value_type& x);
    void insert
    (   const value_type* first,
        const value_type* last
    );
    void erase(iterator position);
    size_type erase(const key_type& x);
    void erase(iterator first, iterator last);
    iterator find(const key_type& x) const;
    size_type count(const key_type& x) const;
    iterator lower_bound(const key_type& x) const;
    iterator upper_bound(const key_type& x) const;
    pair<iterator, iterator> equal_range
        (const key_type& x) const;
};
```

A.3   Adaptors

A.3.1 Container Adaptors

A.3.1.1 Stack Adaptor

```
template <class Container>
class stack
{   friend bool operator==
    (   const stack<Container>& x,
        const stack<Container>& y
    );
    friend bool operator<
    (   const stack<Container>& x,
        const stack<Container>& y
    );
public:
    typedef Container::value_type value_type;
    typedef Container::size_type size_type;
protected:
    Container c;
```

```
public:
   bool empty() const;
   size_type size() const;
   value_type& top();
   const value_type& top() const;
   void push(const value_type& x);
   void pop();
};
```

A.3.1.2 Queue Adaptor

```
template <class Container>
class queue
{   friend bool operator==
    (   const queue<Container>& x,
        const queue<Container>& y
    );
    friend bool operator<
    (   const queue<Container>& x,
        const queue<Container>& y
    );
public:
   typedef Container::value_type value_type;
   typedef Container::size_type size_type;
protected:
   Container c;
public:
   bool empty() const;
   size_type size() const;
   value_type& front();
   const value_type& front() const;
   value_type& back();
   const value_type& back() const;
   void push(const value_type& x);
   void pop();
};
```

A.3.1.3 Priority Queue Adaptor

```
template <class Container, class Compare>
   // Compare = less<Container::value_type> >
   // default argument if available
class priority_queue
{
public:
   typedef Container::value_type value_type;
```

```
      typedef Container::size_type size_type;
protected:
   Container c;
   Compare comp;
public:
   priority_queue(const Compare& x = Compare());
   priority_queue
   (  const value_type* first,
      const value_type* last,
      const Compare& x = Compare()
   );

/* If template members are available:
   template <class InputIterator>
   priority_queue
   (  InputIterator first,
      InputIterator last,
      const Compare& x = Compare()
   );
*/
   bool empty() const;
   size_type size() const;
   value_type& top();
   const value_type& top() const;
   void push(const value_type& x);
   void pop();
};
```

Bibliography

Books and articles

[1] Horstman, *Mastering Object Oriented Design in C++*, Wiley, 1995
[2] Glass and Schuchert, *The STL <primer>*, Prentice-Hall, 1996
[3] Musser and Saini, *STL Tutorial and Reference Guide*, Addison-Wesley, 1996
[4] Nelson, *The C++ Programmer's Guide to the Standard Template Library*, IDG, 1996
[5] Plauger, Stepanov, and Musser, *The Standard Template Library*, Prentice-Hall, 1996
[6] Sedgewick, *Algorithms, 2ed.* Addison-Wesley, 1988.
[7] Zahn, Bergin, "Object-Oriented Lists With Contexts", Journal of Computing in Small
        Colleges, Volume 11, Number 4, March 1996

Information on the web

[8] http://www.cs.rpi.edu/~musser/stl.html
        Information about STL, a reference implementation,
[9] ftp://butler.hlp.hp.com/stl
[10] ftp.cs.rpi.edu/pub/stl
        The HP reference implementation
[11] http://www.sgi.com/Technology/STL/
        The STL Home Page
[12] http://weber.u.washington.edu/~bytewave/bytewave_stl.html
        A page of STL resources. Visit this. A newbie tutorial and more.
[13] ftp://research.att.com/dist/c++std/WP/
        Draft C++ Standard defines the STL
[14] http://csis.pace.edu/~bergin/
        Joseph Bergin, Home Page

Index